I0010362

Implementing Azure Solutions

Eliminate the pain point of implementation

Florian Klaffenbach
Jan-Henrik Damaschke
Oliver Michalski

BIRMINGHAM - MUMBAI

Implementing Azure Solutions

First published: May 2017

Production reference: 2170517

Published by Packt Publishing Ltd.
Livery Place
35 Livery Street
Birmingham
B3 2PB, UK.
ISBN 978-1-78646-785-0

www.packtpub.com

Credits

Authors
Florian Klaffenbach
Jan-Henrik Damaschke
Oliver Michalski

Copy Editor
Madhusudan Uchil

Reviewers
Sebastian Durandeu
Rafael dos Santos

Project Coordinator
Virginia Dias

Commissioning Editor
Pratik Shah

Proofreader
Safis Editing

Acquisition Editor
Prachi Bisht

Indexer
Pratik Shirodkar

Content Development Editor
Amedh Gemraram Pohad

Graphics
Kirk D'Penha

Technical Editor
Vishal Kamal Mewada

Production Coordinator
Shantanu Zagade

About the Authors

Florian Klaffenbach started in 2004 with his IT carrier as 1st and 2nd Level IT Support Technician and IT Salesman Trainee for a B2B online shop. After that, he changed to a small company working as IT Project Manager, planning, implementing, and integration from industrial plants and laundries into enterprise IT. After spending some years, he changed his path to Dell Germany. There he started from scratch as an Enterprise Technical Support Analyst and later worked on a project to start Dell Technical Communities and support over social Media in Europe and outside of the U.S.

Currently he is working as a Solutions Architect and Consultant for Microsoft Infrastructure and Cloud and is specialized in Microsoft Hyper-V, Fileservices, System Center Virtual Machine Manager, and Microsoft Azure IaaS at msg services ag.

In addition to his job, he is active as a Microsoft Blogger and Lecturer. He blogs for example on his own page Datacenter-Flo.de or Azure Community Germany. Together with a very good friend, he founded the Windows Server User Group Berlin to create network of Microsoft ITPros in Berlin.

Florian maintains a very tight network for many vendors such as Cisco, Dell, or Microsoft and Communities. This helps him to grow his experience and to get the best solution for his customers. Since 2016, he is also Co-Chairman of the Azure Community Germany. In April 2016, Microsoft awarded Florian Microsoft Most Valuable Professional for Cloud and Datacenter Management.

With that few lines, I want to thank all people, especially my family and friends who supported me while writing the book. Most of them didn't see me for a long time because I was spending most of my spare time for preparing the next chapter or testing new features which I wanted to mention within the book.

I also want to thank the guys from Microsoft and the coauthors Jan-Henrik and Oliver who support with reviewing and clearing some open questions and misunderstandings.

Hopefully you as reader enjoy the reading the book as much as I writing it.

Jan-Henrik Damaschke is an IT Consultant for Security, Network, and Infrastructure from Germany. He was MVP awarded in the categories of Enterprise Security, PowerShell, and AzureStack. PKI implementation and management is one of his core competencies as well as cloud-related security. He writes articles on security-related topics and is involved in many community events as a speaker as well as an organizer. He is passionate about sharing knowledge with others. For this purpose, he is member of the Microsoft Student Partner program and is engaged on forums and on other platforms. Currently, he is writing a book on Azure infrastructure solutions.

Oliver Michalski started in 1999 with his IT carrier as a Web Developer. Now, he is a Senior Software Engineer for Microsoft .NET and an SOA Architect. He also works as an Independent Enterprise Consultant in the field Microsoft Azure. When he started in 2011 with Microsoft Azure, there was no Azure Community on the German market. Therefore, Oliver founded the Azure Community Germany (ACD).
Oliver is Chairman of the Azure Community Germany, and since April 2016 he has been a Microsoft Most Valuable Professional for Microsoft Azure.

About the Reviewers

Sebastian Durandeu is a senior software engineer with a primary focus on building applications and services for the Cloud using Microsoft technologies. He works at Southworks, a high-end software development company that helps businesses leverage the latest technologies. There he has worked closely with several Microsoft divisions helping the developer community adopt emerging technologies using recommended practices. Sebastian currently lives in Buenos Aires, Argentina where he is an active contributor in the developer community. He shares his knowledge via his Twitter (`@sebadurandeu`) and GitHub accounts (`sdurandeu`).

Rafael dos Santos Christian, Geysla's husband, Ted's father, Entrepreneur, Developer, Cloud specialist. 10 years experience developing and architecting web based solutions.

I would like to thank Lucas Romao for the support and mentoring on learning Microsoft Azure. I also would like to thank all the SDK Team at ITIX, you guys are amazing and I love work with you guys.

www.PacktPub.com

For support files and downloads related to your book, please visit www.PacktPub.com.

Did you know that Packt offers eBook versions of every book published, with PDF and ePub files available? You can upgrade to the eBook version at www.PacktPub.com and as a print book customer, you are entitled to a discount on the eBook copy. Get in touch with us at service@packtpub.com for more details.

At www.PacktPub.com, you can also read a collection of free technical articles, sign up for a range of free newsletters and receive exclusive discounts and offers on Packt books and eBooks.

https://www.packtpub.com/mapt

Get the most in-demand software skills with Mapt. Mapt gives you full access to all Packt books and video courses, as well as industry-leading tools to help you plan your personal development and advance your career.

Why subscribe?

- Fully searchable across every book published by Packt
- Copy and paste, print, and bookmark content
- On demand and accessible via a web browser

Customer Feedback

Thanks for purchasing this Packt book. At Packt, quality is at the heart of our editorial process. To help us improve, please leave us an honest review on this book's Amazon page at `https://www.amazon.com/dp/1786467852`.

If you'd like to join our team of regular reviewers, you can e-mail us at customerreviews@packtpub.com. We award our regular reviewers with free eBooks and videos in exchange for their valuable feedback. Help us be relentless in improving our products!

Table of Contents

Preface

Welcome to our book about implementing Azure solutions. Microsoft Azure is the cloud platform of Microsoft and offers you numerous services to host your existing application infrastructure, deliver services tailored to your individual needs, or even expand your on-premise applications. Azure integrates the cloud services you need to develop, test, implement, and manage your applications and allows you to focus on building great solutions without the need to worry about how the physical infrastructure is assembled.

A very complex field of work and, therefore, the question arises immediately is this: where should I start? Unfortunately, we cannot answer this question, but we can show you the way so that you may find your own answer.

This book provides you with complete solutions that you can follow to learn how to create VMs, virtual networks, storage accounts, and so on as well as best-practice guidance of our consulting work to help you get the most out of your Azure experience. We hope this is a healthy mixture, but are always open to suggestions.

You can send us your feedback at `https://wazcommunity.wordpress.com/feedback/`.

What this book covers

Chapter 1, *Getting Started with Azure Implementation*, provides an overview of cloud service models, cloud deployment models, cloud characteristics, and Azure services.

Chapter 2, *Azure Resource Manager and Tools*, explains all about the Azure Resource Manager and its concepts (Azure Resource Groups, Azure Resource Tags, and Locks). You will also get an introduction to working with the ARM Templates area.

Chapter 3, *Deploying and Synchronizing Azure Active Directory*, gives you an overview of the deployment, management, and functionalities of Azure Active Directory and its relation to a Microsoft Azure subscription.

Chapter 4, *Implementing Azure Networks*, explains how networking in Azure works, how to plan Azure network components, and how to deploy different network components within Azure.

Chapter 5, *Implementing and Securing Azure Storage Accounts*, explains all about Azure Storage Management and its concepts (BLOBs, tables, queues, and files). You will also get some basic storage configurations.

Chapter 6, *Planning and Deploying Virtual Machines in Azure*, demonstrates the difference between the Azure virtual machine types, the common use cases for the different types, and how to deploy virtual machines.

Chapter 7, *Implementing Azure Cloud Services*, explains all about Azure Cloud Services, the Cloud Service architecture, Azure Cloud Services versus Azure App Services, and how to create your first Cloud Service.

Chapter 8, *Implementing Azure Container Service*, provides basic knowledge about the Azure Container Service area and how to create your first container service. You will also learn the necessary steps to work with the service afterward.

Chapter 9, *Implementing Azure Security*, explains all about Azure security concepts (identity management with Azure AD, Role-based Access Control (RBAC), and Azure Storage security) and the Azure Security Center.

Chapter 10, *Skill Wrap Up and Migration Scenario*, provides a basic overview of how classical applications and services can be placed in the Microsoft Cloud ecosystem and which tools can be used for the migration. This chapter is based on a common use case and migration scenario.

What you need for this book

Learning from a book only works if you have the opportunity to implement what you have learned in practice. That's why you need an Azure subscription. To do this at no cost, you can use a free Azure trial from https://azure.microsoft.com/en-us/free/.

To understand parts of the book, you also need an installation of Visual Studio. You can use any edition of Visual Studio. To avoid unnecessary costs, I recommend using the free Visual Studio Community Edition from https://www.visualstudio.com/downloads/.

Who this book is for

This book focuses on providing essential information about the implementation of Azure solutions to software architects, developers, and IT professionals. The technical information will be offered to you in an intermediate and expert level.

Basic knowledge is not necessary, but it is useful for a better understanding of the text. Therefore, some knowledge of programming languages is recommended.

Conventions

In this book, you will find a number of text styles that distinguish between different kinds of information. Here are some examples of these styles and an explanation of their meaning.

Code words in text, database table names, folder names, filenames, file extensions, pathnames, dummy URLs, user input, and Twitter handles are shown as follows: "The current project consists of three artifacts in two solution folders, `Templates` and `Scripts`."

A block of code is set as follows:

```
"parameters": {
    "storageAccountName": {
      "type": "string",
      "metadata": {
        "description": "Storage Account Name"
      }
    }
}
```

Any command-line input or output is written as follows:

```
Resize-AzureVNetGateway -GatewaySKU Basic -VnetName DCF-ANE-GW01
```

New terms and **important words** are shown in bold. Words that you see on the screen, for example, in menus or dialog boxes, appear in the text like this: "In the portal, click on **New**, then click on **Data + Storage**, and then click on **Storage account**."

Warnings or important notes appear in a box like this.

Tips and tricks appear like this.

Reader feedback

Feedback from our readers is always welcome. Let us know what you think about this book—what you liked or disliked. Reader feedback is important for us as it helps us develop titles that you will really get the most out of.

To send us general feedback, simply e-mail `feedback@packtpub.com`, and mention the book's title in the subject of your message.

If there is a topic that you have expertise in and you are interested in either writing or contributing to a book, see our author guide at `www.packtpub.com/authors`.

Customer support

Now that you are the proud owner of a Packt book, we have a number of things to help you to get the most from your purchase.

Downloading the color images of this book

We also provide you with a PDF file that has color images of the screenshots/diagrams used in this book. The color images will help you better understand the changes in the output. You can download this file from `http://www.packtpub.com/sites/default/files/downloads/ImplementingAzureSolutions_ColorImages.pdf`.

Errata

Although we have taken every care to ensure the accuracy of our content, mistakes do happen. If you find a mistake in one of our books—maybe a mistake in the text or the code—we would be grateful if you could report this to us. By doing so, you can save other readers from frustration and help us improve subsequent versions of this book. If you find any errata, please report them by visiting `http://www.packtpub.com/submit-errata`, selecting your book, clicking on the **Errata Submission Form** link, and entering the details of your errata. Once your errata are verified, your submission will be accepted and the errata will be uploaded to our website or added to any list of existing errata under the Errata section of that title.

To view the previously submitted errata, go to `https://www.packtpub.com/books/content/support` and enter the name of the book in the search field. The required information will appear under the **Errata** section.

Piracy

Piracy of copyrighted material on the Internet is an ongoing problem across all media. At Packt, we take the protection of our copyright and licenses very seriously. If you come across any illegal copies of our works in any form on the Internet, please provide us with the location address or website name immediately so that we can pursue a remedy.

Please contact us at `copyright@packtpub.com` with a link to the suspected pirated material.

We appreciate your help in protecting our authors and our ability to bring you valuable content.

Questions

If you have a problem with any aspect of this book, you can contact us at `questions@packtpub.com`, and we will do our best to address the problem.

1
Getting Started with Azure Implementation

Cloud services have come a long way in the last 5 to 10 years. Cloud was and still is one of the biggest trends in **Information Technology (IT)**, with new topics still to be discovered.

In the early 2000s, cloud computing wasn't a widely used phrase, but the concept as well as data centers with massive computing power were already existent and used. Later in that decade, the word *cloud* became a buzzword for nearly anything that was not tangible or online. But the real rise of cloud computing with all its different service models happened before, when the big IT companies started their cloud offers. That was Amazon, Google, and Microsoft in particular. As the cloud offers developed, they enabled companies from startups to Fortune 500s to use cloud services, from web services to virtual machines with billing exact to the minute.

In this chapter, we'll explore the following topics:

- Cloud service models
- Cloud deployment models
- Cloud characteristics
- Azure services overview

Service models

Cloud computing the new trend model for enabling workloads, that use resources from a a normally extreme huge resource pool, that is operated by a cloud service provider. These resources include servers, storage, network resources, applications, services or even functions. These can be rapidly deployed, operated and automated with a low effort and the prices are calculated on a minute base. This cloud model is composed of five essential characteristics, three service models, and four deployment models.

Cloud offers are mainly categorized into the following service models:

- **Infrastructure as a Service** (**IaaS**): Infrastructure as a Service describes a model in which the cloud provider gives the consumer the possibility to create and configure resources from the computing layer upwards. This includes virtual machines, networks, appliances, and many other infrastructure-related resources:
  - The most popular IaaS resources in Azure contain virtual machines, virtual networks (internal and external), container services and storage.
- **Platform as a Service** (**PaaS**): Platform as a Service gives the consumer an environment from the operating system upwards. So, the consumer is not responsible for the underlying IaaS infrastructure. Examples are operating systems, databases, or development frameworks:
  - Microsoft Azure contains many PaaS resources such as SQL databases, Azure app services, or cloud services.
- **Software as a Service** (**SaaS**): Software as a Service is the model with the lowest levels of control and required management. A SaaS application is reachable from multiple clients and consumers, and the owning consumer doesn't have any control over the backend, except for some application related management tasks.
- Examples of SaaS applications are Office 365, Visual Studio Online, Outlook website, OneDrive, and even the Amazon website itself is a SaaS app with Amazon as its own consumer.

A comparison of service model responsibilities is as follows:

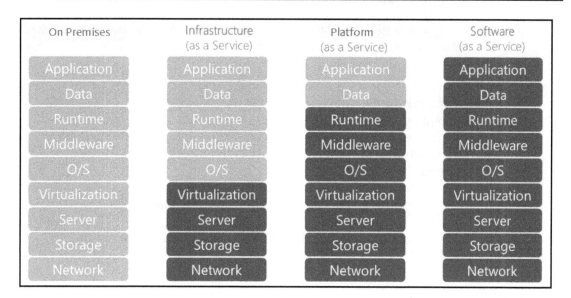

Cloud service models

Deployment models

Furthermore, there are a number of deployment models for cloud computing that need to be discussed. These deployment models cover nearly all common cloud computing provider scenarios. They describe the group of consumers that are able to use the services of the cloud service, rather than the institution or the underlying infrastructure:

- **Public Cloud**: A Public Cloud describes a cloud computing offer that can be accessed by the public. This includes individuals as well as companies.
    - Examples of a Public Cloud are Microsoft Azure and Amazon AWS.
- **Community Cloud**: A Community Cloud is only accessible by a specified group. These are, for example, connected by location, an organization membership, or by reasons of compliance.
    - Examples of a Community Cloud are Microsoft Azure Germany (location) or Microsoft Azure Government (organization and compliance) for US Government authorities.
- **Private Cloud**: Private Cloud describes an environment/infrastructure built and operated by a single organization for internal use. These offers are specifically designed for the different units in the organization.

- Examples are Microsoft **Windows Azure Pack (WAP)** or Microsoft Azure Stack, as well as OpenStack, if they are used for internal deployments.

- **Hybrid Cloud**: The Hybrid Cloud combines the Private and Public Clouds. It is defined as a Private Cloud environment at the consumer's premises as well as Public Cloud infrastructure that the consumer uses. These structures are generally connected by site-to-site VPNs or **Multiprotocol Label Switching (MPLS)**. A Hybrid Cloud could also exist as combination of any other models such as Community and Public Clouds.

  - Examples are Azure VMs connected to an on-premises infrastructure via ExpressRoute or site-to-site VPN.

Below is a comparison between a related example, in this case between Azure (Public Cloud) and Azure Pack (Private Cloud):

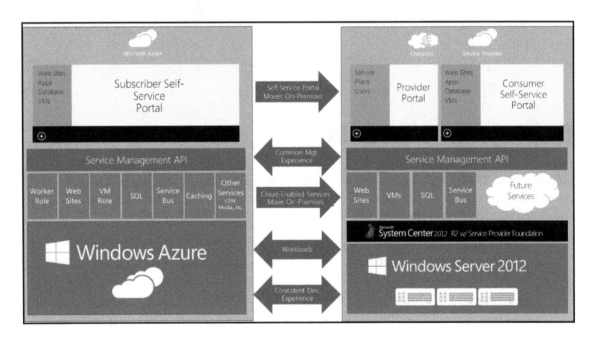

Comparison of Microsoft Azure (Stack) to Azure Pack

With Summer 2017 Microsoft will release the new version of the private cloud adoption from Azure Resource Manager. The new version will be named Azure Stack and will sooner or later be equal to the Azure Resource Manager Framework.

Cloud characteristics

Microsoft Azure is one of the biggest cloud service providers worldwide, offering a wide range of services from IaaS to PaaS to SaaS. It fulfills all the characteristics that the **National Institute of Standards and Technology (NIST)** describes for cloud computing. These are as follows:

- **On-demand self-service**: An automated deployment of resources that a consumer orders through an interface such as a consumer portal.
- **Broad network access**: Providing availability of cloud services through a standardized network interface that are, at best, accessible by several endpoint devices.
- **Resource pooling**: This means that the automated assignment and reassignment of diverse resources from various resource pools for individual customers is possible.
- **Rapid elasticity**: It is also known as rapid scaling, and describes the ability to scale resources in a massive way. The automatic and fast assignment and reassignment of resources, and rapid up- and down-scaling of single instances are keywords when talking about **rapid elasticity**. The adjustment of web server resources depending on the demand is an example of rapid elasticity.
- **Measured service**: All usage data for consumer resources is monitored and reported to be available for consumers and the cloud provider. This is one of the requirements for minute-based billing.

Microsoft Azure

When Windows Azure came online to the general public in February 2010 there were solely database services, websites, and virtual machine hosting available. Over time, Microsoft constantly added features and new services to Azure, and, as there were more and more offers for Linux and other non-Windows services, Microsoft decided in April 2014 to rename Windows Azure as Microsoft Azure. This supported Microsoft's commitment to transform itself into a services company, which means that, in order to be successful, you have to offer as many services as possible to as many clients as possible. Since then, Microsoft has constantly improved and released new services. Additionally, it constantly builds and expand its data centers all over the world.

The service updates happen very frequently. That is the reason why you need to keep yourself informed. For example, the database offer you are using could have improved storage or performance capabilities. Information sources are the official Microsoft Azure Blog and the Azure Twitter channel. Furthermore, information can be found on the websites of several Azure MVPs.

Azure services overview

Azure offers many services in its cloud computing platform. These services include the following:

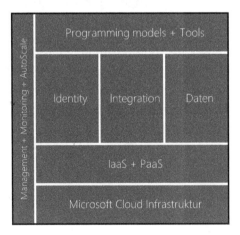

The service categories, differentiated between platform services and infrastructure services, are as follows:

- **Platform Services**:
    - **Management**: The management services include the management portal, the marketplace with the services gallery, and the components to automate things in Azure.
    - **Services compute**: Services compute are the Azure cloud services that are basically PaaS offers for developers to quickly build and deploy highly scalable applications. The service fabric and Azure RemoteApp are also in this category.
    - **Security**: Containing all the services that provide identity in Azure, such as the Azure Active Directory, multi-factor authentication, and the key vault that is a safe place for your certificates.
    - **Integration**: The integration services include interface services such as BizTalk and Azure Service Bus, but also message helpers such as storage queues.
    - **Media and CDN**: These are basically two services. One is the CDN that makes it possible to build your own content delivery network based on Azure. The other is the media services that make it very easy to use and process different media with the help of Azure.
    - **Web and mobile**: These include all the services that assist in creating apps or backend services for web and mobile; for example, web apps and API apps.
    - **Developer services**: These are cloud-based development tools for version control, collaboration, and other development-related tasks. The Azure SDK is a part of the developer services.
    - **Data**: The data services contain all the different database types that you can deploy in Azure (SQL, DocumentDB, MongoDB, Table storage and so on) and diverse tools to configure them.
    - **Analytics and IoT**: As the name suggests, analytics services are tools to analyze and process data. This offers a broad range of possibilities from machine learning to stream analytics. These can, but don't have to, build on certain data services. **Internet of Things (IoT)** services include the fundamental tools needed to work with devices used for the IoT such as the Raspberry Pi 2.

- **Hybrid operations**: This category sums up all the remaining services that could not clearly be categorized. These include backup, monitoring, and disaster recovery as well as many others.
- **Infrastructure services**:
  - **Operating system and server compute**: This category consists of compute containers. It includes virtual machine containers and, additionally, the container services that are quite new to the product range.
  - **Storage**: Storage services are the two main storage types: **BLOB** and **file storage**. They have different pricing tiers depending on the speed and latency of the storage ordered. Storage is looked at in detail in Chapter 6, *Planning and Deploying Virtual Machines in Azure.*
  - **Networking**: This category consists of the basic networking resources. Examples are Load Balancer, ExpressRoute, and VPN Gateways.

The important thing is to remember that we are talking about a rapidly changing and very agile cloud computing platform. After this chapter, if you have not already done so, you should start using Azure by experimenting, exploring, and implementing your solutions, while reading the correlating chapters.

For testing purposes, you should use the **Azure Free Trial** (https://azure.microsoft.com/en-in/offers/ms-azr-0044p/), **Visual Studio Dev Essentials** (https://www.visualstudio.com/dev-essentials/) or the included Azure amount from a MSDN subscription.

Azure basics

In the following section, we will take a look at the basic Microsoft Azure key concepts. This should provide an overview and an idea of how to use Azure.

Azure Resource Manager

In the previous major version of Azure, a deployment backend model called **Azure Service Manager** (**ASM**) was used. With higher demand on scaling, being more flexible and more standardized a new model called the ARM was introduced and is now the standard way of using Azure.

This includes a new portal, a new way of looking at things as resources and a standardized API that every tool, including the Azure portal, that interacts with Azure uses.

With this API and architectural changes, it's possible to use such things as Azure Resource Manager templates for any size of deployment. ARM templates are written in **JavaScript Object Notation** (**JSON**) and are a convenient way to define one or more resources and their relationship to another programmatically. This structure is then deployed to a resource group. With this deployment model, it's possible to define dependencies between resources as well as being able to deploy the exact same architecture again and again. The next part will dive a little deeper into resources.

Resources

Azure resources are the key to every service offering in Azure. Resources are the smallest building blocks and represent a single technical entity like a VM, a Network Interface Card, a storage account, database or a website.

When deploying a web app, a resource called **App service** will be deployed along with a service plan for billing.

When deploying a Virtual Machine from Azure Marketplace template a VM resource will be created as well as a storage account resource holding the virtual hard disks, a Public IP Address resource for initial access to the VM, a Network Interface card and a Virtual Network resource.

Every resource has to be deployed to one specific resource group. A resource group can hold multiple resources, while a single resource can only exist in one resource group. Resource groups also can't contain another resource group, what leads to a single layer of containers regarding resources.

One resource group can contain all resources of a deployment or multiple resources of different deployments. There are no strong recommendations on structuring resource groups, but it's recommended to organize either resource of one project/enrollment/deployment in separate resource groups or distribute resources based on their purpose (networking, storage, and so on) to resource groups.

Azure regions

Azure as a global cloud platform provides multiple regions to deploy resources at. One region consists of at least one highly available data center or data center complex.

The (at the time of writing) 34 regions are distributed all over the world and include community clouds like Azure Germany or government clouds like US Gov Virginia. Additionally, to the implicit high availability inside a region and a data center, it's possible to select a region and creation of most resources. This region represents a set of data centers that are connected through Microsoft owned high-speed network to replicate the data in near real-time between the specific data centers.

Regions can also have an impact on the performance and availability of some resources. Some services may be not or only partially available in a specific region.

The costs of offered services also vary by region. For reduced latency, it's recommended to choose a region next to the physical location of the consumer. It might also be important which legal requirements must be met. This could, for example, result in a deployment only in EU regions or even regions in specific countries.

- The available Azure regions are listed here: `https://azure.microsoft.com/en-us/regions/`
- This list lists all the services available in specific regions: `https://azure.microsoft.com/en-us/regions/services/`

Azure Portal

The Azure Portal is a web application and the most straightforward way to view and manage most Azure resources. The Azure portal can also be used for identity management, to view billing information and to create custom dashboards for often used resources to get a quick overview of some deployments.

Although it's easy to start with using and deploying services and resources, it's highly recommended to use some Azure Automation technologies for larger and production environments.

The Azure portal is located at `https://portal.azure.com`.

Azure automation

Azure automation is a service and a resource as well an Azure concept in the context of cloud computing.

It's very important to see automation as an essential concept when it comes to cloud computing. Automation is one of the key technologies to reduce operational costs and will also provide a consistent and replicable state. It also lays the foundation to any rapid deployment plans.

As Azure uses very much automation internally, Microsoft decided to make some of that technology available as a resource called **automation account**.

Azure Automation tools

Azure provides several ways of interacting and automating things. The two main ways to interact with Azure besides the portal are the Azure PowerShell and the **Azure Command-Line Interface (CLI)**.

Both are basically just wrappers around the Azure API to enable everyone not familiar with REST APIs, but their specific scripting language to use and automate Azure. The Azure PowerShell module provides cmdlets for managing Azure services and resources through the Azure API. Azure PowerShell cmdlets are used to handle Account management and Environment management like creating, updating and deleting resources.

These cmdlets work completely the same on Azure, Azure Pack and Azure stack, Microsoft's private cloud offerings.

Azure PowerShell open source and maintained by Microsoft. The project is available on GitHub at the following link:
```
https://github.com/Azure/azure-powershell
```
The Azure CLI is a tool that you can use to create, manage, and remove Azure resources from the command-line. The Azure CLI was created for administrators and operators that are not that experienced with Microsoft technologies, but with other Server technologies like Unix or Linux.

The Azure CLI is an open source project as well and is available for Linux, macOS, and Windows here:

```
https://github.com/Azure/azure-cli
```

REST APIs

All Azure Services, including the Azure Management Portal, provide their own REST APIs for their functionality. They can, therefore, be accessed by any application that RESTful Services can process.

In order for software developers to write applications in the programming language of their choice, Microsoft offers wrapper classes for the REST APIs.

These are available as a so-called Azure SDK for numerous programming languages (for example, .NET, Java, Node.js) here:

```
https://github.com/Azure
```

Summary

In the last chapter, we learned that the classic model had changed a lot. In the classic world, you had complete control over the hardware and software that is deployed. This has led to hardware decisions that focus on massive scaling. An example is purchasing a server with more cores to satisfy peak performance needs. Unfortunately, this infrastructure might be underutilized outside the demand window. With Azure, you can deploy only the infrastructure that you need, and adjust this up or down at any time. This leads to a focus on scaling out through the deployment of additional compute nodes to satisfy a performance need. Although this has consequences for designing an appropriate software architecture. These days it's sure that scaling out cloud services is more cost-saving than scaling up through racks and servers.

Microsoft has built many Azure datacenters around the globe. There are even more planned, especially sovereign clouds in regions like China and Germany. Only the largest global enterprises can deploy datacenters in this manner, so using Azure makes it easy for enterprises of any size to deploy their services close to their customers.

For small businesses, Azure allows for a low-cost entry point, with the ability to scale on demand. This prevents a large capital investment in infrastructure and provides the flexibility to architect and re-architect systems as needed. Using cloud technologies supports the startup mentality of growing fast and failing fast.

In the next chapter, we will take a look at Azure Resource Manager and the Azure resource manager tools.

2
Azure Resource Manager and Tools

The Azure platform consists primarily of three parts: part 1, called **Azure Execution Model**, denotes the areas where you can provide your services and applications in the cloud; parts 2 and 3, called **Azure Application Building Blocks** and **Azure Data Services**, refer to services that extend the platform to common capabilities and functionalities.

I could actually quit the description of the platform, because most users get only these three parts to see, but there are still more. Many other services are working under the hood of the platform and ensure the ongoing operation. These services include, for example, the Azure traffic manager, the Azure load balancer, and the Azure resource manager. All of these services can be customized using various interfaces for your personal needs.

In this chapter, I'll introduce you to the Azure resource manager in detail and we'll explore the following topics:

- Azure resource manager and Azure resource groups
- Azure resource tags
- Azure resource locks
- Working with ARM templates and the Azure resource explorer
- Creating your own ARM template

Understanding the Azure resource manager

With the classic Azure system management, you could previously manage only one resource on the Azure platform at the same time. But what about more complex applications, as are common today? The infrastructure of today's applications typically consists of several components - a virtual machine, a storage account, a virtual network, a web app, a database, a database server, or a third-party service. To manage such complex applications, with the first preview of the Azure management portal 3.0, the concept of resource groups was introduced.

You now see your components no longer as separate entities, but as related and interdependent parts of a single entity. So you will be able to manage all the resources of your application simultaneously.

As an instrument for this type of management, the Azure resource manager (and the Azure resource manager tools) was introduced, and can be accessed via a variety of different technologies and interfaces. These access options include the following:

- The traditional way via the Azure management portal (portal version 3.0 and newer)
- The script-based way via Azure PowerShell (look for PowerShell modules with the prefix AzureRM) or via the cross-platform command-line interface Azure CLI
- For developers, there are also SDKs available (.NET and some other programming languages) and, as with all Azure services, an extensive REST API

Functionalities provided by the Azure resource manager

In this section, I would like to give you a brief overview of the functionalities of the Azure resource manager. The list, however, is only a selection and is limited to the most frequently used features. You will find detailed information on the use of the features in the following sections of this chapter.

Let us have a look at the list:

- Access control with Azure **Role-Based Access Control (RBAC)**.
- Logical organization of all the resources of a subscription, with Azure resource tags (for example, for each project and tenant).
- Improved cost control. You can view the costs for the whole group or for a group of resources with the same tag.
- Use of Azure resource manager templates (ARM templates):
    - As a deployment template, in the provision of individual solutions on the Azure platform (the most popular example is deploying a SharePoint server farm).
    - As a resource provider template, for the implementation of measures (for example, configuration) within the resource groups.
- By using templates, you have the ability to define dependencies between resources, so that they are provided in the correct order.

- Through the use of templates, you have the possibility to repeatedly and securely provide your application and resources throughout the entire lifecycle, and this always in the same form
- You can modify the templates (JSON data files) to your own needs and even create your own templates.

Working with the Azure resource manager

We now know that the Azure resource manager serves as the technical base for the provision of resources. How are we going to continue? First, we will deal with the basic workflows in Azure resource manager. Then, in the second part, we will look at working with templates.

Before we begin, I want to introduce some very important facts that are important for all workflows:

- All of the resources in your resource group have the same life cycle. You will deploy, update, and delete them at the same time.
- Each resource can only exist in one resource group.
- You can add or remove a resource to a resource group at any time. You can also move a resource from one resource group to another.

- A resource group can contain resources that exist in different locations.
- A resource can interact with a resource in another resource groups when the two resources are related but they do not share the same life cycle (for example, a web app connecting to a database).

OK, let's start with the first workflow.

Creating an Azure resource group

The **Creating an Azure resource group** workflow is the first in a series of basic workflows, but also the most important. Why? Simple answer: an Azure resource group is the central element of the Azure resource manager concept. Without an existing resource group, nothing works, and I mean not only individual services, but your complete Azure subscription. To create an Azure resource group, perform the following steps:

1. Open your Azure management portal at `https://portal.azure.com`.
2. In the portal, click on **Resource groups**:

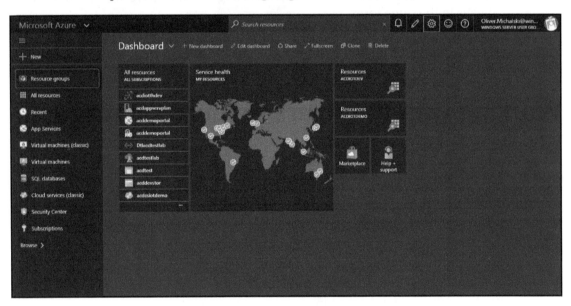

3. On the **Resource groups** blade, click on the **Add** option:

4. On the **Resource groups** blade, type the following values, and then click on the **Create** button:

- **Resource group name**: `acdppbook` (or the name of your choice)
- **Subscription**: Use the default subscription

- **Resource group location**: Select your preferred location:

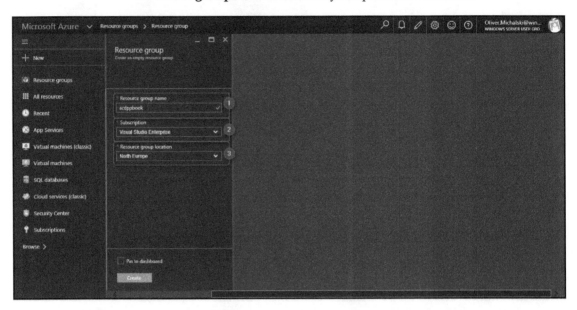

5. You can see the progress when creating the resource group, in the notification service of the portal:

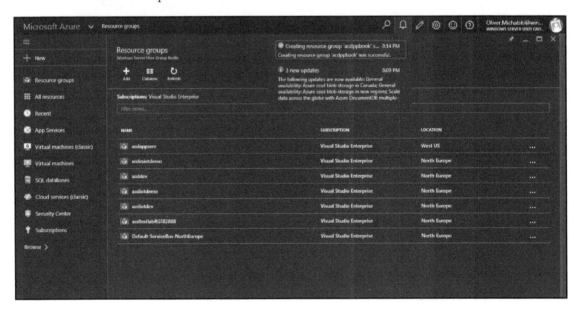

6. As soon as the resource group has been created, you can find it in the list:

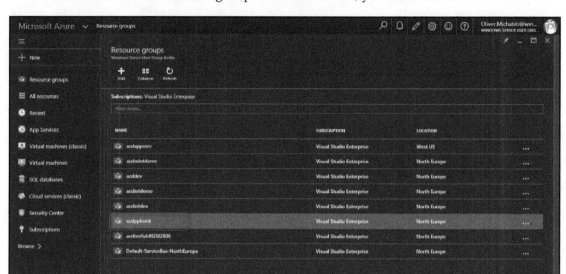

Adding a resource to an Azure resource group

We have just learned how to create an Azure resource group. Now we'll fill the new resource group with life and add a resource. To complete this process, the Azure platform has a total of three possible approaches. I will now introduce you to them one by one.

For all approaches, I will show the necessary work steps on the example of adding an Azure storage account. But note that the description of the procedure applies also to all other resource types in the same or slightly modified form.

First approach - adding a storage account to your Azure resource group

To add a storage account to your Azure resource group, perform the following steps:

1. Open your Azure management portal at https://portal.azure.com.

2. In the portal, click on **New**, then click on **Data + Storage**, and then click on **Storage account**:

3. On the **Create storage account** blade, type a unique name for the storage account you are creating in the **Name** textbox. If the name is unique, you will see a green tick:

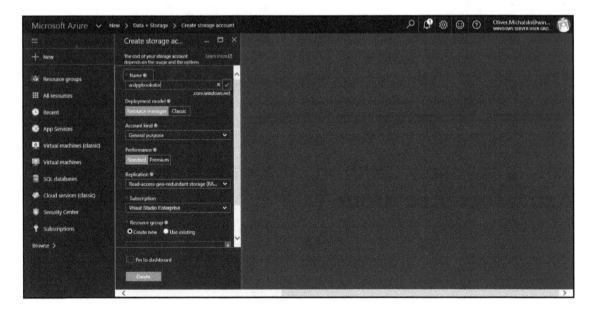

4. In the **Resource group** section, click the **Use existing** checkbox, then search and select **acdpppbook** in the drop-down list:

5. In the **Location** list, select the same location you have been using for the Azure resource group, and then click on the **Create** button:

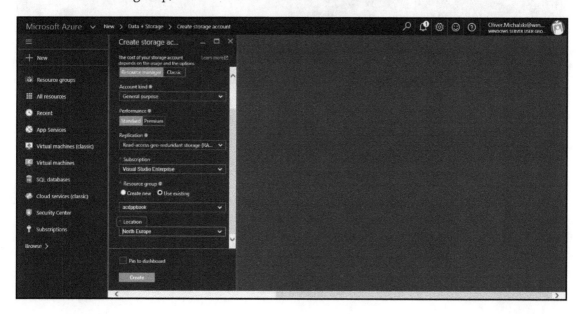

Second approach - adding a storage account to your Azure resource group

The first approach is the default path for adding Azure resources and usually suffices in most cases. There is a second possibility available, which is also applicable for all types of Azure resources but was originally intended for offers from third-party companies: the way over the Azure marketplace. Let's have a look:

1. In the portal, click on **Resource groups**:

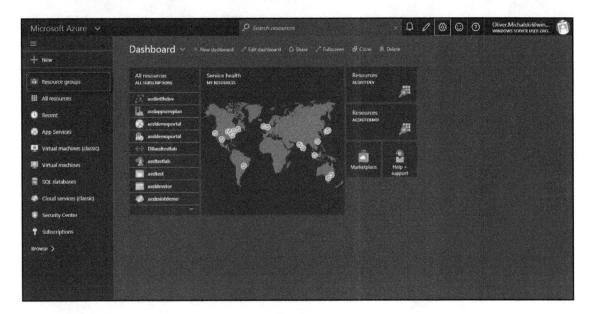

2. On the **Resource groups** blade, click on the**acdppbook** name field:

3. On the **Resource groups** dashboard, click on the **Add** option:

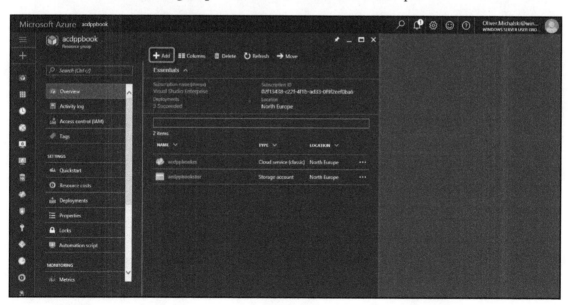

4. Now the Azure marketplace opens. Select a resource and create it as described in the previous section:

Third approach - adding a storage account to your Azure resource group

From the second approach (the way over the Azure space), a special case is still available: template deployment. This is, however, at the time of writing this section, still a preview. Changes in the procedure and functionality are possible at any time. Let's have a look at this:

1. In the portal, click on **New** and then click on **See all** in **MARKETPLACE**:

2. Now the Azure marketplace opens. Select the **Template deployment** offer:

3. If you don't see the entry immediately, simply enter `Template deployment` into the search field:

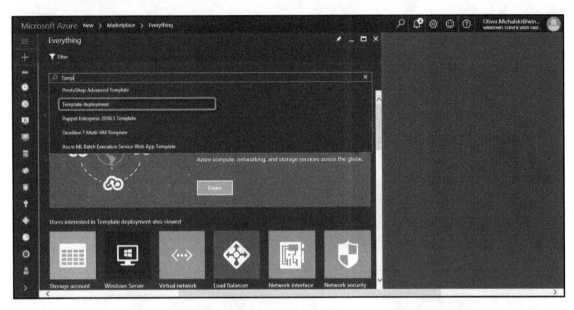

4. Now the info page of the offer opens; press the **Create** button here:

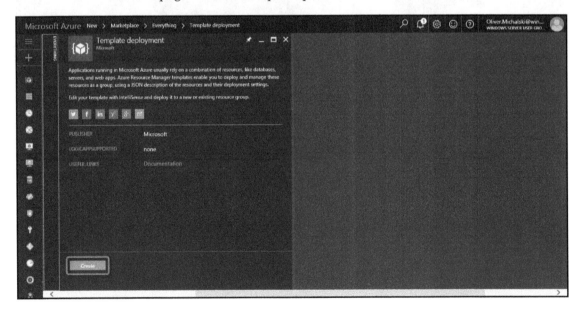

5. Next, the **Custom deployment** blade opens. By default, however, there are no resources, so you must first press the **Edit** button:

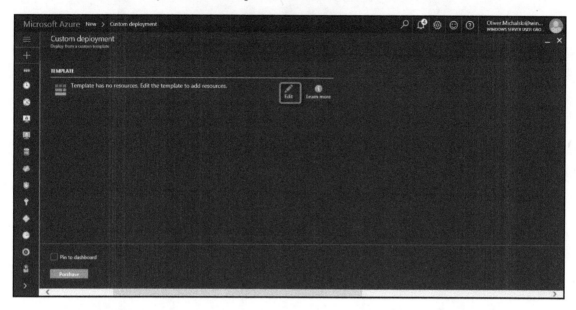

6. Next, the **Edit template** window will open with a default template. For your work with this, you will find the two buttons **Add resource** and **Quickstart templates**:

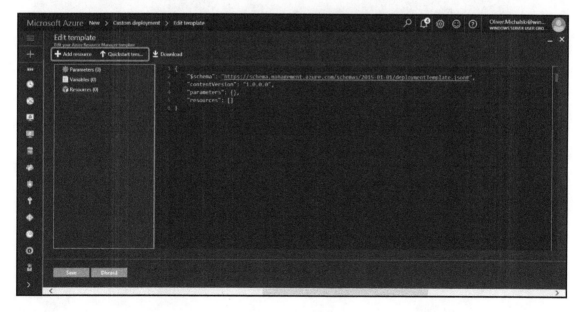

7. With the **Add resource** button, you can select an Azure resource from a list and add it to your template:

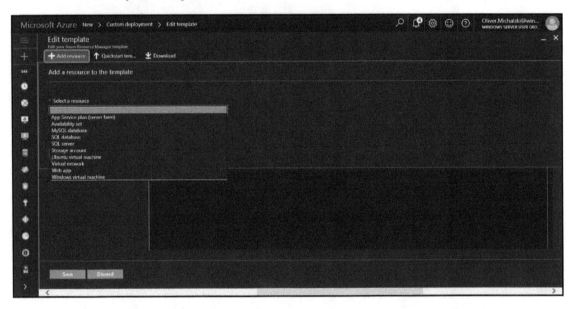

8. With the **Quickstart template** button, you can load a more complex template, from the constantly growing collection of community templates:

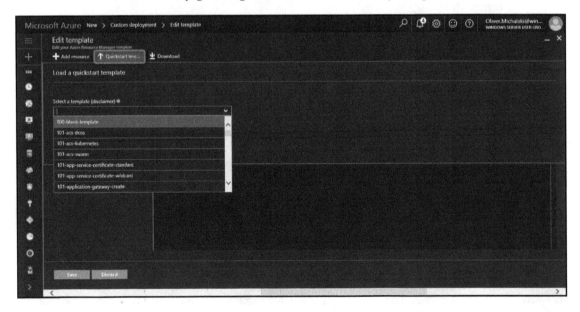

9. For our small demo, I selected **Storage** account in the **Select a resource** list. Depending on the selected resource, additional input fields will appear (usually at least one input field for the resource **Name**). When you have filled everything in, press the **OK** button:

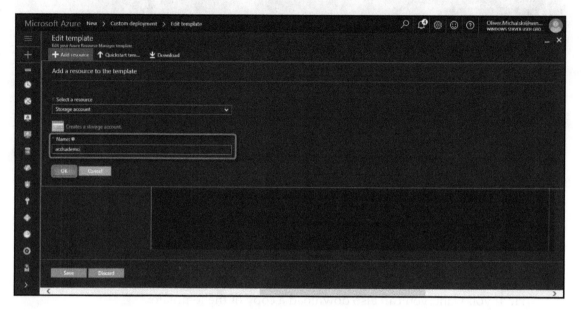

10. Now the **Edit template** window opens again, but this time with a template for your resource. If necessary, you can add more resources to your template by repeating the previous working step:

11. If you want, you can also download a copy of the template:

12. When everything is ok, press the **Save** button:

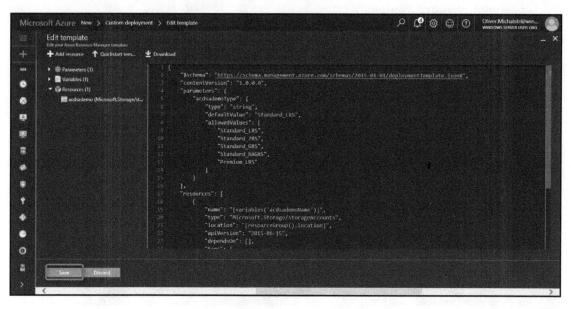

13. We are back in the **Custom deployment** blade. Here you have to make a few final entries. First, select a **Resource group**:

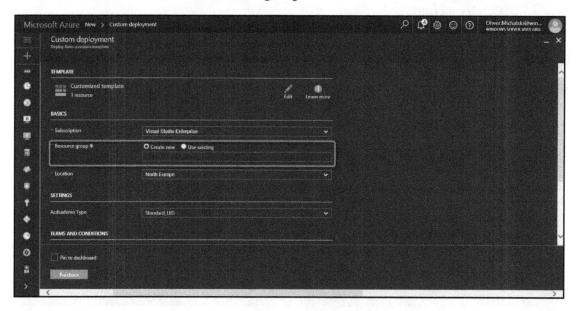

14. Then you can change, depending on the selected resource type, the **SETTINGS** of your resource (optional):

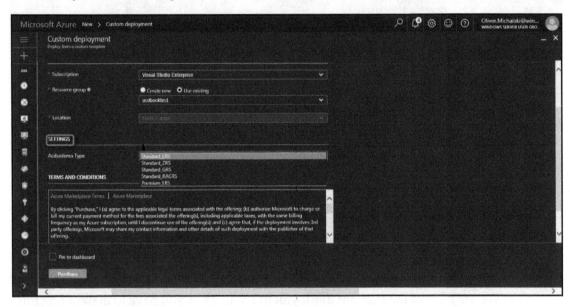

15. Finally, you must accept the Azure marketplace license, and then press the **Purchase** button:

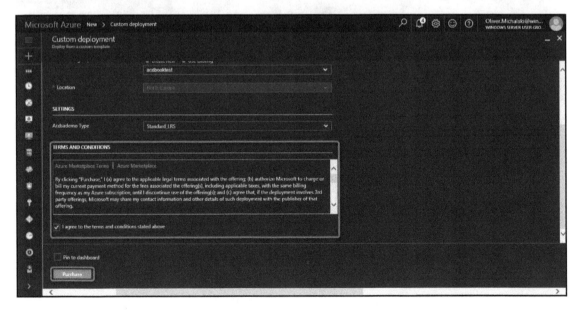

This is not really a purchase!

Now the deployment of the template is running.

Tagging in the Azure resource manager

We have just learned how to create an Azure resource group, and how to add an Azure resource. What we are still missing? Short answer: we still need a way to organize our resources logically, for example, for the calculation of cost or for a targeted tracking.

The Azure resource manager offers a solution for this—Azure resource tags. Azure resource tags are any key/value pairs that appear useful to describe a resource.

Let's see an example:

Key	Value
Department	Management
Project	ppbook
Tenant	ACD

Once you have defined a resource tag, you can use this as a filter in Azure PowerShell or in the Azure Billing APIs (Azure Usage API, Azure RateCard API). Up to 15 tags can be defined per resource.

I will show you the necessary work steps on the example of tagging an Azure storage account, but note that the description of the procedure applies to all other resource types in the same form:

1. Open your Azure management portal at `https://portal.azure.com`.

2. In the portal, click on **Resource groups**:

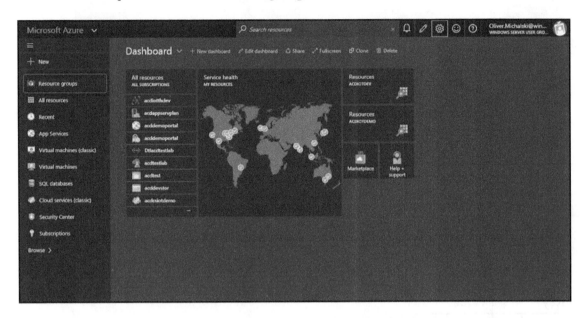

3. On the **Resource groups** blade, click the **acdppbook** name field:

4. In the navigation section on the **Resource groups** dashboard, click on the **Tags** button:

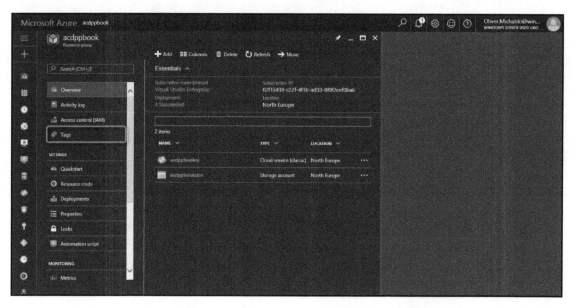

5. Now open the **Tags** blade. In the **Key** textbox, type Name, and then in the **Value** textbox, type ppbook. After this, click on **Save**:

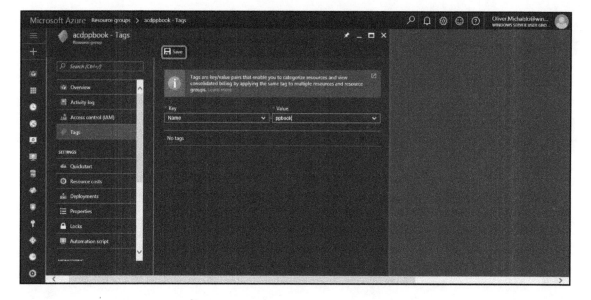

6. Go back to the **Resource groups** dashboard. In the resource grid, select the **acdppbookstor** row, and then click the **...** field:

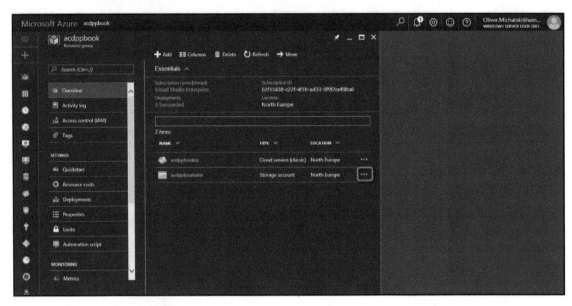

7. In the navigation section of the **Resources** dashboard (**acdppbookstor**), click the **Tags** button:

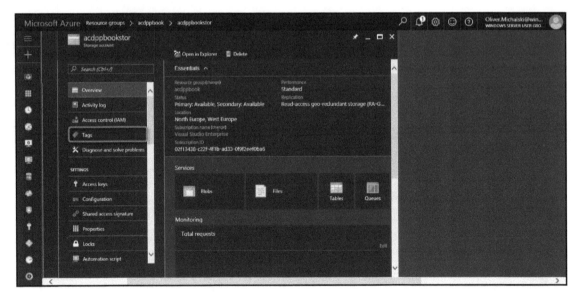

8. On the **Tags** blade, in the **Key** box, type again Name, and then in the **Value** box, type ppbook. Click **Save**:

9. In the portal, click on **More services**, scroll down the list, and then click on **Tags**:

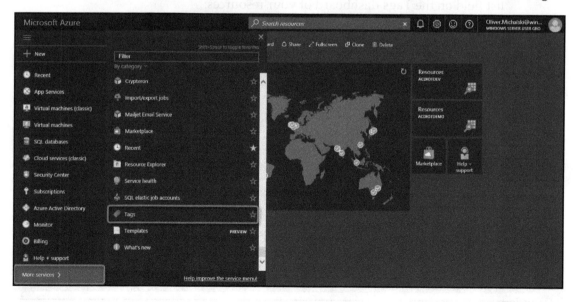

10. In the **Tags** blade, search the row for your tag **Name: ppbook**, and then click the ... field. Now you can see all the resources that are associated with the tag:

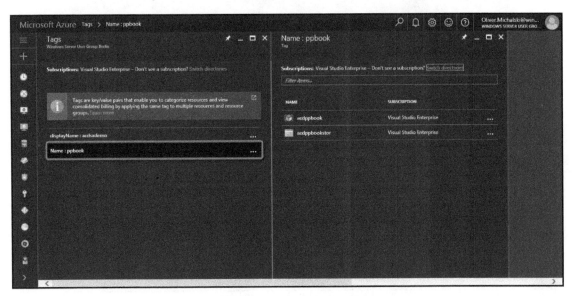

11. You can also see all the resources that are associated with the tag, by clicking the list field on the **Tags** dashboard of your resources:

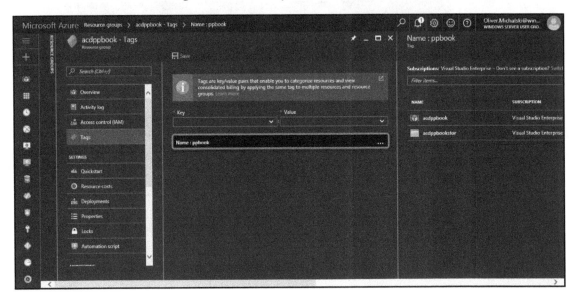

Locking Azure resources

Now you know how to organize your resources, but for working with the resources, there is still another functionality that is important, which I will introduce now.

Azure resource locks

What does this mean? As an administrator, you may need to lock a resource group, or resource to prevent other users from accidentally deleting or modifying critical resources. The Azure resource manager offers a mechanism with two levels (**CanNotDelete** or **ReadOnly**) to be able to make appropriate settings.

Let's take a look at this:

1. In the portal, click on **Resource groups**:

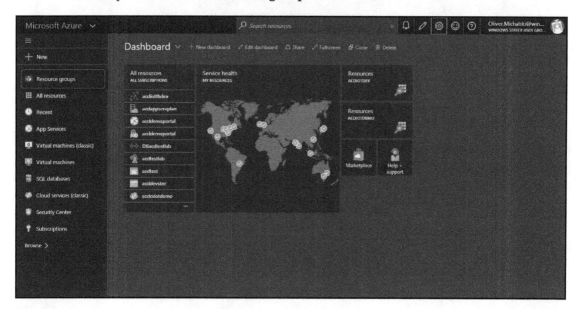

2. On the **Resource groups** blade, click the **acdppbook** name field:

3. In the navigation section on the **Resource groups** dashboard, click on the **Locks** button:

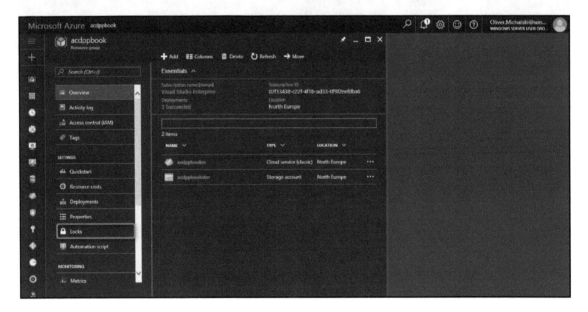

4. On the **Locks** blade, click on the **Add** button:

5. Now type `ppbookdemo` in the **Lock name** textbox, select a **Lock type**, and click on **OK**:

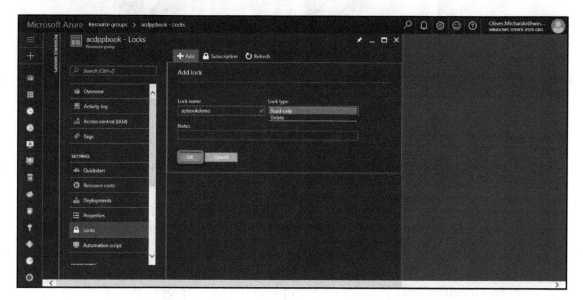

6. Your first lock is ready.

Attention!

I have put in my example **Read-only** as a **Lock type** on **Resource groups**. This lock is automatically inherited to all subordinate resources. This has the consequence, however, that the functionality of individual resource types is no longer guaranteed.

7. For example, no keys can be retrieved for a **Storage account** (this is a read and write operation). The operation is, however, mandatory for access:

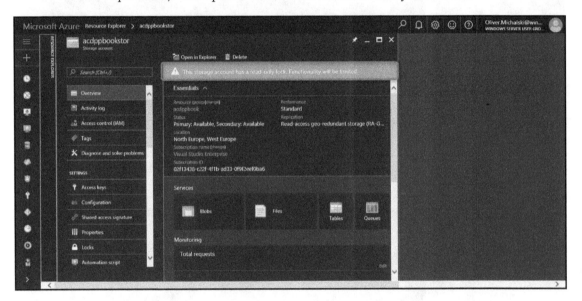

Working with ARM templates

Now we come to the more advanced section of the explanations on the subject of working with the Azure resource manager. The content of this section is also divided into two parts.

In part 1, we consider the issue from the view of an IT professional. IT pros are less interested in developing their own templates but want to reuse their existing deployments in template form.

The corresponding feature in Azure resource manager is to export a deployment as an ARM template. This feature allows you to create templates of your deployment, download the templates to secure them in a source code repository, modifying your templates and of course the redeployment.

Part 2 (from the perspective of the developer) is easier to explain. This section deals with the topic of authoring an ARM template.

Exporting a deployment as an ARM template (for IT pros)

always roll out the same basic configuration in Azure? Then the following procedure, in the future, can make the work easier:

You often realize demos or customer projects and always roll out the same basic configuration in Azure? Then the following procedure, in the future, can make the work easier: Open your Azure management portal at `https://portal.azure.com`.

1. In the portal, click on **Resource groups**:

2. On the **Resource groups** blade, click on the**acdppbook** name field:

Now we will export our deployment to an ARM template.

Example 1: exporting a resource group to an ARM template

other resources. To export a resource group, perform the following steps:

1. The first example is about the export of a complete resource group, that is a resource container and any number of other resources. To export a resource group, perform the following steps: In the navigation section of the Resource groups dashboard, click on Automation script:

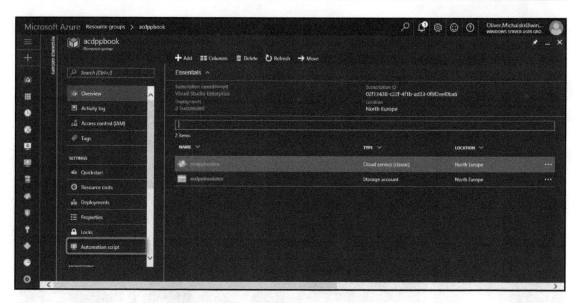

2. Now you can see the resource group template. Click on **Download** to save the template to finalize your work:

3. In addition to the template in the JSON data format, special scripts (or classes) are also provided for Azure CLI, Azure PowerShell, NET, or Ruby. You will see this by pressing one of the links in the navigation area. These scripts help you to deploy the template:

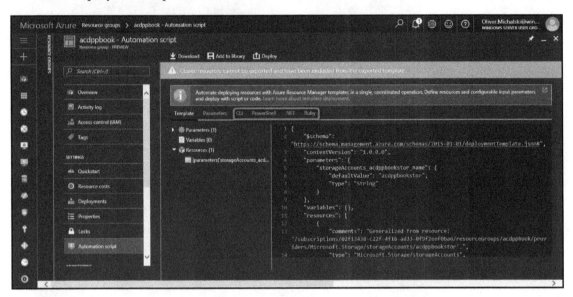

 Not all resource types support the export template function. If your resource group only contains a storage account, a virtual machine, or a virtual network, you will not see an error. However, if you have created other resource types, you may see an error stating that there is a problem with the export.

Example 2: exporting a resource (from the deployment history) to an ARM template

In the second example, we only want to export a single resource (app, database, etc.). For this, we usually use the deployment history list to select the version that works best for us. To export a resource from the deployment history, perform the following steps:

1. Go back to the **Resource group** dashboard for **acdppbook**. In the navigation section, click on **Deployments** or use the link **Deployments**, shown in the field **Essentials**:

2. Select the deployment that you want to export. Click on the field. Now the deployment properties site opens. Click on **View template**:

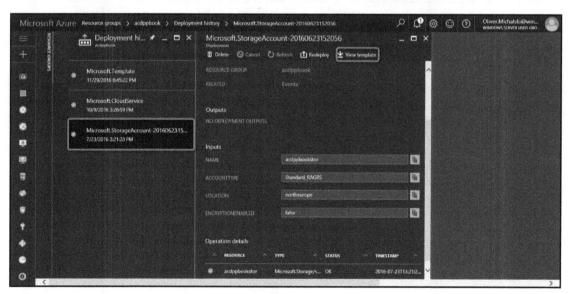

3. Now you can see the resource template. Click on **Download** to save the template to finalize your work:

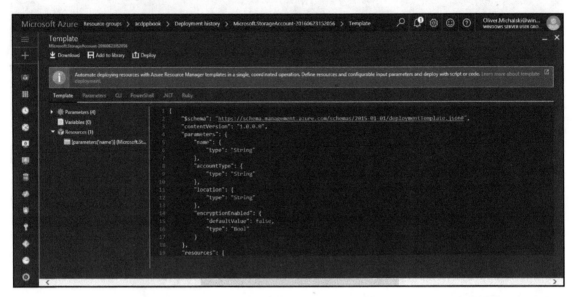

Example 3: exporting a resource (classic) to an ARM template

Also in the third example, we want to export a single resource (app, database, etc.). This time, however, on the so-called classical way. This is different from Example 2 by the fact that only the most recent version of the resource is exportable. To export a resource on the classical way, perform the following steps:

1. Go back to the **Resource groups** dashboard for **acdppbook**. In the resource grid, select the **acdppbookstor** row, and then click the **...** field:

2. On the **Resource** dashboard, click on **Settings**, and then click on **Automation script**:

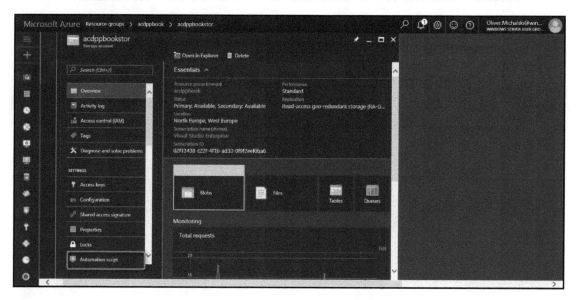

3. Now you can see the resource template. Click on **Download** to save the template to finalize your work:

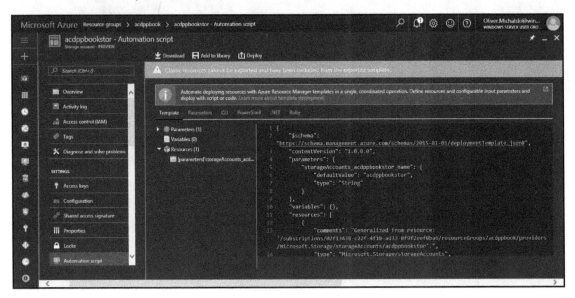

Modifying an ARM template

We have finished the topic of exporting to an ARM template. Now the question arises: what is missing? As I said earlier, the feature supports the ability to redeploy and modify templates. We shall take a look now:

1. Go back to the **Export resource group template** view. Click on **Deploy**:

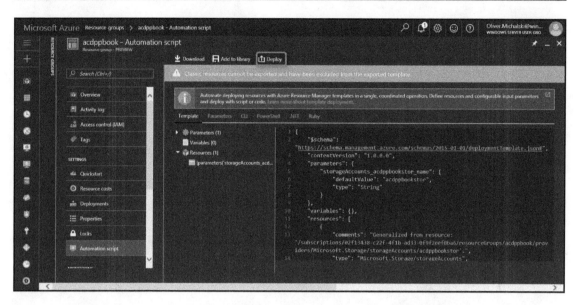

2. Next, the **Custom deployment** blade opens. This time, there is one resource available. To start the working process, you must press the **Edit** button:

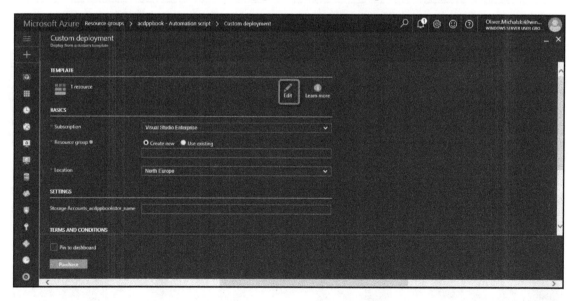

3. The next window is the **Edit template** view. Here you can edit your template directly in the text:

4. You can add another resource to your template (for example, a virtual network to a virtual machine). Click on **Add resource** and then select the desired resource from the list:

5. You can select any resource from the **Select a resource** drop-down list:

6. You can also take a **Quickstart template** as a reference for your work. Click on **Quickstart template** and then select the desired template from the list:

7. You can select any desired quick start template from the **Select a template** drop-down:

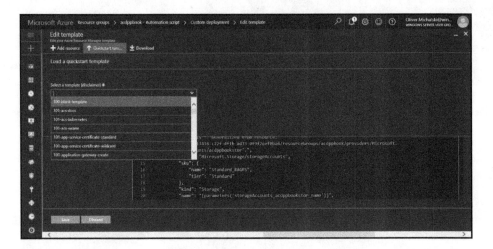

Azure **Quickstart template** are a collection of ARM community templates (with solutions for many workloads) and you can find them here: https://github.com/Azure/azure-quickstart-templates.

8. When everything is ok, press the **Save** button:

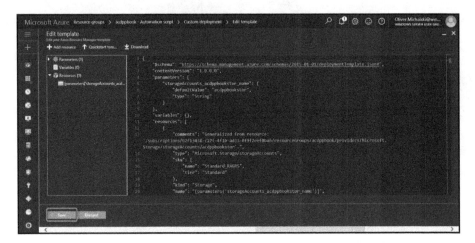

9. We are back in the **Custom deployment** blade. Here you have to make a few final entries. First, define a **Resource group** and a **Location**:

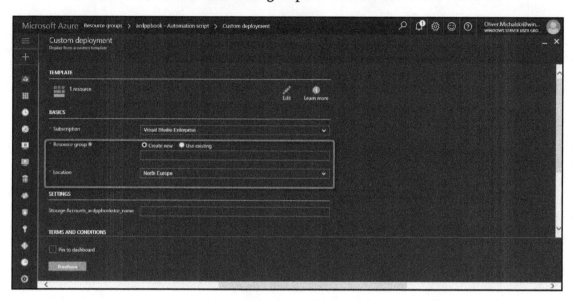

10. In the **SETTINGS** section, you must type a new name for your resource:

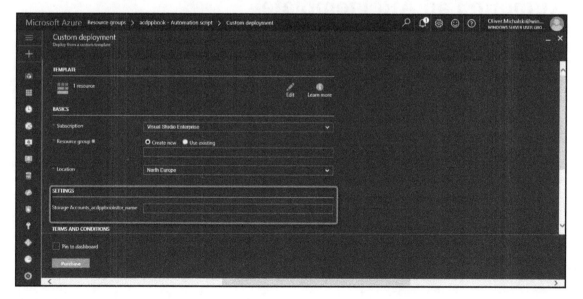

11. Finally, you must accept the**Azure Marketplace Terms**, and then press the **Purchase** button:

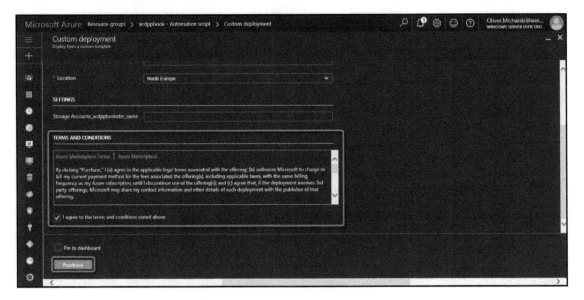

Authoring an ARM template

Before you can create a template, some planning tasks are required:

- What are the types of resources to be provided?
- What are the locations of resources?
- What is the version of the resource provider API used to deploy resources?
- Must some resources be provided for other resources?
- What values should be passed during the deployment, and what values would you define directly in the template?
- Do you need to return values from the deployment?

Once you have answered these questions, you can get started. Ok, at least theoretically, you can start. Before you can start, we should clarify the software requirements.

Because a JSON data file is an XML-based text file, you really need only a simple text editor (for example, Notepad). I recommend you still use Visual Studio (with an excellent JSON editor). To prevent unnecessary expense, the Visual Studio Community edition is sufficient for our purposes completely.

There is still an alternative available - **Azure Resource Manager Template Visualizer (ArmViz)**. With ArmViz, you can create templates with purely graphic means. ArmViz has one weakness, however - it is a preview and only available outside the platform.

Let's take a look at it:

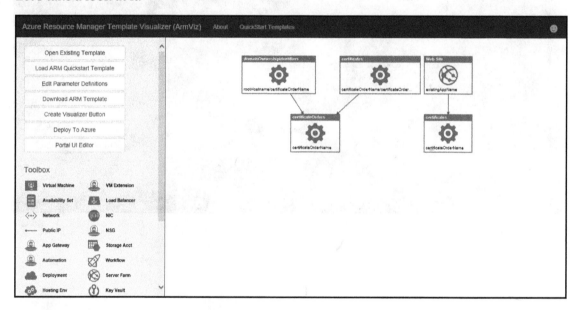

You can find ArmViz at `http://armviz.io/#/`.

Creating your own ARM template (for developers)

To create an ARM template, perform the following steps:

1. Open your Visual Studio, and click on the **New Project...** link:

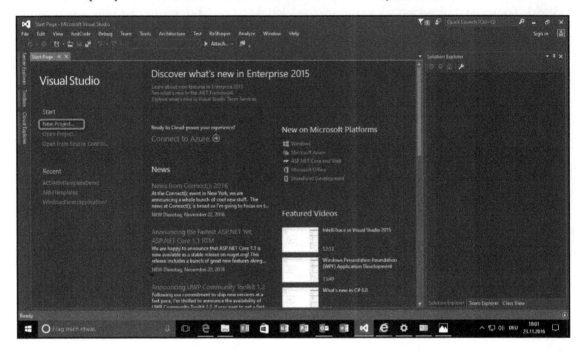

2. Now the selection dialog opens with the available project templates. The required template, **Azure Resource Group**, can be found in the **Cloud** area:

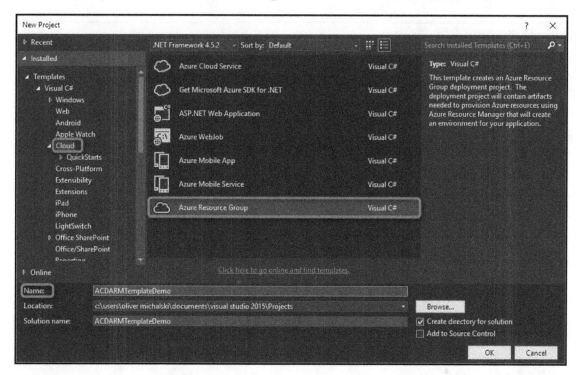

If you do not find the entry there, you have forgotten to install the Azure SDK and Azure VS tooling.

3. If everything is clear, specify a project **Name**, for example, `ARMTemplateDemo`, and press the **OK** button.

4. Now another selection dialog opens, this time with a list of available Azure templates:

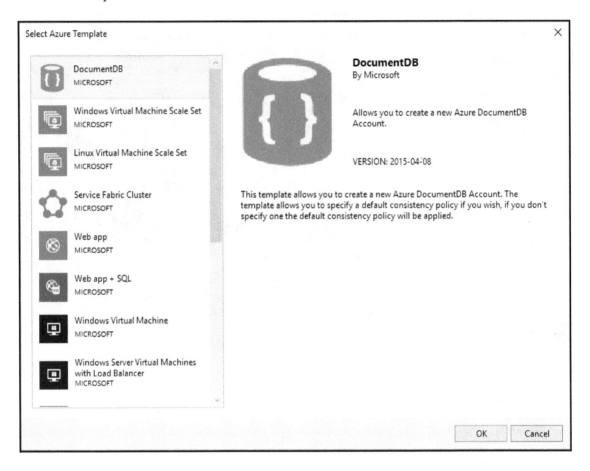

5. The template **Blank Template** that we need for our demo can be found as the last entry in the list. Select the entry and press the **OK** button:

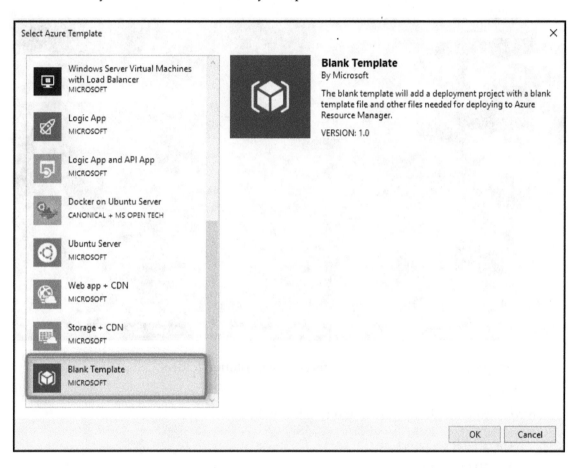

6. Wait briefly until the project has been loaded. You should now see the following screen:

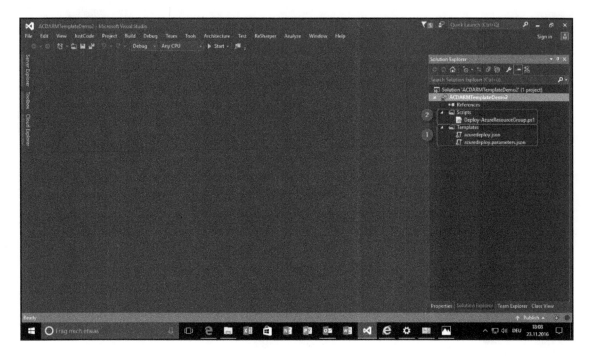

The current project consists of three artifacts in two solution folders, `Templates` and `Scripts`.

In the `Templates` folder, you will find two JSON files:

- `azuredeploy.json`
- `azuredeploy.parameters.json`

`azuredeploy.json` is the template for the real template and `azuredeploy.parameters.json` is used as a store for the required parameter values. The name `azuredeploy` you can change in any way. but the endings `.json` and `.parameters.json` must be maintained. In the Scripts folder, you will find a PowerShell script that will help you to perform the final deployment..

Let's have a look at `azuredeploy.json`:

```json
{
    "$schema":
"http://schema.management.azure.com/schemas/2015-01-01/deploymentTemplate.json#",
    "contentVersion": "1.0.0.0",
    "parameters": {},
    "variables": {},
    "resources": [],
    "outputs": {}
}
```

This is the simplest form of an ARM template but I should like to point out that in this form, the template is not valid and cannot be executed.

Here is the reason, some of these fields are required and others are optional. The following table shows whether a field should be filled in:

Field	Required
$schema	Yes
contentVersion	Yes
parameters	No
variables	No
resources	Yes
output	No

As you can see, the fields `$schema`, `contentVersion`, and `resources` need to be filled in. For the fields `$schema` and `contentVersion`, you can continue to use the pre-enclosed values, so you must add at least one resource.

Now let's add a resource. Once again, I chose a storage account as the resource type. The relevant section in the `azuredeploy.json` file looks like this:

```json
"resources": [
  {
    "type": "Microsoft.Storage/storageAccounts",
    "name": "[parameters('storageAccountName')]",
    "apiVersion": "2015-06-15",
    "location": "[resourceGroup().location]",
    "properties": {
      "accountType": "Standard_LRS"
    }
```

```
    }
  ]
```

There's one thing I need to point out: the use of parameters is not necessary but without parameters, your template would always deploy the same resources with the same names, locations, and properties.

In order to avoid this situation, in the presented code segment, a parameter for the resource name is used.

For the parameters, we have to provide the corresponding definition. The relevant section in the azuredeploy.json file looks like this:

```
"parameters": {
    "storageAccountName": {
        "type": "string",
        "metadata": {
            "description": "Storage Account Name"
        }
    }
}
```

The template is now ready, valid, and executable. The complete code for azuredeploy.json looks like this:

```
{
    "$schema":
"https://schema.management.azure.com/schemas/2015-01-01/deploymentTemplate.
json#",
    "contentVersion": "1.0.0.0",
    "parameters": {
        "storageAccountName": {
            "type": "string",
            "metadata": {
                "description": "Storage Account Name"
            }
        }
    },
    "resources": [
        {
            "type": "Microsoft.Storage/storageAccounts",
            "name": "[parameters('storageAccountName')]",
            "apiVersion": "2015-06-15",
            "location": "[resourceGroup().location]",
            "properties": {
                "accountType": "Standard_LRS"
            }
```

```
        }
    ]
}
```

Azure resource explorer

The authoring of an ARM template is a difficult process. Especially when it comes to the individual components of the template and the use of valid values, many users have an information gap. But also for this problem, there is a solution on the Azure platform: the Azure resource explorer.

The Azure resource explorer is a tool for looking at your resources or at the resources of the Azure platform. By using this tool, you can see how the resources are structured, and it enables you to view the properties for resources.

How can I find the Azure resource explorer?

1. Open your Azure management portal at `https://portal.azure.com`.
2. In the portal, click on **More services**, scroll down the list, and then click the **Resource Explorer** button:

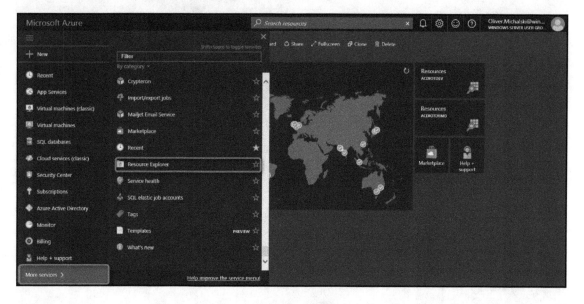

3. In **Resource Explorer**, you can find two nodes:

- **Providers** (the resources from the Azure platform itself)
- **Subscriptions** (your resources):

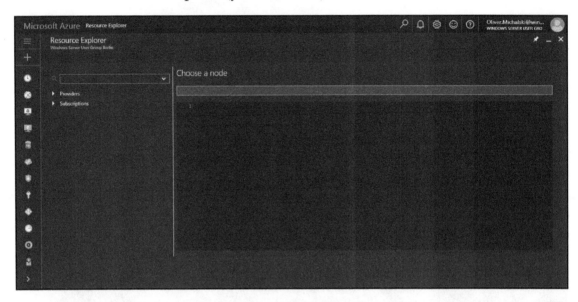

4. By clicking the nodes, you can search for the information you want:

Summary

In this chapter, we learned all about the Azure resource manager and therefore the basics for implementing Azure solutions.

In the first part of this chapter, we saw the creation of an Azure resource group, how to add resources to this group, and last but not least, how to organize the work with the resources in this group.

In the second part of this chapter, there followed detailed information for developers and IT professionals.

In the following chapters, we will use this knowledge and deal with the concrete implementation.

3
Deploying and Synchronizing Azure Active Directory

As the quantity of cloud services increase, identity management and security as well as access policies within cloud environments and cloud services is becoming even more essential and important.

The Microsoft central instance for this is Azure Active Directory. Every security policy or identity Microsoft provides for their cloud services is based on Azure Active Directory.

Within this chapter, you will learn the basics about Azure Active Directory, how you implement Azure AD and hybrid Azure Active Directory with connection to Active Directory Domain Services.

We are going to explore the following topics:

- Azure Active Directory overview
- Azure Active Directory subscription options
- Azure Active Directory deployment
- Azure Active Directory user and subscription management
- How to deploy Azure Active Directory hybrid identities with Active Directory Domain Services
- Azure Active Directory hybrid high availability and non-high availability deployments

Azure Active Directory

Azure Active Directory or Azure AD a multi-tenant cloud based directory and identity management service developed by Microsoft.

Azure AD also includes a full suite of identity management capabilities including:

- Multi-factor authentication
- Device registration
- Self-service password management
- Self-service group management
- Privileged account management
- Role based access control
- Application usage monitoring
- Rich auditing
- Security monitoring and alerting

Azure AD can be integrated with an existing Windows Server Active Directory, giving organizations the ability to leverage their existing on-premises identities to manage access to cloud based SaaS applications. An organization is also able to easy implement Single Sign-On an multi factor authentication through Azure AD without adding third party software into their environment.

After this chapter you will know how to setup Azure AD and Azure Connect. You will also able to design a high available infrastructure for identity replication.

The following figure describes the general structure of Azure AD in a hybrid deployment with Active Directory Domain Services.

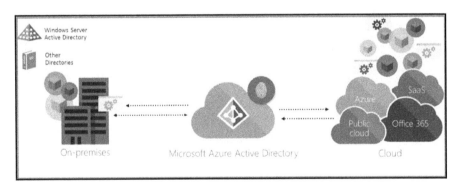

Source: https://docs.microsoft.com/en-us/azure/active-directory/active-directory-hybrid-identity-design-considerations-overview

Customers using different Microsoft services like Office 365, CRM online, or Intune are already using Azure AD for their service. You can easily identify if you use Azure AD if you have a username like `user@domain.onmicrosoft.com`. Other top-level-domains like `.de` or `.cn` are also possible if you are using Microsoft Cloud Germany or Azure China.

Azure AD is a multi-tenant, Geo-distributed, high availability service running in every Microsoft data center around the world. Microsoft has implemented automated failover with a minimum of two copies of your Azure Directory Service in other regional or global data centers.

Your directory is running in your primary data center, is regularly replicated into another two in your region. If you only have two Azure data centers in your region, as in Europe, the copy will distribute to another data center in another region:

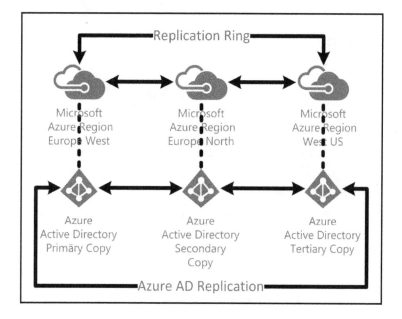

Azure Active Directory options

There are currently three selectable options for Azure Active Directory with different features to use. There will be a fourth option, **Azure Active Directory premium P2** available since late 2016.

Azure AD free

Azure AD free supports common features such as:

- Up to 5,00,000 directory objects which could be user, devices, applications, or groups
- User/group management (add/update/delete), user-based provisioning and device registration
- **Single Sign-On (SSO)** for up to ten applications per user
- Self-service password change for the cloud users
- Connect and sync with on-premises Active Directory Domain Services
- Up to three basic security and usage reports

Azure AD basic

This supports all the common features from free Azure AD and more, such as:

- Same features like free and additional Group-based access management/provisioning
- Self-service password reset for the cloud users
- Company branding (logon pages / access panel customization)
- Application proxy
- Service level agreement 99.9%

Azure AD premium P1

Supports common features from free and basic Azure AD such as:

- Group-based access management/provisioning
- Self-service password reset for the cloud users
- Company branding (logon pages / access panel customization)
- Application proxy
- Service level agreement 99.9%

Premium features such as:

- Self-service group and app management / self-service application additions / dynamic groups
- Self-service password reset/change/unlock with on-premises write-back
- Multi-factor authentication (cloud and on-premises (MFA server))
- MIM CAL plus MIM server
- Cloud app discovery
- Connect health
- Automatic password rollover for group accounts

Since Q3/2016 Microsoft has also enabled customers to use the Azure Active Directory P2 plan, which includes all the capabilities in Azure AD premium P1 as well as the new **Identity Protection** and **Privileged Identity Management** capabilities. This was an important step for Microsoft to extend its offering for Windows 10 Device Management with Azure AD.

Currently Azure AD enable Windows 10 customers to join a device to Azure AD, implement SSO for desktops, Microsoft passport for Azure AD, and central administrator BitLocker recovery.

Depending on what you plan to do with your Azure environment, you should choose your Azure Active Directory option.

Deploying a custom Azure AD

To understand how you deploy an Azure Active Directory you need to understand that Azure Active Directory is directly connected to your Azure subscription. So, the Azure accountsubscription administration is always the first service administrator for your Azure environment. There can only be one account administrator per Azure subscription. The account administrator is the only one who can manage Azure AD and subscription connections. If you lose your administrator credentials or lose access to the administrator account, you can no longer manage your subscription.

You should therefore plan who will create your subscription and which account is the account administrator. To create a subscription, the subscription administrator must have a Microsoft Accounts or former named Live ID or Microsoft Account, Azure Active Directory account. This can be created, for example, via Office 365 before adding Azure agreements and subscription payments or could be an account created and synchronized via the Active Directory Domain Service to Azure. What you shouldn't do is to use a personal account of an employee to function as an account administrator and Global Azure Administrator. If there is any change with that employee, you could lose Azure AD access. In any case, you should work with group accounts or service accounts, so that a minimum of two people are able to access the subscription.

Normally an Azure Active Directory is created when you create an Azure subscription or you subscribe to a Microsoft Cloud service like Office 365.

As an Azure account administrator you can create a new Azure AD and change your Azure subscription to the new Azure AD.

Let's begin by creating an Azure AD:

1. First you need to log in to `https://manage.windowsazure.com/`:

Currently Microsoft offers two portals: `https://manage.windowsazure.com` which represents the old deployment engine based on **Microsoft Service Manager**; and the modern portal `https://portal.microsoft.com`, which is based on the Microsoft resource manager engine and should be the preferred portal. As soon as all service are migrated to resource manager engine, the old portal will be disabled.

2. Navigate to Azure **ACTIVE DIRECTORY** on the lower left site of the navigation bar.

3. When you click on it, you see the Azure AD which are already deployed. With a fresh subscription, you normally see the **Default Directory**. What you also see is the **DATACENTER REGION** where your directory is deployed, and which region your subscription is in:

4. To create a new directory, you need to click on **NEW** in the lower left corner and navigate as shown in the following screenshot:

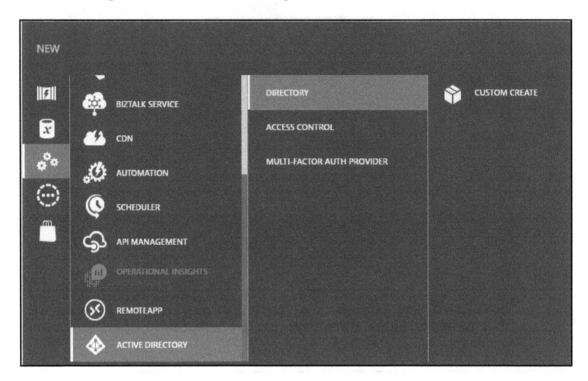

5. Click on **CUSTOM CREATE** to start the wizard that will show guide you through the installation. Within the wizard you will define the **DIRECTORY**, **NAME** and **COUNTRY OR REGION** for your Active Directory. Every Azure AD name is unique, so you cannot create one which is already in use:

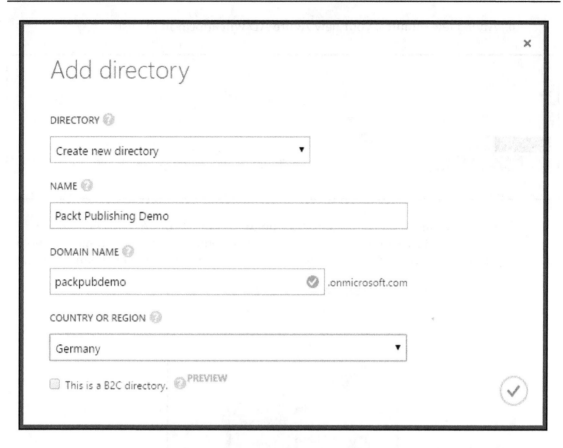

Microsoft also added the option to use a business to customer Azure Active Directory. Azure Active Directory B2C is a cloud identity management solution for your consumer-facing web and mobile applications.

You can find more information in the Azure Documentation: `https://docs.microsoft.com/en-us/azure/active-directory-b2c/active-directory-b2c-overview`.

6. After a few minutes, your new Azure AD will appear in the list:

7. Now you can change your subscription to the new Azure Active Directory and you can add co-administrators, who can also connect to Azure and manage your resources. You need to navigate to **SETTINGS** on the left lower site in the menu:

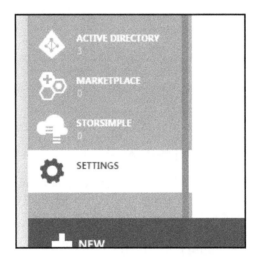

In this menu, you can select the **SUBSCRIPTIONS** which should be changed to the new Azure AD.

8. In the lower half of the page you see the **EDIT DIRECTORY** button:

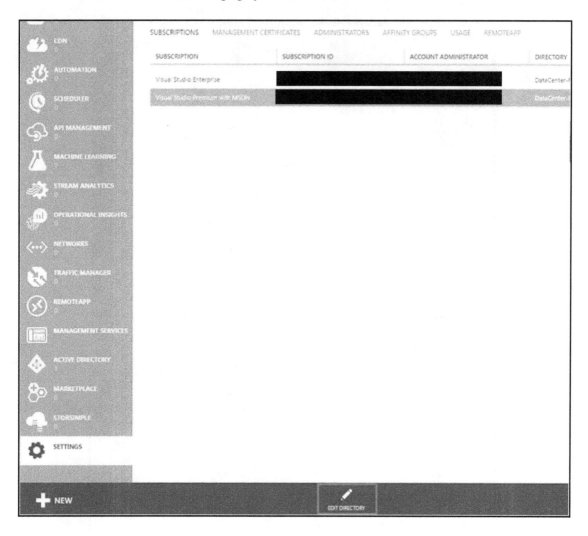

9. Within the upcoming wizard, you can change the **DIRECTORY**:

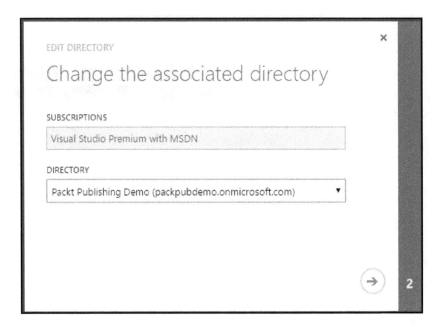

10. And confirm the directory mapping:

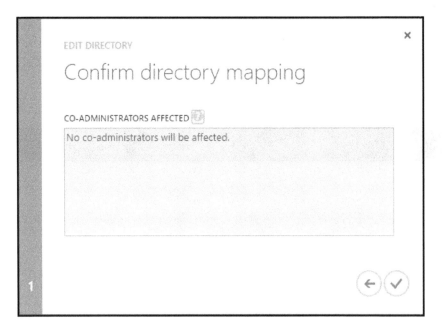

TIP

After you agreed that the directory is mapped to the new subscription all Co-Admins will be removed and you can use the subscription within the new Azure AD.

11. If you wish or need to add additional administrators on your subscription, you need to navigate to **ADMINISTRATORS**:

12. There you can **ADD**, **EDIT** or **REMOVE** additional administrators to within the subscription:

13. You can add the following account types as co-administrators:

- Microsoft Accounts or Live IDs
- Azure Active Directory accounts within that subscription

Adding accounts and groups to Azure AD

First you need to understand what accounts can be added to Azure AD. Basically there are two types of accounts:

- **Cloud accounts**: Accounts that are created via Azure Active Directory or other Microsoft Cloud services, like Office 365.
- **Hybrid accounts**: Accounts that are created and located in on-premises Microsoft Active Directory Domain Services. Those accounts are deployed via the Azure Active Directory connect and synchronization tool.

To create cloud accounts, you have several options. Most Azure AD users start with **Office 365** and do not natively add users via Azure. If you've used **Office 365** before, that would be the simplest for you.

The example shown in the following screenshot guides you how to add a user from the **Office 365** preview portal via `https://portal.office.com`:

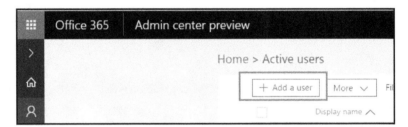

Alternatively, to create new users in Azure AD via the Azure Portal you need to follow these steps:

1. Visit the `https://manage.windowsazure.com/` Azure Portal.

2. Scroll down to Azure Active Directory and select the AD where you want to create the user:

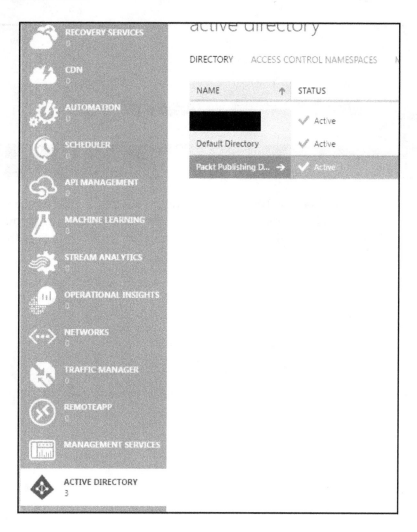

3. In the menus for **USERS** and **GROUPS** you can add new users or groups to your Azure AD:

Users can have different roles and access to applications or parts of Azure via **Microsoft Azure Resource Manager Security** and **Access Roles**. You will get more detail on the security features within the following chapters.

4. By August 2016 Microsoft started to migrate all Azure AD Service into Azure resource manager engine. So, you will need to become familiar with the new interface. Browse to `https://portal.azure.com`:

5. Click on**More services** on the sidebar and look for**Azure Active Directory**:

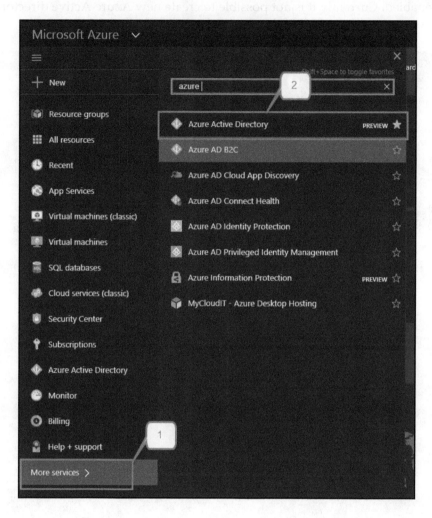

6. The new **Azure Active Directory** interface does not yet have all the features enabled. Currently it is not possible to create new Azure Active directories but you can perform most of the user and application operations:

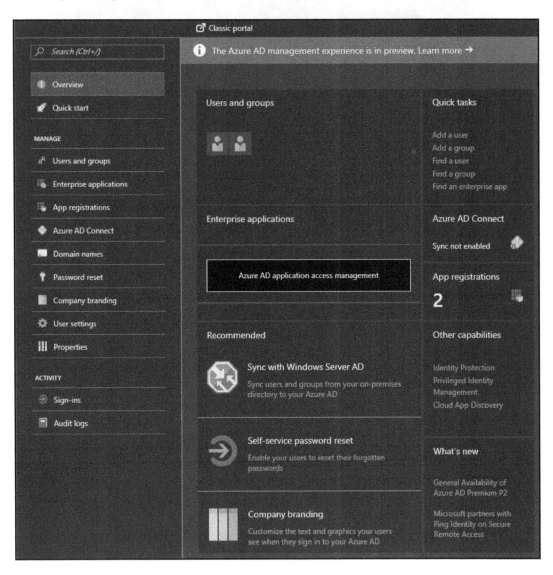

7. In addition to the new portal Microsoft also extended the user management to the **Azure AD management** portal. While writing the book the new user and group management is still in preview, so changes are still possible. To add or change user accounts, you now have different opportunities. The first one would be to open user and group management via Azure Active Directory interface:

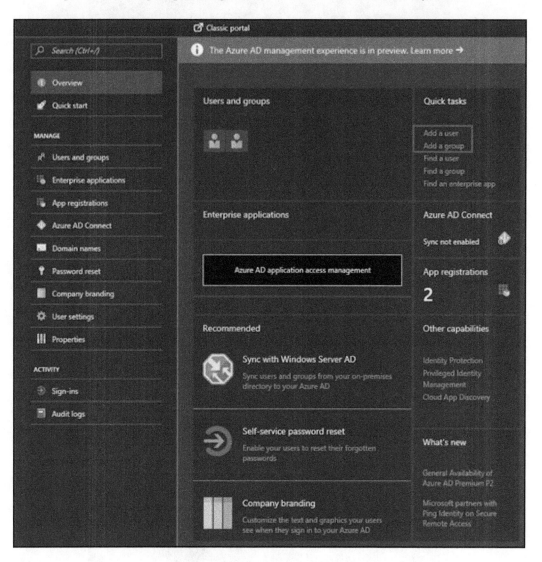

8. Or look for **Users and groups** with the Microsoft resources:

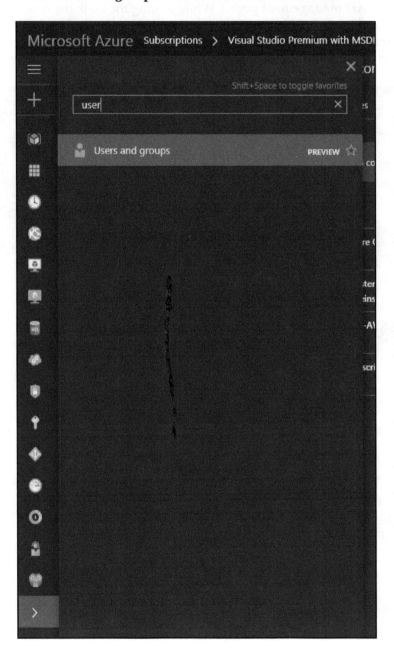

9. Both ways will bring you to the same blade with options to create **Users and groups**:

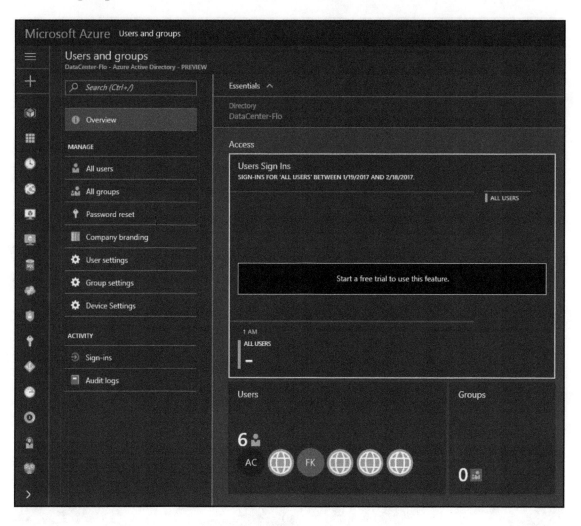

10. To add a user within the new UI, you click on **All users** as shown in the following screenshot:

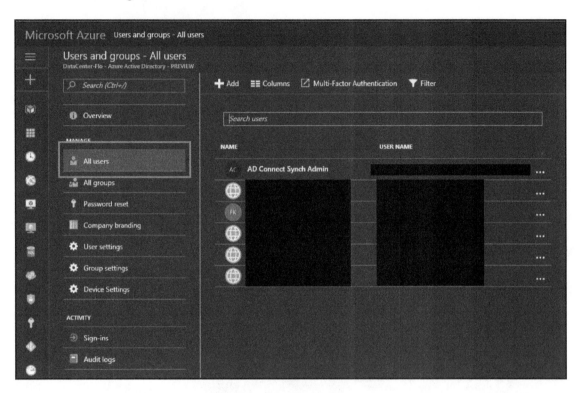

11. There you click on**Add** and follow the instructions shown in the following screenshot:

12. The blade will ask you to provide a username, as shown here:

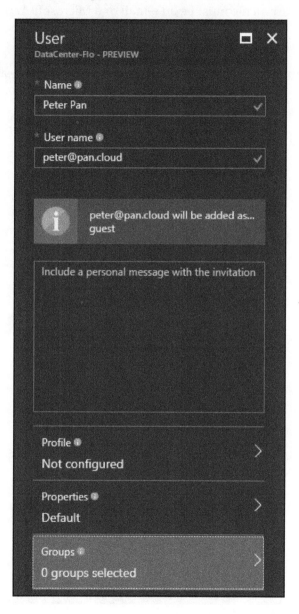

Please be aware that with Azure AD free without Office 365 the username must be an e-mail or a Microsoft Account (former Microsoft Live account) to be able to receive the invitation for Azure AD.

13. While creating the user, you have different options for pre-staging information about the user, including **First name**, **Last name**, **Job title** or **Department**:

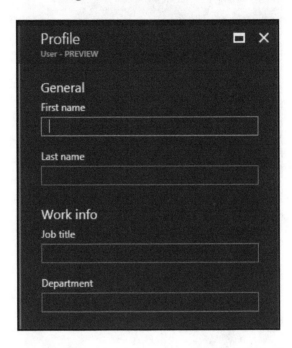

14. With a synced Active Directory Domain Service and other joined services, you can change the **Source of Authority**:

15. You can also join the account directly to Azure AD **Groups** during creation:

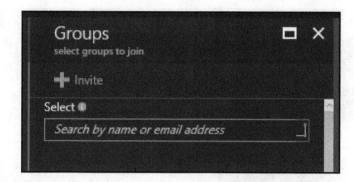

16. The new UI for Azure AD included a new option to join users as account admins (formerly know as co-administrators). To do this, change the admin rights of the user by clicking on the relevant user to open the user blade:

17. Then, click on **Directory role** to open the role options:

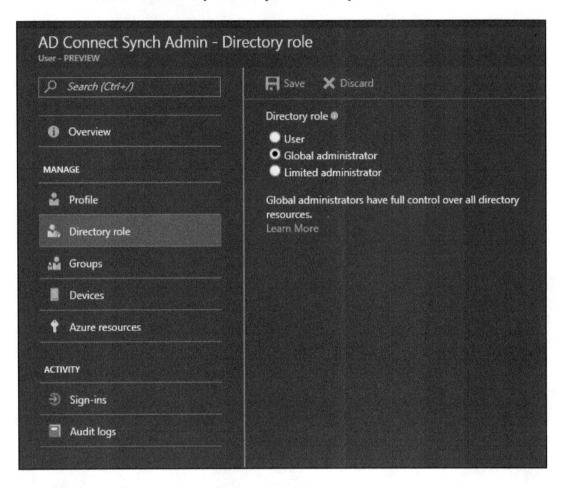

18. Not every user needs to be **Global administrator** to be able to fulfill his job. Mostly, one of or more of the options of a **Limited administrator** should be enough.

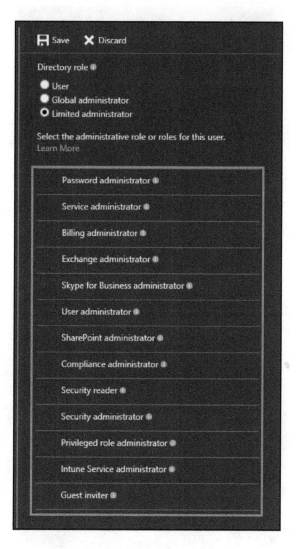

19. After you add the user to his admin role, you need to go to **Subscriptions** within the Azure resources:

20. There you select the **Subscriptions** for which the user should be the co-administrator:

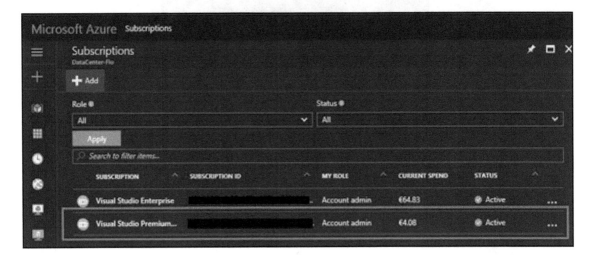

21. In the following blade, you click on **Access control (IAM)** and then on **Add**:

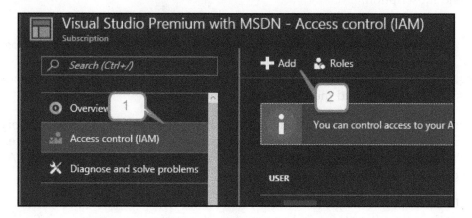

22. Now **Select a role** for the user. To make him a co-administrator, we need to give him **Owner** rights:

As an **Owner**, he has full access to the subscription resources, which would enable him to do all operations that need to be done on a subscription. As a **Reader**, he can see billing and resources of a subscription but not change things inside the subscription. That is the option most billing tools like **Cloud Cruiser** or **Azure Costs** need to create their statistics.

23. can now manage the subscription:

Next, select the user or group which should have the permissions. This user can now manage the subscription:

 You can also invite Microsoft Accounts to your subscription without creating a user first. When it comes to best practice or how it would be done in the field, you wouldn't add any single accounts into the subscription. You should give permission on the subscription or resource to a group, and then add users to the group.

The other option to create new users and groups, is to sync them via Active Directory Domain Service from your connected on-premises Active Directory Domain Service. To do this, you'll need an additional tool named Azure Active Directory Connect, Azure AD Connect or short AAD Connect.

Azure AD Connect will integrate your on-premises directories with **Azure Active Directory**. This allows you to provide a common identity for your users for Office 365, Azure, and SaaS applications integrated with Azure AD:

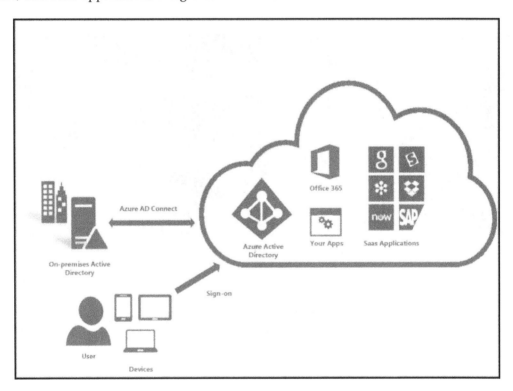

Source: https://azure.microsoft.com/en-us/documentation/articles/active-directory-aadconnect/

Azure AD Connect is the central tool to implement hybrid identities in Azure which enables you to license your software or implement identity and access management like Single Sign-On, Multi-factor authentication or the AD Rights Management Service.

Azure AD Connect brings five programs with different purposes for Azure AD Connect:

- **Azure AD Connect**: Azure AD Connect is the configuration tool with an integrated and detailed wizard to configure Azure AD and on-premises Active Directory Domains Services synchronization.
- **Synchronization Rule Editor**: Is a basic tool to configure and customize synchronizations between Azure AD and on-premises Active Directory Domains Services:

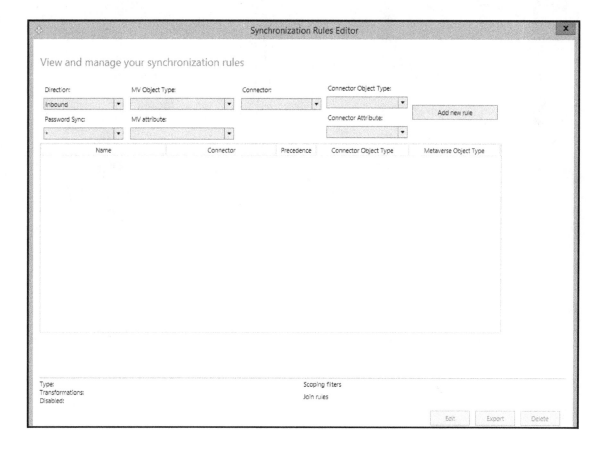

- **Synchronization Service**: The **Synchronization Service** is a tool to basically monitors and logs the synchronization between Azure AD and on-premises Active Directory Domains Services. You can supervise the synchronization process:

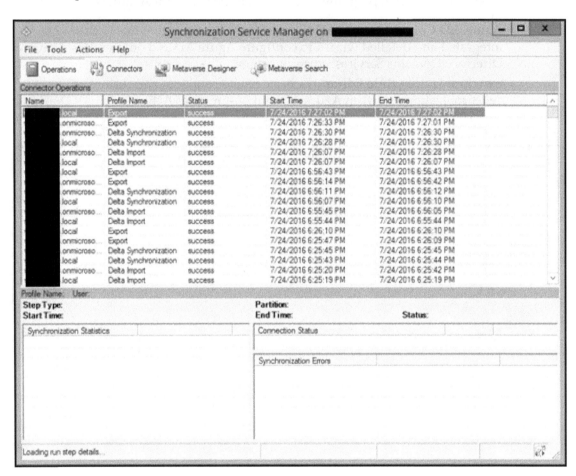

- **Synchronization Service Key Manager**: Helps to manage security keys to encrypt data transferred between Azure AD and on-premises Active Directory Domains Service:

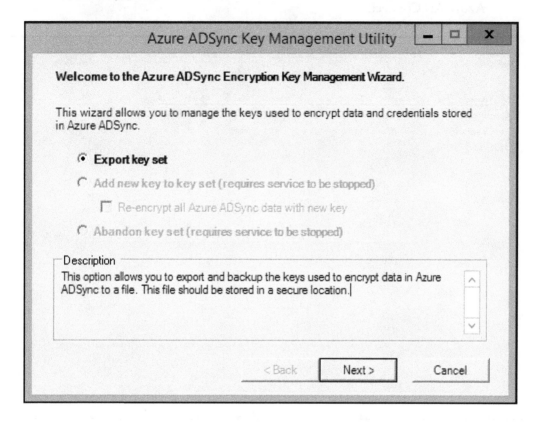

- **Synchronization Service Web Service Configuration Manager**: This came with the version 1.1.189.0 from Azure Active Directory Connect in June 2016. It is used to configure **Microsoft Account Entity Management** (**MIM**) endpoints with Azure AD Connect:

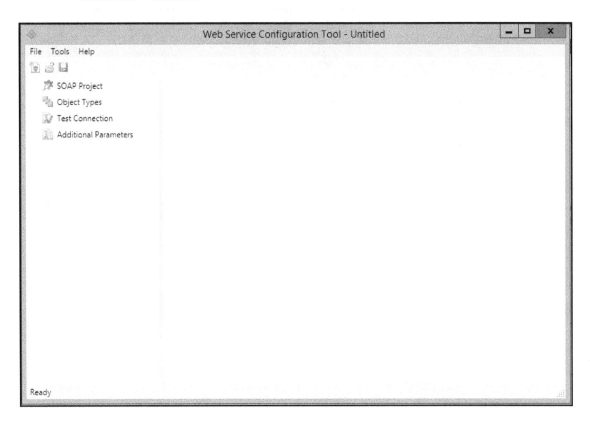

Azure AD Connect and all components are freely available and can be downloaded from Microsoft:
`https://www.microsoft.com/en-us/download/details.aspx?id=47594.`

You can deploy Azure AD Connect in three different ways for the users. Each method gives different kinds of integration levels and is more or less dependent to your Azure AD subscription level:

The first solution is to use **Password Synchronization**. This option transfers user passwords as hashed values to the cloud. The option is also that one which enables the basic Single Sign-On option for your users to Azure AD-based applications in your organization. The password synchronization is only based on user account and password replication. So changes within Azure AD will take some time or be manual. This option is also only practical for small environments with less than 300 users. For larger environments, you would have too much replication traffic and too many changes within Azure AD, which would take too long. As an example, a replication of around 4,000 users could take up to 12 hours before it is visible in the Azure AD:

The following screenshot shows you the tooltip you get when you hover over the question mark at **PASSWORD SYNCHRONIZATION**:

The second option is to select the new **PASS-THROUGH AUTHENTICATION**. With this option, your AD Connect and Azure AD will not store any identity data, and they will send all requests directly to your environment.

The following screenshot shows you the tooltip you get when you hover over the question mark at **PASS-THROUGH AUTHENTICATION**:

The third and most complex solution is to implement an **Active Directory Federation Services** (**ADFS** or **AD FS**) with Azure AD, in the interface named federation with AD FS. That will enable full Single Sign-On and add multifactor authentication. The organizations and implementations. If you want to implement ADFS you need also to have Public and Private Key infrastructure and certificates from a trusted agency in place. For ADFS you need good response times so you might need to upgrade your Internet access and/or wide area network connectivity.

The following screenshot shows you the tooltip you get when you hover over the question mark at **Federation with AD FS**:

The fourth and easiest way is to not configure user sign-in. This option enables only license and user replication from local to cloud and vice versa. There is no option to replicate passwords, and your users will not be able to sign in or use Azure AD resources. Users would be able to use, for example, Office 365 or Azure remote app.

The following screenshot shows you the tooltip you get when you hover over the question mark at **DO NOT CONFIGURE**:

DO NOT CONFIGURE

This option allows your users to do federated sign in using a solution not managed by this wizard.
While logged in to the corporate network, your users can access cloud resources without entering their passwords again.

With the new enhancements in Windows 10 and with Azure AD, you can now also configure Single Sign-On directly from your on-premises Windows systems. To enable this feature, you need to mark **Enable single sign on**:

Single sign on

This option enables users on the corporate network to get a single sign on experience when accessing cloud services from their domain joined desktop machines.

Installing Azure AD Connect - prerequisites

For those who haven't worked with AD FS before, Federations offer a standard-based service that allows the secure sharing of identity information between trusted business partners (known as a **federation**) across an extranet. When a user needs to access a web application from one of its federation partners, the user's own organization is responsible for authenticating the user and providing identity information in the form of *claims* to the partner that hosts the web application. The hosting partner uses its trust policy to map the incoming claims to claims that are understood by its web application, which uses the claims to make authorization decisions. So, basically Azure AD and Microsoft become your business partner in AD FS.

From a planning perspective, the following prerequisites must be in place:

- An Azure subscription or an Azure trial subscription-this is only required for accessing the Azure Portal and not for using Azure AD Connect. If you are using Azure PowerShell or Office 365 you do not need an Azure subscription to use Azure AD Connect.
- An Azure AD global administrator account for the Azure AD tenant you wish to integrate with.
- An AD Domain Controller or member server with Windows Server 2008 or newer (see the following for the appropriate sizing for that machine)

The Domain Controller or member server you will be using as the Azure AD Connect machine in your environment must meet the following minimum specifications:

Number of objects in AD	CPU	Memory	Hard drive size
Fewer than 10,000	1.6 GHz	4 GB	70 GB
10,000 to 50,000	1.6 GHz	4 GB	70 GB
50,000 to 100,000	1.6 GHz	16 GB	100 GB
For 100,000 or more objects the full version of SQL Server is required otherwise Windows internal database or SQL Express can be used.			
100,000 to 300,000	1.6 GHz	32 GB	300 GB
300,000 to 600,000	1.6 GHz	32 GB	450 GB
More than 600,000	1.6 GHz	32 GB	500 GB

First before you start the installation of the AD Connect you need to configure two user accounts. The first one should be a service account with enterprise admin rights or for subdomains with domain admin rights within your on-premises Active Directory Domain Service. The other one must be a global administrator in Azure Active Directory.

The following screenshot shows you the **User** settings you need for the Azure AD `synch` administrator:

These two accounts will perform actions on both directories. So, the on-premises user won't have access to Azure AD, and the Azure AD admin won't have access to the on-premises AD:

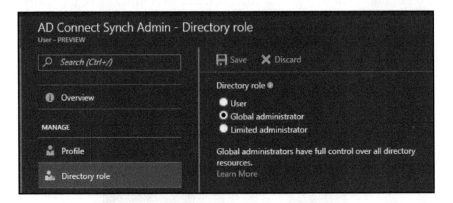

The following diagram shows you the basic workflow behind the communication from Azure AD, AD Connect and on-premises Active Directory Domain Service:

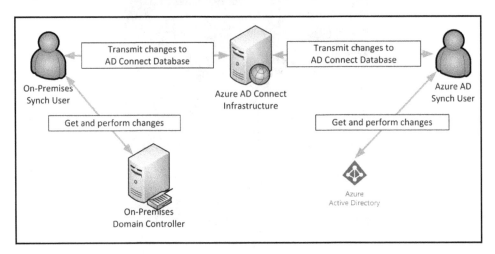

After you choose which type of user sign-on you want to use for your Azure AD users implementation, the wizard changes and adds or removes configuration options. For the ADFS implementation you need to perform some more steps to get the federation running. For the ADFS implementation, you will need at least one **ADFS Server** and one **ADFS Proxy** additionally as well as additional service accounts. The connection will work automatically based on **Windows Remote Management (WinRM)**. As explained earlier, the Azure AD will authenticate against your on-premises ADFS implementation.

The following diagram reflects the more complex environment:

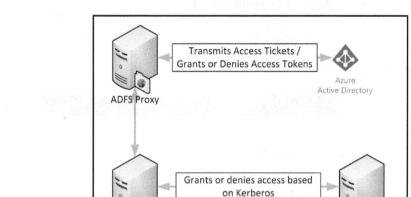

Installing basic Azure AD Connect environment

As an example, I will show you how to implement Azure AD Connect with password synchronization. The other options for the setup are similar:

1. First you need to download **Azure AD Connect**. Within the setup you will have to do the configurations for the synchronization but you can redo your setup by looking for **Azure AD Connect** in the Windows Start menu:

To be aware, your AD Connect Server must be joined to the on-premises Active Directory Domain.

2. Accept the license terms and click on **Continue**:

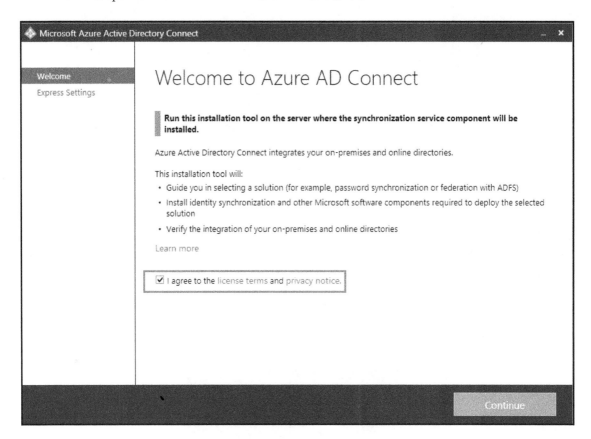

3. Choose **Customize** to continue:

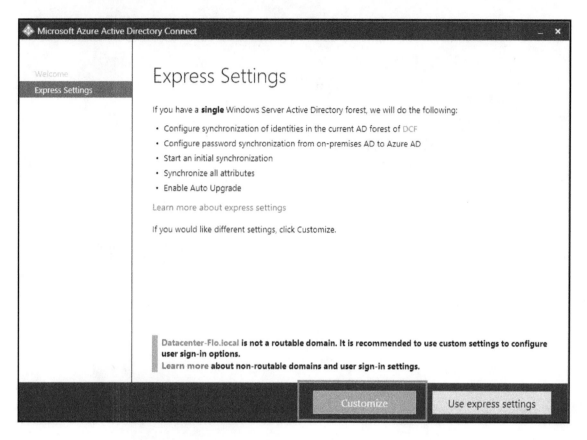

4. Choose **Password Synchronization** and click on **Next**:

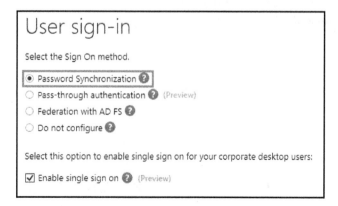

5. In the next window enter the credentials of your Azure AD `synch` account:

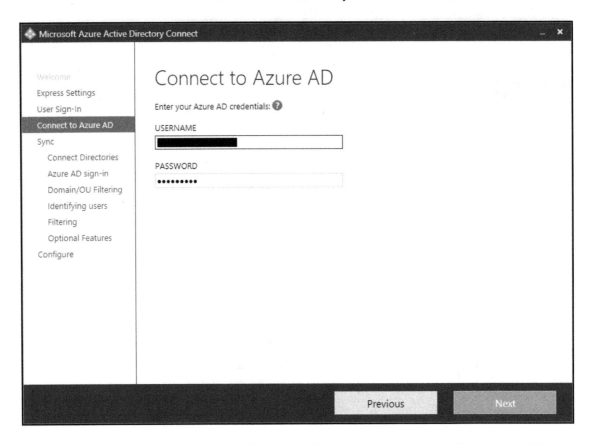

6. On many websites and also Microsoft documentations you will find terms like **DirSync** and AD **Sync**. Both are out of support since Azure AD Connect reached production state. Please visit this website for more information `http://blog.azureandbeyond.com/2017/04/06/dirsync-azure-ad-sync-end-of-support/?fb_action_ids=1199177306847421&fb_action_types=news.publishes` .

7. Next, you need to add your on-premises administrator account:

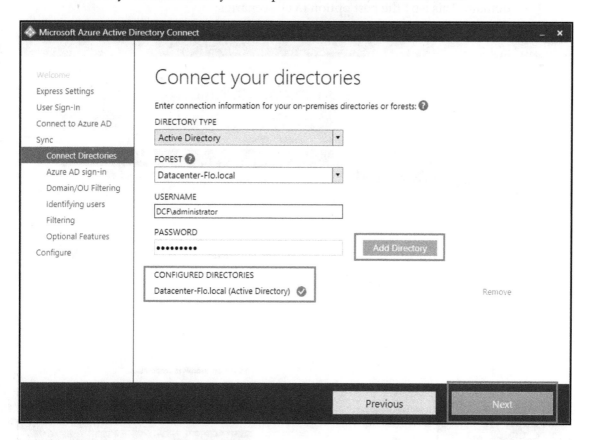

For multi domain forest Active Directory infrastructures, your admin account on-premises need to be an *enterprise administrator*. If you only have a single domain forest, you can use a regular domain admin.

8. For the next step, you need to select the attribute in your on-premises domain which identifies the **User Principal Name** (**UPN**) in the Azure AD.

The UPN is an Internet-style login name for a user based on the Internet standard RFC 822.

9. Microsoft best practice is to select the user principal name of your on-premises domain. This isn't the best option in all scenarios:

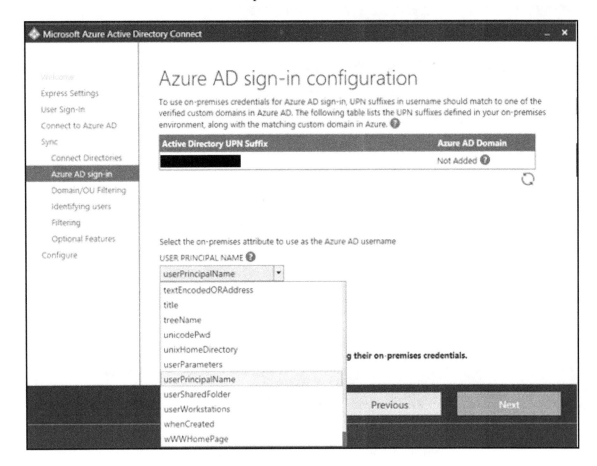

Just from the field, it is not always helpful to choose the user principal. Depending on the domain, sometimes it is better to choose the e-mail instead of the user principal name in Azure AD. That's because the primary e-mail in a synced scenario is always the login name. So, if your login name is @company.onmicrosoft.com the primary e-mail would become this domain too.

10. The following diagram shows you an example for a decision path, when to choose UPN and when an e-mail address. It's very basic but helps in most cases:

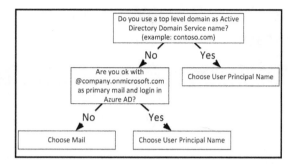

11. After you select which attribute that will be your identifier, you need to set the AD filter. It isn't recommended to parse the whole ADDS for synchronization, because that would take a lot of time, unless you have a large on-premises Active Directory. For faster synchronization, it is recommended to select only a subset of the on-premises Active Directory objects; for example, select only the **organizational units** or **OUs** that contains the requested objects:

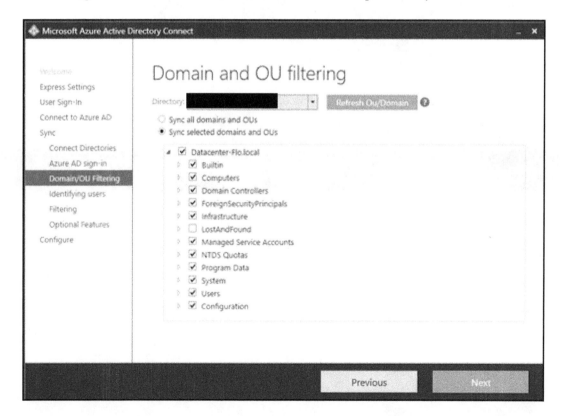

12. Now choose how your users should be identified over your domain. Depending of your decision you now select user principal name or e-mail:

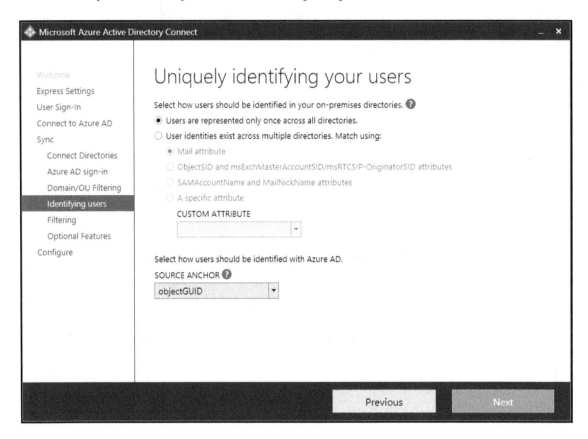

13. Afterwards configure the filter for your accounts. You can either synchronize all users and device or use a filter group. Here the best way is to have specified group for your users. From a security and resource perspective you shouldn't select all users otherwise you would sync unnecessary or possibly restricted accounts to Azure AD:

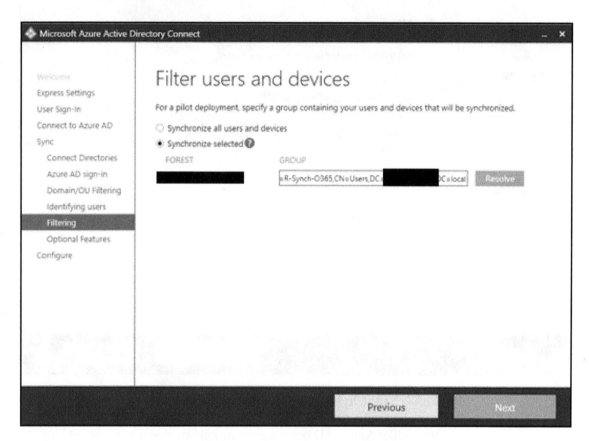

14. In the next steps, you choose which features you want to have synced in addition to the attributes:

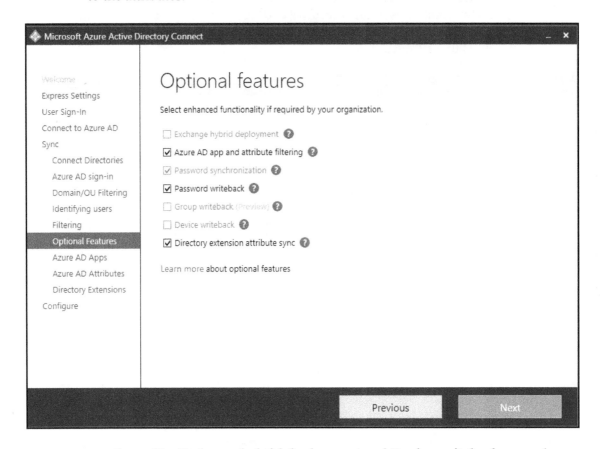

Some, like **Exchange hybrid deployment** and **Device writeback,** are only available with certain Active Directory extensions or with additional subscriptions like Azure AD premium or mobile device management like Intune. Best field practice is to at least sync the **Azure AD app and attribute filtering**. That will enable you to sync allowed apps and license attributes between Azure AD and Active Directory, which is, for example, necessary if you license your Microsoft Office in your Terminal server environment with Office 365 E3 or E5 plans. If you do not choose to enable the feature, it could be possible that some applications will not appear to be licensed. Office 365 installed on a Citrix Terminal Server is a good example for that. Without synchronization, Citrix does not know about the license details and the user receives an Office licensing login every time he starts his Office applications on the Terminal Server.

15. In the next few windows, you can decide which **Azure AD apps** will be synced:

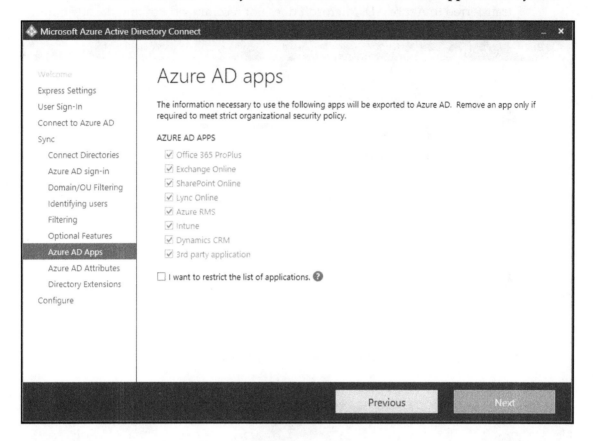

16. Afterwards you can limit the attributes from Active Directory that will be transferred to Azure AD. Microsoft does not recommend limiting the attributes:

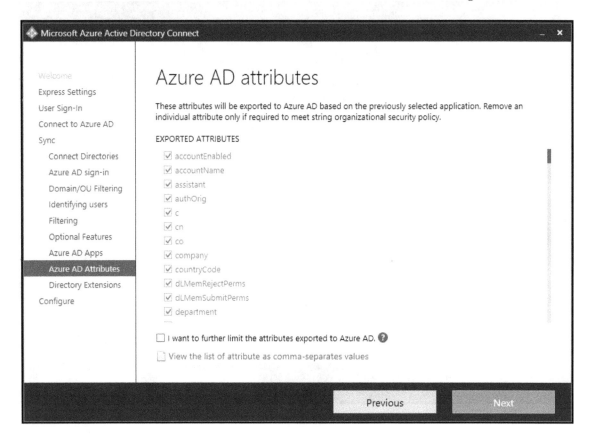

17. Now you can select which **Directory extension** attributes from your on-premises environment are transferred to Azure AD. This is important for certain applications running in the cloud. In this walkthrough, we will not select any attribute:

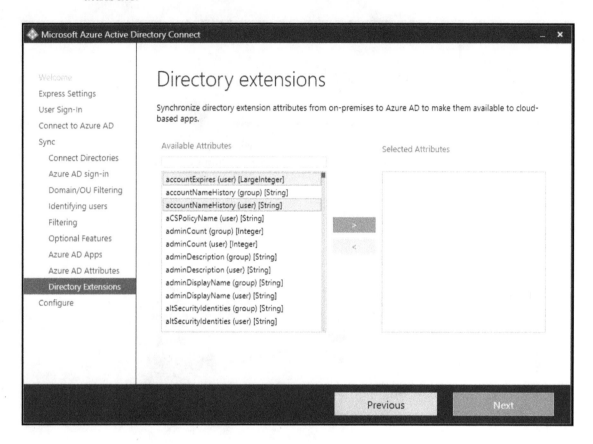

18. Once you've run through these steps, you can complete the installation. Outside of a migration scenario, or as long as you don't want to enable high availability for Azure AD Connect, you can start synchronization. Otherwise you should stage your installation first and start the first synchronization after:

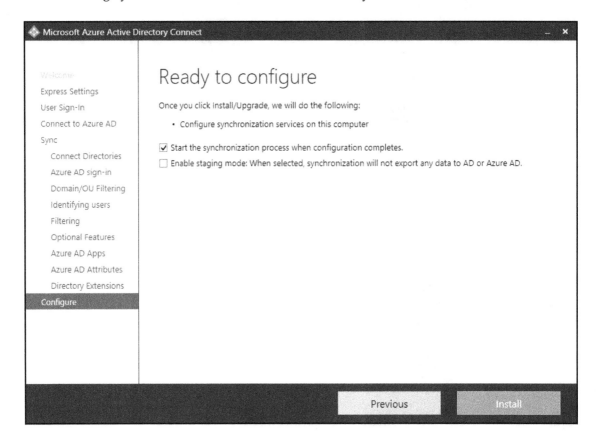

19. To disable the staging mode, you need to start Azure AD Connect from the Start menu again. It will act like a regular Azure AD Connect, except that the second wizard option is to disable the staging mode:

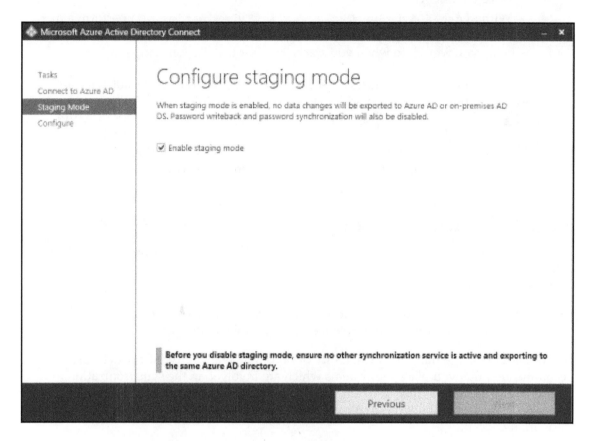

You have now implemented a simple SSO-enabled Azure AD and Active Directory synchronization.

After you've started synchronization, Azure AD Connect will replicate changes every hour between Azure AD and Active Directory.

You can either trigger synchronization manually by using following PowerShell commands:

- With `Start-ADSyncSyncCycle -PolicyType Delta`, you sync all changes since the last sync.
- With `Start-ADSyncSyncCycle -PolicyType Initial`, you perform a full sync with all settings you have configured in Azure AD Connect. It's likely to be what you would do when you start *sync* after installation.

 From a common practice a security standpoint, you should not sync any on-premises domain admin account in Azure AD or shouldn't give the personal Azure AD account of you IT people any admin rights in Azure AD. Anytime you should create cloud only accounts for your admins, which also only serve as admin accounts in Azure AD. That protects both directory from capturing if any of the admins is corrupted.

Azure AD Connect high available infrastructure

Now you know how to set up a basic AD synchronization without considering availability infrastructure, and now we'll look at how you can achieve Azure AD synchronization in a high availability environment.

The first thing you should know is that the Azure AD Connect tool cannot be clustered, so you need to use the *staged mode* to implement it in passive mode.

So, for placement in either high availability or non-high availability infrastructures, it is recommended that you place the systems which are involved in the synchronization in Azure virtual machines. This is so that you do not transfer as much data through the open Internet. More details about these concept will be explained in the next chapter about Azure networking.

In our high availability scenario, every active and primary source of synchronization is placed into Azure. The backup and passive parts are based into the on-premises data center and connected via VPN or MPLS to Azure.

So, to have a user and password synchronization option in a high availability environment, we need the following system:

- Two Active Directory domain controllers with Global Catalogue and DNS
- Two SQL server database servers within an application cluster
- Two Azure AD Connect servers, one in active and one in staged mode

For the domain controllers and database servers, both will automatically fail-over if one system falls out. For the Azure AD Connect server you need to disable the staged mode and perform the fail-over manually.

The following diagram shows you how such an infrastructure could look:

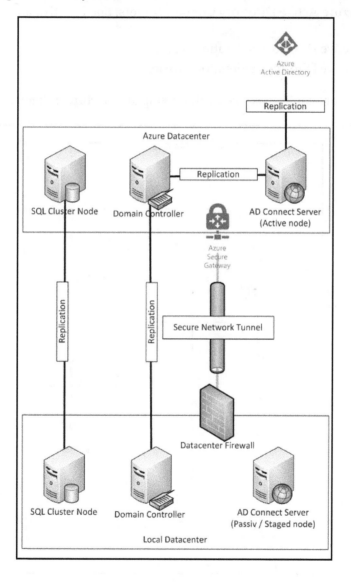

Looking at a more complex scenario, if you want to implement a high availability ADFS infrastructure some additional systems are needed:

- Two Active Directory domain controllers with Global Catalogue and DNS
- Two SQL Server database servers within an application cluster
- Two Azure Active Directory Connect servers, one in active and one in staged mode
- Two Active Directory federation servers
- Two Active Directory federation proxies

Such an infrastructure could look like the following architectural schema:

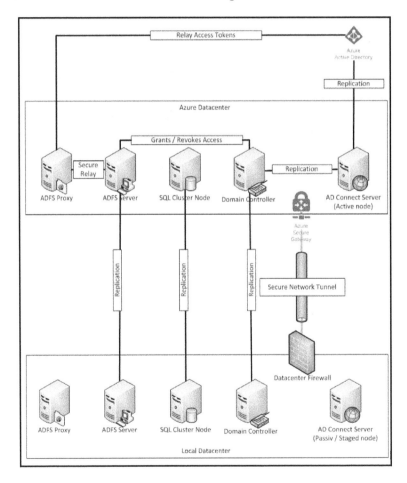

Summary

You should have learned how Azure AD works and what feature each subscription level of Azure AD offers to you. You should also be familiar with creating users in Azure AD and syncing them with your on-premises Active Directory. You saw also other options for user sign in with ADFS and how to make your Azure Hybrid environment highly available.

Within the next chapter, we will cover the internal, external and hybrid networking with and within Azure.

4
Implementing Azure Networks

Just as you plan the network in your data center or company, you need to do it in Azure also. Networking is essential in Azure and if you do not plan it right you could force outages or bottlenecks for deployed services.

Depending on what you plan with Azure, you should put some effort in planning your network and connections into Azure.

Within this chapter, you will learn the basics about Azure networking, how to implement Azure networking, and how to decide which WAN and connectivity solution you should use.

We are going to explore the following topics:

- Azure virtual networks
- Azure VPN gateways
- Azure local gateways
- Azure site-to-site and point-to-site VPN
- Azure ExpressRoute
- Azure connections and routes
- Azure DNS
- Azure application gateway

We will also set up a basic network configuration during this chapter.

Azure networking limits

Before we start deep diving into the Azure components, let us take a view on the networking limits in Azure:

Resource	Default limit	Maximum limit
Virtual networks per subscription	50	500
DNS servers per virtual network	9	25
Private IP addresses per virtual network	4,096	4,096
Concurrent TCP connections for a virtual machine or role instance	500k	500k
Network interfaces	300	10k
Network security groups	100	400
NSG rules per NSG	200	500
User defined route tables	100	400
User defined routes per route table	100	400
Public IP addresses (dynamic)	60	Limit can be increased by support
Public IP addresses (static)	20	Limit can be increased by support
Load balancers (internal and Internet facing)	100	Limit can be increased by support
Load balancer rules per load balancer	150	150
Public frontend IP per load balancer	5	Limit can be increased by support
Private frontend IP per load balancer	1	Limit can be increased by support
Application gateways	50	50

There are additional limits for Azure ExpressRoute. We will take a look at them when we are talking about ExpressRoute later on.

Azure networking components

To start with Azure networking, you need to know and understand the components which are needed to set up an Azure solution.

Let us start from the easiest part to the more difficult ones.

Azure virtual networks (VNet)

An Azure VNet is a logical isolated network for your services connected to your subscription in Azure. You have full control about the IP address blocks, DNS settings, security policies, and route tables within this network. You can also split your VNet into subnet and launch Azure IaaS virtual machines and cloud services within these subnets. By using Azure virtual gateways and WAN solutions, you can also connect your virtual networks to the Internet or your on-premises environment.

When you look for Azure VNet in Azure, you basically search for the network and you should see the symbol shown in the following screenshot:

Normally you're setting up a network like you do in your on-premises network. You create a network with an IP range such as 10.0.0.0/16 and split it up into different subnetworks. Every Azure VNet has at least a minimum of two subnets. The first is the **gateway subnet**, which is basically a router network where every internal network router for the other Azure VNet subnetworks is in. We personally prefer to use the first subnet of the Azure VNet as the gateway subnet but you can choose any subnet you like. The only thing you need to know is that the gateway subnet needs a minimum of /29 CIDR IPs. I normally recommend /24 CIDR. You would never use it but it's logical and you can follow up with a /24 CIDR subnet design. The second one is the network for your services or servers depending on your own design, normally it is /24 CIDR.

 As of September 2016, Azure started to support IPv6 to be used in Azure. The deployment and support of IPv6 is still in progress while writing the book.

The following diagram shows you an example for a network configuration:

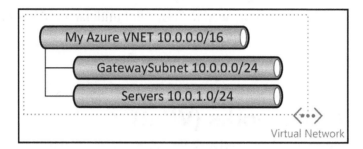

All subnetworks are fully routed to each other. That is not the best situation in most of the cases. One example is when you need a **Frontend** and a **Backend** network in Azure, as shown in the following diagram:

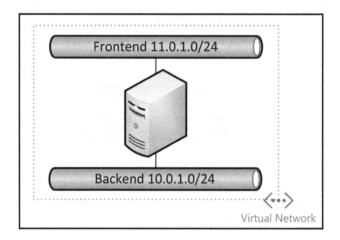

Currently there are only two ways to resolve that issue:

- The first one is to create two VNets and put a virtual machine with two network adapters in both networks and route within the virtual machine.
- The other way is to implement custom routes and send packages for the frontend network into the either of your other Azure or on premises networks.

There is a great *nice to know* within the VNet setting. Under **Monitoring,** you can see a detailed networking diagram of your Azure network.

The following screenshot shows an example of a **Diagram**:

VNet peering

There is also an option to connect different Azure VNet works in the same Azure data center. This option is called **Azure VNet peering**. VNet peering for Azure virtual network lets you directly link two virtual networks in the same region via private IPs. VNet peering routes packets between virtual networks through the internal Azure backbone network. There is no Azure gateway between these networks. This allows a low-latency, high-bandwidth connection between virtual machines in the virtual networks.

VNet peering also allows transit through the peered virtual networks, so a network virtual appliance or a VPN gateway in one virtual network can be used by a virtual machine in another peered virtual network. Peering works across virtual networks in different subscriptions. So you are able to connect, for example, subscriptions paid by different departments or subscription owners. Later in this chapter, I will show you how to set up VNet peering. In the future, it may also be possible to connect Azure services such as Azure SQL or Azure Storage directly via VNet peering to Azure VNets. That would allow you to use Azure PaaS resources without using a public network or connection in Azure.

 As of September 2016, Microsoft allows VNet peering between **Azure Resource Manager** (**ARM**) environments and **Azure Service Manager** (**ASM**) environments. That would enable customers to migrate from ASM to ARM more easily.

Azure VPN gateways

Azure VPN gateways are basically your core routers and firewalls within your Azure environment.

An Azure gateway can serve different purposes:

- Internet gateway
- Site-to-site VPN gateway
- Point-to-site VPN gateway
- ExpressRoute gateway
- VNet-to-VNet gateway

We won't be able to cover the deployments of point-to-site VPN gateways in this book but you can find a detailed guide in the Microsoft documentation at
`https://azure.microsoft.com/en-us/documentation/articles/vpn-gat`
`eway-howto-point-to-site-rm-ps/`.

The following screenshot shows the Azure service you need to look for when you want to implement an Azure VPN gateway:

Every VNet can have at least one VPN gateway. VPN gateways are available in different service offerings with different features and available services.

The following table shows a short summary:

	VPN gateway throughput	VPN gateway max IPSEC tunnels	Active - Active VPN	ExpressRoute gateway throughput	VPN gateway and ExpressRoute coexist
Basic	100 Mbps	10	No	No	No
Standard	100 Mbps	10	No	1000 Mbps	Yes
High Performance	200 Mbps	30	Yes	2000 Mbps up to 10000 Mbps	Yes

The following diagram shows how the basic **VPN Gateway** is connected to your Azure network:

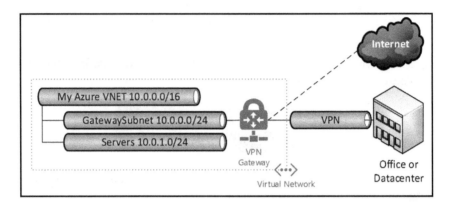

With the standard or performance gateway it would look like the following diagram:

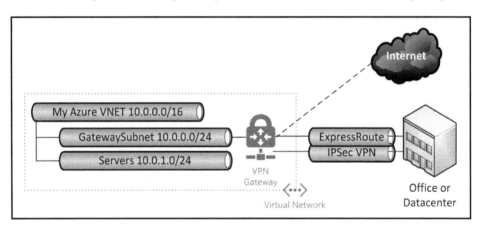

When you start the setup of a gateway, you need to decide what kind of gateway you want to deploy. The basic offering can be deployed via Azure GUI; for the other offerings, you need to do some PowerShell. The following screenshot shows the GUI version:

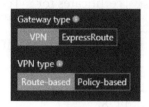

Depending on your WAN solution, you choose either **VPN** or **ExpressRoute**. For **ExpressRoute,** you need an MPLS solution in place. I will explain that later. For the VPN solution, you need to decide between a **Route-based** or **Policy-based** VPN, which means you need to decide if you want to enable dynamic routing with IPSEC IKEv2 or static IPSEC IKEv1.

The decision as to which VPN type you need must be done based on your on-premises VPN device. Not every device can speak **Route-based** VPN. Microsoft has published a list of supported devices. You can see them here at
`https://azure.microsoft.com/en-us/documentation/articles/vpn-gateway-about-vpn-devices/`.

There are also some more additional requirements you need to think of when choosing your VPN gateway in Azure. The following table shows you those provided by Microsoft:

	Policy-based basic VPN gateway	Route-based basic VPN gateway	Route-based standard VPN gateway	Route-based high performance VPN gateway
Site-to-site connectivity (S2S)	Policy-based VPN configuration	Route-based VPN configuration	Route-based VPN configuration	Route-based VPN configuration
Point-to-site connectivity (P2S)	Not supported	Supported (can coexist with S2S)	Supported (can coexist with S2S)	Supported (can coexist with S2S)

Authentication method	Pre-shared key	Pre-shared key for S2S connectivity, certificates for P2S connectivity	Pre-shared key for S2S connectivity, certificates for P2S connectivity	Pre-shared key for S2S connectivity, certificates for P2S connectivity
Maximum number of S2S connections	1	10	10	30
Maximum number of P2S connections	Not supported	128	128	128
Active routing support	Not supported	Not supported	Supported	Supported

In summary, you can basically have the following gateway configurations:

- The policy-based basic **VPN Gateway** with site-to-site VPN is shown in the following diagram:

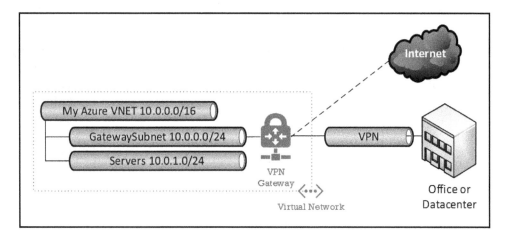

Looking on the current WAN developments and most of the customer infrastructures, a policy-based VPN Gateway should only be used if there is absolutely no other option. Most enterprise grade Firewalls are able to work with route-based VPN. Otherwise you can switch to a virtual network device in Azure.

- Route-based standard **VPN Gateway** with **ExpressRoute** shown in the following diagram:

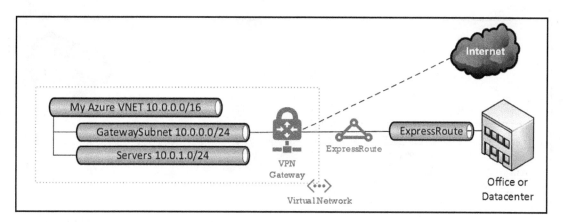

- Route-based basic **VPN Gateway** with a **Site 2 Site VPN** and **Point 2 Site VPN** or a **Route-based** standard or performance **VPN Gateway** with a **Site 2 Site VPN** and **Point 2 Site VPN**:

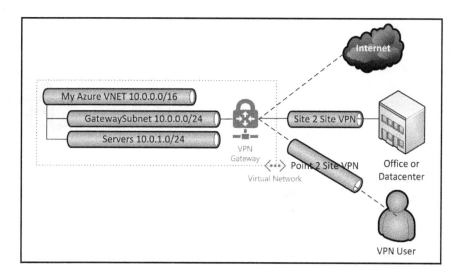

- Route-based standard or performance **VPN Gateway** with site-to-site or ExpressRoute:

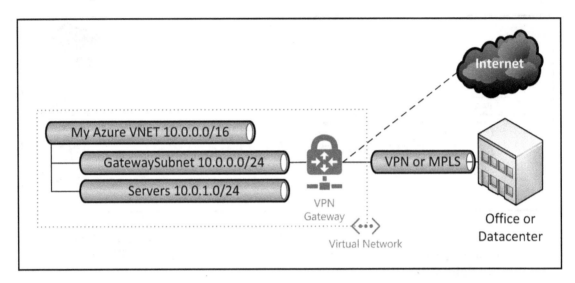

- Route-based standard or performance **VPN Gateway** with a site-to-site VPN and **ExpressRoute**:

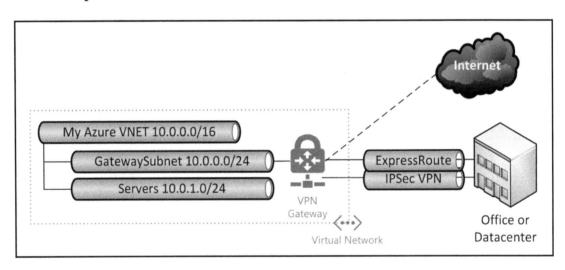

Later in the chapter, you will learn how to configure a VPN Gateway with ExpressRoute and a basic VPN with a site-to-site VPN and how to upgrade that VPN to standard or performance. You will also learn what you need to do to implement a point-to-site VPN.

Azure local gateway

Local network gateways represent the configuration of your local firewall environment. Within a local network gateway, you configure the public IP of your firewall device as well as the IP spaces you manage within a local environment. The following screenshot shows the Azure service you need to look for when you want to implement an Azure local network gateway:

The following screenshot shows you how to configure a local network gateway:

Currently, it is not possible to work with DNS entries or dynamic public IPs. Azure is also not supporting IPv6 within the environment as a local network gateway at the present time. So you definitely need a public IPv4 IP for your production environment. That may change in the near future when the IPv6 deployment is moving on in Azure.

 There is an option to work with dynamic public IPs but I only recommend that for test environments or home labs. You can use a dynamic DNS provider such as DynDNS to collect your changing IP address. Afterwards, you can recreate your Azure local gateway with the newly obtained IP. MVP Florent Appointaire wrote a little script for the Azure Resource Manager to configure to help you with that; please refer to https://gallery.technet.microsoft.com/Update-AzureRM-S2S-VPN-c46 cc39e.

Azure ExpressRoute

When we are talking about ExpressRoute, we are talking about a common **Internet Service Provider** (**ISP**) technology called **Multi Protocol Label Switching** (**MPLS**) or ISP IP VPN.

MPLS is a type of data-carrying technique for telecommunications networks that directs data from one network to the next based on short path labels rather than long network addresses. This technology avoids long and complex routing tables. The labels identify virtual links between distant nodes. MPLS can encapsulate packets of various network protocols; that's why it is named *multiprotocol*. MPLS supports nearly all common access technologies, including T1/E1, ATM, frame relay, and dark fiber connects, into points of presence or DSL.

The routing within those networks is based on **Border Gateway Protocol** (**BGP**) routing. BGP is a standardized gateway protocol designed to exchange routing and reachability information among autonomous systems on the Internet. The protocol is often classified as a **path vector** protocol but is sometimes also classed as a **distance-vector routing** protocol. The BGP makes routing decisions based on paths, network policies, or rule sets configured by a network provider and makes core routing decisions.

Normally you see MPLS when connecting a range of offices or data centers with very complex routing or mashed networks between the network sites. MPLS also does not terminate Quality of Service settings at the gateway; all settings can be transported from network site to network site. The following diagram shows an example for such a mashed environment:

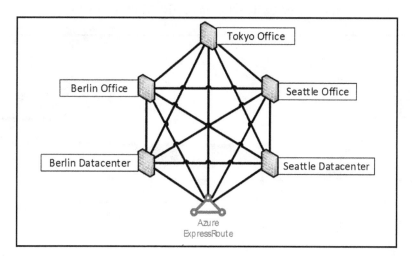

Microsoft offers with ExpressRoute the option to connect your Azure and Office 365 environment directly to your MPLS network.

When you configure, you will be able to configure the different peering's. The three peering types are:

- **Private peering**: Azure compute services, namely virtual machines and cloud services that are deployed within a virtual network can be connected through the private peering domain. The private peering domain is considered to be a trusted extension of your core network into Microsoft Azure. You can set up bidirectional connectivity between your network and Azure virtual networks.
- **Public peering**: Services such as Azure Storage, SQL databases, and websites are offered on public IP addresses. You can privately connect to services hosted on public IP addresses, including VIPs of your cloud services, through the public peering routing domain. You can connect the public peering domain to your DMZ and connect to all Azure services on their public IP addresses from your WAN without having to connect through the Internet.

- **Microsoft peering**: Connectivity to all other Microsoft online services (such as Office 365 or Dynamics CRM) will be through the Microsoft peering. You can enable bi-directional connectivity between your WAN and Microsoft cloud services through the Microsoft peering routing domain.

The following diagram shows the basic schema on the Microsoft site:

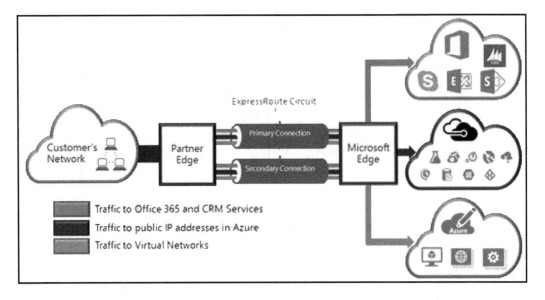

Source:
https://azure.microsoft.com/en-us/documentation/articles/expressroute-introduction/

What basically happens is that your ISP connects your network to the network of Microsoft. Those connections happen at most of the **Point of Presence(PoP)** or Internet exchange hubs all over the globe. The following diagram shows how this happens within the Azure data center:

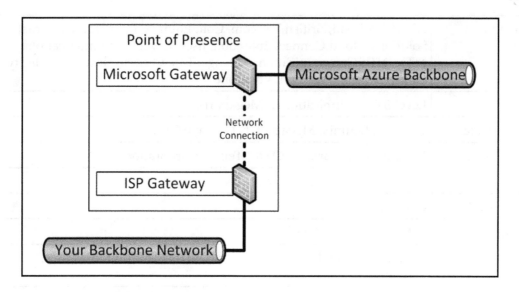

Azure global Points of Presence

The following table shows you the list of PoPs Microsoft and partner ISPs peer at the moment:

Location	Service providers
Amsterdam	Aryaka Networks, AT&T NetBond, British Telecom, Colt, Equinix, euNetworks, GÉANT+, InterCloud, Internet Solutions-Cloud Connect, Interxion, Level 3 Communications, Orange, Tata Communications, TeleCity Group, Telenor, Verizon
Atlanta	Equinix
Chennai	Tata Communications
Chicago	AT&T NetBond, Comcast, Equinix, Level 3 Communications, Zayo Group
Dallas	AT&T NetBond, Equinix, Level 3 Communications, Megaport
Dublin	Colt
Hong Kong	British Telecom, China Telecom Global, Equinix, Megaport, Orange, PCCW Global Limited, Tata Communications, Verizon

London	AT&T NetBond, British Telecom, Colt, Equinix, InterCloud, Internet Solutions-Cloud Connect, Interxion, Jisc+, Level 3 Communications, MTN, NTT Communications, Orange, Tata Communications, Telecity Group, Telenor, Verizon, Vodafone
Las Vegas	Level 3 Communications+, Megaport
Los Angeles	CoreSite, Equinix, Megaport, NTT, Zayo Group
Melbourne	Equinix, Megaport, NEXTDC, Telstra Corporation
New York	Equinix, Megaport, Zayo Group
Montreal	Cologix+
Mumbai	Tata Communications
Osaka	Equinix, Internet Initiative Japan Inc.-IIJ, NTT Communications, Softbank
Paris	Interxion
Sao Paulo	Equinix, Telefonica
Seattle	Equinix, Level 3 Communications, Megaport
Silicon Valley	Aryaka Networks, AT&T NetBond, British Telecom, CenturyLink+, Comcast, Equinix, Level 3 Communications, Orange, Tata Communications, Verizon, Zayo Group
Singapore	Aryaka Networks, AT&T NetBond, British Telecom, Equinix, InterCloud, Megaport, Orange, SingTel, Tata Communications, Verizon
Sydney	AT&T NetBond, British Telecom, Equinix, Megaport, NEXTDC, Orange, Telstra Corporation, Verizon
Tokyo	Aryaka Networks, British Telecom, Colt, Equinix, Internet Initiative Japan Inc.-IIJ, NTT Communications, Softbank, Verizon
Toronto	Cologix, Equinix, Zayo Group
Washington DC	Aryaka Networks, AT&T NetBond, British Telecom, Comcast, Equinix, InterCloud, Level 3 Communications, Megaport, Orange, Tata Communications, Verizon, Zayo Group

National Azure Points of Presence

For the National Azure environment or Azure environment disconnected from Azure global, Microsoft offers different PoPs to connect to. Those PoPs are completely disconnected from the Azure Global PoPs. The internet services providers to connect to are in the following table.

National Azure	Location	Service providers
US Government	Chicago	AT&T NetBond, Equinix, Level 3 Communications, Verizon
US Government	Dallas	Equinix+, Verizon+
US Government	New York	Equinix, Level 3 Communications+, Verizon
US Government	Washington DC	AT&T NetBond, Equinix, Level 3 Communications, Verizon
China	Beijing	China Telecom
China	Shanghai	China Telecom
Germany	Berlin	Colt, e-shelter, Megaport
Germany	Frankfurt	Colt, Equinix, Interxion

If your provider is not directly listed, you need to get in contact with your ISP to find the right location and partner for deployment.

To find information about the Azure PoPs and peering partners, you can visit the Azure documentation website at `https://azure.microsoft.com/en-us/documentation/articles/expressroute-locations-providers/`.

Microsoft also started to maintain a list of direct through ISPs, those ISP who leverage Equinix, Interxion, e-shelter etc. to connect to Azure ExpressRoute. The list can be found in the Azure Documentation visiting following website `https://docs.microsoft.com/en-us/azure/expressroute/expressroute-locations-providers#a-namec1partnersaconnectivity-through-service-providers-not-listed`.

Another point Microsoft also started is to name certified and qualified Solution Integrator for ExpressRoute which support customers with planning, deploying and maintaining ExpressRoute in a customer environment. Microsoft maintains the list of those Partners on their Azure documentation website `https://docs.microsoft.com/en-us/azure/expressroute/expressroute-locations-providers#expressroute-system-integrators`.

Microsoft offers ExpressRoute in the following two service levels: **Standard SLA** and **Premium SLA**. As described next, the premium offering expands the standard offering in the following limits:

- Increased routing table limit from 4k routes to 10k routes for private peering.
- Increased number of VNets that can be connected to the ExpressRoute circuit (default is 10).
- Global connectivity over the Microsoft core network. You will now be able to link a VNet in one geopolitical region with an ExpressRoute circuit in another region. Example: You can link a VNet created in Europe West to an ExpressRoute circuit created in Silicon Valley.
- Connectivity to Office 365 services and CRM Online.

Depending on the bought ExpressRoute service level there are different limitations:

Resource	Default limit
ExpressRoute circuits per subscription	10
ExpressRoute circuits per region per subscription for ARM	10
Maximum number of routes for Azure private peering with ExpressRoute standard	4,000

Maximum number of routes for Azure private peering with ExpressRoute premium add-on	10,000
Maximum number of routes for Azure public peering with ExpressRoute standard	200
Maximum number of routes for Azure public peering with ExpressRoute premium add-on	200
Maximum number of routes for Azure Microsoft peering with ExpressRoute standard	200
Maximum number of routes for Azure Microsoft peering with ExpressRoute premium add-on	200

Depending on the ISP and network location, Microsoft offers the following bandwidths and connections:

Circuit size	Number of VNet links for standard	Number of VNet links with premium add-on
50 Mbps	10	20
100 Mbps	10	25
200 Mbps	10	25
500 Mbps	10	40
1 Gbps	10	50
2 Gbps	10	60
5 Gbps	10	75
10 Gbps	10	100

ExpressRoute is highly recommended for enterprise environments which need a guarantee for latency and bandwidth for their Azure and Office 365 environment.

Microsoft will also enable a high performance ExpressRoute circuit. The high performance ExpressRoute will enable customers to throughput 10 Gbps from the WAN directly to their VM's.

An Azure ExpressRoute circuit is represented in the Azure portal with the following symbol:

Later on in the chapter, I will explain how to deploy an ExpressRoute circuit.

Azure connections

Azure connections are the *wire* between the internal VNet gateway and your Azure VPN gateway or ExpressRoute circuit. With these connections, you can establish the tunnel through the Azure network and establish the connection to your on-premises environment or other VNets.

You can find the Azure connections by searching for **Connections,** as shown in the following screenshot :

An Azure connection offers the options shown in the following screenshot:

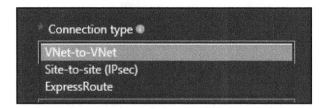

Later on in the chapter, we will use Azure connections to build up a connection between VPN and MPLS gateways.

Azure routes

With routes in Azure, you can change the default *Any to Any* routing within Azure to meet your needs.

The following screenshot shows the Azure service you need to look for when you want to implement an Azure route:

With routes, you can basically redirect traffic from one subnet to another location. The following screenshot shows the current offerings of that Azure service:

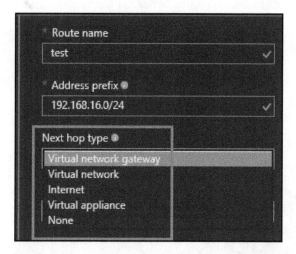

Within the setup part of this chapter, I will explain how to configure a custom route:

- **Virtual network gateway**: The traffic will be forwarded to another Azure gateway. This option can be used if you maybe want to send traffic via another gateway or route to its target. Or you have redirected all traffic to a Virtual Appliance and want specific traffic to bypass the appliance.
- **Virtual network**: Transfers traffic directly into another VNet. That could be used to transfer traffic from one VNet to another which can't be reached directly.
- **Internet**: Traffic will be send directly into the Internet.
- **Virtual appliance**: The traffic will be sent to a third-party virtual network device hosted in your Azure environment. That can be a Barracuda Next Generation Firewall or a Cisco Nexus device, for example.
- **None**: Traffic will be dropped and will not be routed.

Azure third-party network devices

Some vendors such as Cisco, Barracuda, or F5 offer VPN and network devices such as firewalls or load balancers as Azure virtual appliances via the Azure marketplace. Those devices can be directly integrated in your Azure infrastructure.

If you want to use one of these devices, you can look after them in the Azure marketplace and deploy them out like regular virtual machines.

The following screenshot shows an example search for `barracuda`:

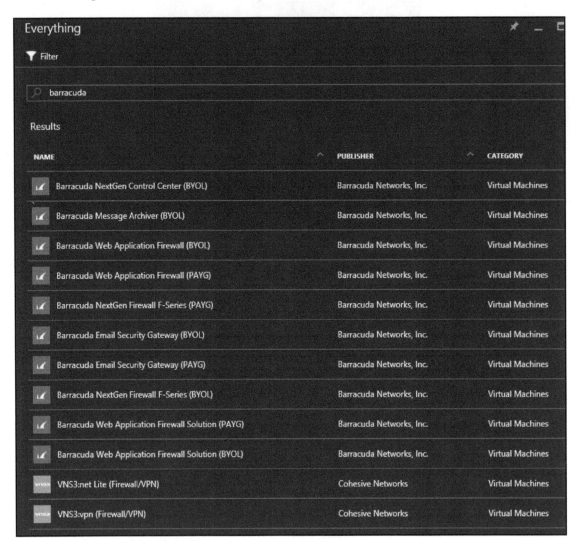

To integrate one of these devices into your environment, you need to implement Azure routes to pass traffic to the third-party devices, as shown in the next diagram.

Normally there is no need to implement a third-party device because the Microsoft standard services offer approximately 80% of all services that are needed by most customers. Sometimes there are cases where you need to implement special systems such as a load balancer in Azure. Under certain circumstances, your target application has to use a load balancer feature that is not supported by the Azure load balancer.

The following diagram shows another case where you have the requirements for additional data encryption on a transfer level. In that case you implement a VPN Tunnel or other encryption technology within an **ExpressRoute** and Azure VPN gateway. The following diagram is based on the Barracuda Next Generation Firewall design:

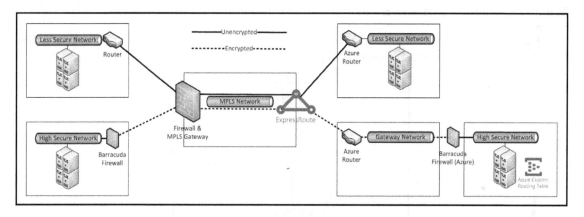

One thing you need to be aware of is that most of the third-party network solutions need an additional license and have some additional costs which might be not covered by you Microsoft Azure Subscription. So please read the introduction page of the product carefully.

Normally you should see information as shown in the following screenshot:

In the text, there should be additional information, as shown in the example screenshot :

> • This Barracuda NextGen Control Center is licensed using the Bring-Your-Own-License (BYOL)
> model. Fill out the evaluation form to receive a 30-day evaluation license or purchase one of
> the licenses depending on your requirement.

Azure load balancer

The Azure load balancer is a layer 4 (TCP, UDP) load balancer which distributes incoming traffic among healthy instances of a service or among virtual machines in Azure. You can compare it with well-known load balancers such as Citrix Netscaler, Microsoft TMG or Windows server load balancer.

The Azure Resource Manager load balancer can distribute traffic that works with public IPs and Azure DNS entry. The following diagram shows the basic load balancing mechanism:

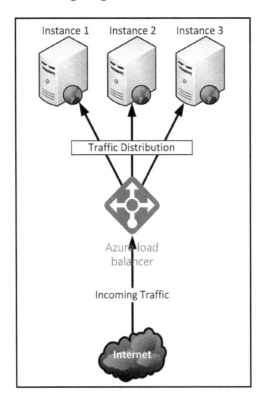

The feature list of an Azure load balancer is shown in the following sections.

Hash-based distribution

The load balancer uses a hash-based distribution algorithm. By default, it uses a 5-tuple hash to map traffic to available services and servers. It provides stickiness only within a transport session. Packets in the same TCP or UDP session will be directed to the same instance behind the load balancer. When the sender site closes, and reopens the session or starts a new session from the same source IP, the source port changes. This may result in a redirection of the traffic to a different data center and load balancer endpoint.

Port forwarding

The load balancer gives you control over how inbound communication is managed. This communication can include traffic that's initiated from Internet hosts or virtual machines in other cloud services or virtual networks.

An input endpoint listens on a public port and forwards traffic to an internal port. You can map the same ports for an internal or external endpoint or use a different port for them.

You can use port forwarding to redirect traffic from an incoming port to another port your server listens to. For example, your endpoint listens to port 443 and you have a web application on the server listening to port 8443. You can configure the endpoint to redirect the traffic from port 80 to port 8443 on the server.

Automatic reconfiguration

The load balancer instantly reconfigures itself when you scale instances up or down. That happens, for example, when you add or remove new servers or instances into the same load balancer set.

Service monitoring

The load balancer can probe the health of the various server instances. When a probe fails to respond, the load balancer stops sending new connections to the unhealthy instances. Three types of probes are currently supported:

- **Guest agent probe (on PaaS VMs only)**: The load balancer utilizes the Azure guest agent inside the virtual machine. The guest agent listens and responds with an HTTP 200 response only when the instance is ready and healthy. If the agent fails to respond with an HTTP 200 response, the load balancer marks the instance as unresponsive and stops sending traffic to that instance. The load balancer will continue to ping the instance until it responds again or the instance is removed from the load balancer set. Attention: If you are running a website, the code is typically running the process w3wp.exe. This processes are not monitored by the guest agent so the load balancer will never informed when the instance fails.

- **HTTP custom probe**: This probe overrides the default (guest agent) probe. You can use it to create your own custom logic for your application to determine the health of the role instance. As an example, the HTTP probe could login to a page and changes some values as a result of the logic. If the when fine without issues, the probe is good, otherwise it will generate an alert. The load balancer will regularly probe your endpoint (every 15 seconds, by default).

- : This probe relies on successful TCP session establishment to a defined probe port.

TCP custom probe: This probe relies on successful TCP session establishment to a defined probe port. Source NAT

All outbound traffic to the Internet comes from your instances and services that go through **source NAT (SNAT)**. The VMs and Services use the same **virtual IP (VIP)** address as the incoming traffic. SNAT provides different benefits:

- It enables upgrade and disaster recovery of services, since the VIP can be dynamically mapped to another instance of the service.
- It reduces the access control list easier. ACLs expressed in terms of VIPs do not change as services scale up, down, or get redeployed.

The load balancer configuration supports full NAT for UDP. Full NAT is a type of NAT where the port allows inbound connections from any external host.

 To learn more about the Azure network load balancer, you should visit the Microsoft MSDN source at https://azure.microsoft.com/en-us/documentation/articles/load-balancer-overview/.

Azure application gateways

The Azure application gateway is another form of load balancing in Azure. Application load balancing enables Azure Customers to create routing rules for network traffic based on HTTP protocols like for publishing Websites on the same IP Address.

Application gateways currently support layer-7 application delivery for the following application-based load balancing algorithms:

- HTTP load balancing
- Cookie-based session affinity
- **Secure Sockets Layer (SSL)** offload
- URL-based content routing
- Multi-site routing

Application gateways currently offer the sizes **small**, **medium**, and **large**.

You can create up to 50 application gateways per subscription. Each application gateway can have up to 10 instances each, which makes up to 500 instances depending on the gateway site.

Please note that the small size is only for testing purpose and shouldn't be used in production.

Every gateway has a limited throughput performance. The following table shows the performance per gateway:

Back-end page response	Small	Medium	Large
6 K	7.5 Mbps	13 Mbps	50 Mbps
100 K	35 Mbps	100 Mbps	200 Mbps

The Azure application gateway is represented in the Azure portal with the symbol shown in the following screenshot:

We will not cover Azure application gateways further in this book, but to get more information, you can access the Azure application gateway documentation at
`https://azure.microsoft.com/en-us/documentation/articles/applica`
`tion-gateway-introduction/`.

Azure Traffic Manager

Like the application gateway or the load balancer, the **Traffic Manager** is a mechanism to distribute incoming traffic among different Azure data centers. Unlike the load balancing of the other Azure balancers, the Traffic Manager works based on distribution via DNS entries, which means you deploy an DNS Name for the traffic manager. The clients connect directly to the endpoint for the application which has the best response time for his location. Traffic manager is mostly used as a frontend for Content Delivery Networks or Applications distributed over different Azure Regions. The following table summarizes the differences between all three load balancers:

Service	Azure load balancer	Application gateway	Traffic Manager
Technology	Transport level (OSI layer 4)	Application level (OSI layer 7)	DNS level
Application protocols supported	Any	HTTP and HTTPS	Any (An HTTP/S endpoint is required for endpoint monitoring)

Endpoints	Azure VMs and cloud services role instances	Any Azure internal IP address or public internet IP address	Azure VMs, cloud services, Azure web apps and external endpoints
VNet support	Can be used for both Internet facing and internal (VNet) applications	Can be used for both Internet facing and internal (VNet) applications	Only supports Internet-facing applications
Endpoint monitoring	Supported via probes	Supported via probes	Supported via HTTP/HTTPS GET request

The Azure Traffic Manager is symbolized with the following item in the Azure portal:

Azure DNS

With Azure DNS, you can host your DNS domains in Azure and manage your DNS records using the same credentials you use for other Azure services. So Azure DNS offers basically the same services as GoDaddy or UnitedDomains and other DNS providers.

Setting up Azure networks

Let us start deploying our Azure network infrastructure. We will start from the basics and then go up with different external and internal connections. All steps we do are also possible to do via PowerShell but we will stay with the Portal GUI within this guide.

Setting up Azure VNet

The following are the steps to set up Azure VNet:

1. First of all, we navigate in our **Resource group** and use**Add** to open the Azure marketplace:

2. In the next step, we look for Virtual network within the Azure marketplace and click **Virtual network**:

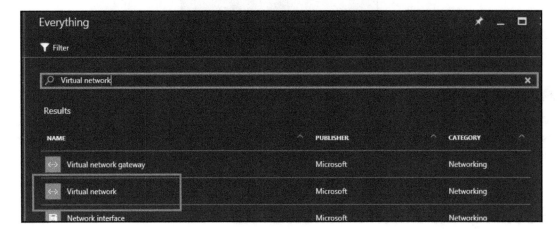

3. In the Azure blade afterwards you need to decide between Resource Manager and Classic. You should only choose **Resource Manager**. The Classic is based on the old **Azure Service Manager** (**ASM**) environment and has certain limitation. Microsoft is currently migrating all services left in ASM. After the migration Microsoft will some when remove ASM and all resources deployed within it:

4. In the next interface, we need to configure the network details:
    - **Name**: The name of your Azure network.
    - **Address space**: The IP address range you want to use within your Azure environment.
    - **Subnet name**: The name of your first subnet that could be either the gateway subnet or another one. We will stay with our server network for now and add the gateway network later.
    - **Subnet address range**: The IP range of the subnet you want to use.

The rest should be predefined by your resource group:

5. After the creation, the **Virtual Network** (**VNet**), should be listed in your resource group. You maybe need to click on **Refresh**:

6. Now we will add our gateway subnet. Therefore, we select the VNet to open the settings:

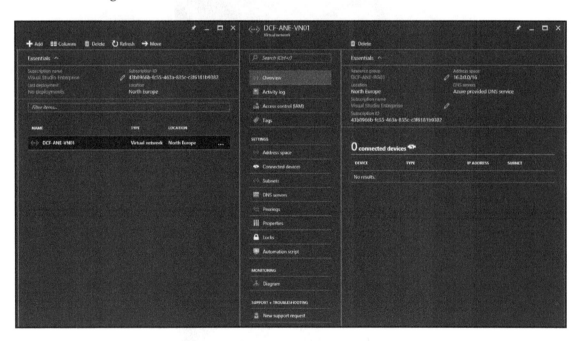

7. Yet we want to add the gateway subnet. Click on **Subnets** to open the subnet blade:

8. Afterwards you select the **+ Gateway** subnet button and another blade with the creation details will open:

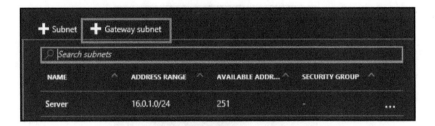

9. Within that blade, you need to define the subnet mask that the gateway uses. As explained earlier, we need a minimum of /29 CIDR addresses:

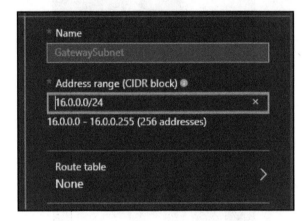

10. After clicking **OK**, the gateway subnet will be deployed in Azure. If you want to add more subnetworks, you can use the **Subnet** button:

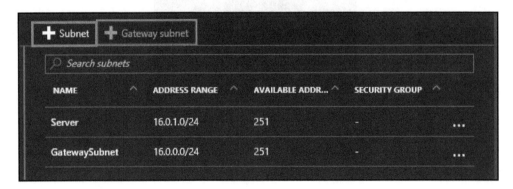

11. In the VNet settings, there is another option that could come in handy. Azure deploys every system with DHCP and by default configures Microsoft DNS servers as default DNS to the virtual machine. In most scenarios, you will need to change this setting to your own DNS server. Therefore, you can do this manually within the VM or change the default configuration within your Azure VNet. To do so, you need to select the **DNS servers** option in the **Settings**:

12. There you have a switch which changes between **Azure DNS** and **Custom DNS**:

13. We need to change it to**Custom DNS** and then we can add our DNS servers and **Save** the change:

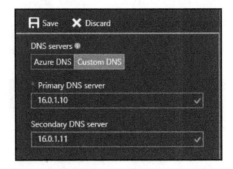

14. Now every system within that VNet will use the **Custom DNS** server settings.

Setting up Azure virtual network site-to-site VPN

After we have deployed our network, we can now start to deploy our VPN gateway. At first we deploy a site-to-site VPN to one of your sites. We will use the Azure portal to deploy the gateway and later update it via PowerShell.

Configuring local network gateway

network gateway follow the given steps:

1. To configure the local network gateway follow the given steps: At first we need to deploy the Local network gateway. Therefore, we click +Add in our resource group and search after local network in the Azure marketplace:

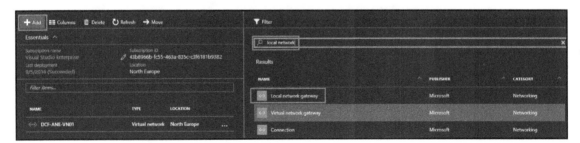

2. In the upcoming menu, you need to click on **Create**, afterwards the set up for the local gateway configuration appears:

- **Name**: The name of your Azure local gateway
- **IP address**: The public IPv4 address of your local firewall or router device
- **Address space**: The IP ranges you use behind your local firewall and router device

3. That's all from for the local network gateway. Now we go on with the configuration of our VPN gateway in Azure.

Configuring Azure virtual network gateway

To configure the virtual network gateway, follow the given steps:

1. At first, we need to deploy the **Virtual network gateway**. Therefore, we click **Add** in our resource group and search after `virtual network` in the Azure marketplace:

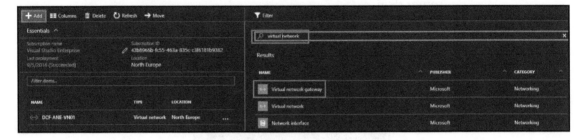

2. After changing to the next blade, you need to configure your gateway. Therefore, you need to proceed as follows:

3. First you need to give your gateway a **Name**:

4. Then extend the **Virtual network** blade and connect your gateway to the gateway network we previously created in the VNet:

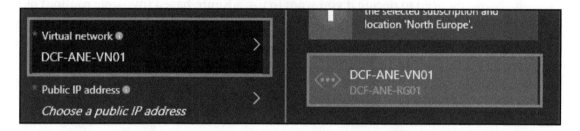

5. Now we need to create a public IP for our gateway. Extend the **Public IP address** blade and click on **Create new**:

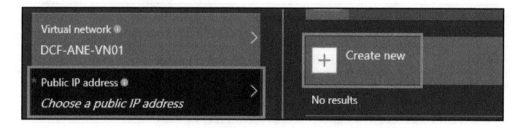

6. Another blade opens and you need to give the new **Public IP address** a name for the resource and need to save with **OK**:

7. After you created the public IP, you need to decide which gateway type you want to use. To deploy a site-to-site VPN based on IPSEC, you need to choose the gateway type **VPN**:

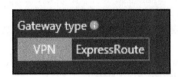

8. Now you need to decide if you want to use a **Route-based** (dynamic routing) or **Policy-based** (static routing) VPN:

9. Which type of VPN you can use is based on your on-premises firewall. The following table shows the configuration you need to do on your on-premises firewall. IKE phase 1 setup:

Property	Policy-based	Route-based and standard or high performance VPN gateway
IKE version	IKEv1	IKEv2
Diffie-Hellman group	Group 2 (1024 bit)	Group 2 (1024 bit)
Authentication method	Pre-shared Key	Pre-shared Key
Encryption algorithms	AES256 AES128 3DES	AES256 3DES
Hashing algorithm	SHA1(SHA128)	SHA1(SHA128), SHA2(SHA256)
Phase 1 **Security Association** (**SA**) lifetime (time)	28,800 seconds	10,800 seconds

10. IKE phase 2 setup:

Property	Policy-based	Route-based and standard or high performance VPN gateway
IKE version	IKEv1	IKEv2
Hashing algorithm	SHA1(SHA128)	SHA1(SHA128)
Phase 2 SA lifetime (time)	3,600 seconds	3,600 seconds
Phase 2 SA lifetime (throughput)	102,400,000 KB	-
IPSEC SA encryption and authentication offers (in the order of preference)	1. ESP-AES256 2. ESP-AES128 3. ESP-3DES 4. N/A	See Route-based gateway IPSEC SA offers
Perfect forward secrecy (PFS)	No	No (*)
Dead Peer Detection	Not supported	Supported

Microsoft maintains a list of test and supported VPN devices which can be used by customers. You can find the list of devices and more information about the VPN setup at https://azure.microsoft.com/en-us/document ation/articles/vpn-gateway-about-vpn-devices/.
If you don't have any of these devices or you didn't want to use a Windows server as VPN gateway, there is also the option to use free firewall solutions such as pfSense. Bart Decker wrote a great blog about the topic. You can find the blog at http://www.hybrid-cloudblog.com/p fsense-azure-hybrid-cloud/.

11. To finish the setup, we click **Create**. Now it will take around 45 minutes until our gateway is deployed:

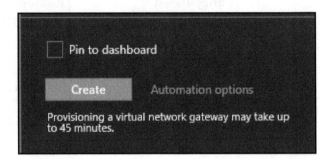

 During the deployment process, Microsoft is deploying several virtual machines and VXLAN tunnels within their environment. Microsoft also integrates the new gateway and public interfaces into their security system, which includes honey potting and DDoS prevention for the gateways. This process takes some time.

12. After the deployment is finished, we have created an Azure virtual network gateway as with the SKU *basic*. If you want to upgrade the gateway to standard or performance, you only need to run following PowerShell script against your Azure environment:

```
Resize-AzureVNetGateway -GatewaySKU <gatewaysize>
 -VnetName <gatewayname>
```

13. PowerShell command example to resize to high performance gateway:

```
Resize-AzureVNetGateway -GatewaySKU HighPerformance
 -VnetName DCF-ANE-GW01
```

14. PowerShell command example to resize to standard gateway :

```
Resize-AzureVNetGateway -GatewaySKU Standard -VnetName
 DCF-ANE-GW01
```

15. The same works also with downsizing a gateway:

```
Resize-AzureVNetGateway -GatewaySKU Basic -VnetName
 DCF-ANE-GW01
```

16. Besides the PowerShell way of resizing the gateway, Microsoft started to include the feature into the portal GUI. Therefor you need to navigate to the **Gateway** and open the detail blade:

17. Within the detail blade you go to **Configuration** and change the **SKU**. Afterwards you need to save the new SKU. Please be aware that the change of the SKU will take again up to 45 minutes:

Configuring connection between local and virtual network gateways

enable the routing:

1. Now we need to establish a connection between gateways and enable the routing: Please go back to your Resource group and click Add again. Now we look for Connection in the marketplace. Then select Connection:

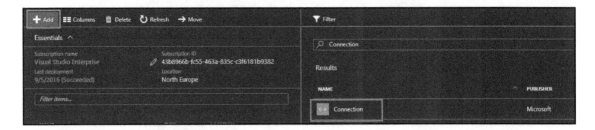

2. Now change the **Connection type** to **Site-to-site (IPsec)**:

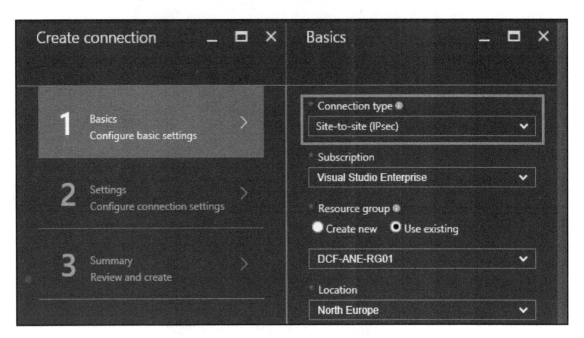

3. In the **Settings** phase, we first select the Azure **Virtual network gateway**:

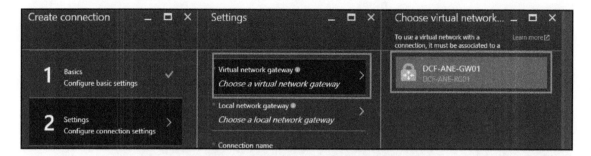

4. Afterwards, we select the **Local network gateway**:

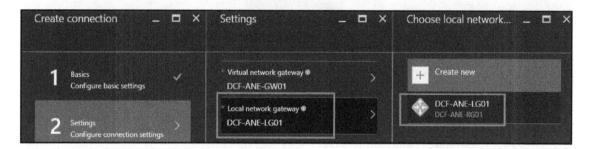

5. The **Connection name** will be created automatically but you can change it if necessary:

6. You then need to create a **pre-shared key** (**PSK**) secret for both gateways to share:

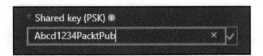

7. You can check the **Summary** and deploy the connection:

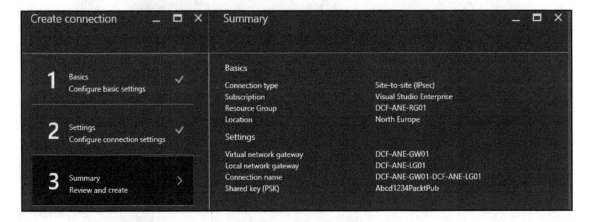

8. To check if the connection is deployed and working fine, you need to leverage the connection item in your **Resource group**:

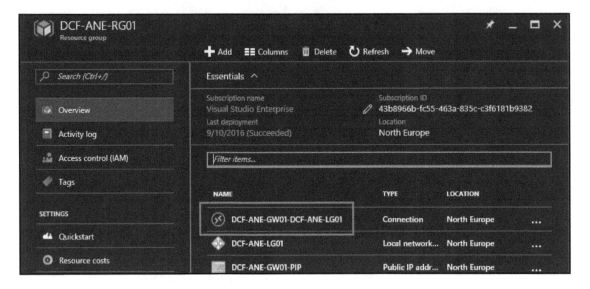

9. There is an **Overview** within the detail blade of the connection. When the connection is successful the **Status** will change to **Successful**:

In most of the cases when the Status of the connection is not changing to connected, there are misconfiguration on the on premises Firewall or Network device. Mostly it's because there are different configurations of timeouts or encryption. For most of the VPN Devices you can find configuration guides on within the Azure documentation. `https://docs.microsoft.com/en-us/azure/vpn-gateway/vpn-gateway-about-vpngateways`If you still have issues, please contact the support of your VPN device manufacturer.

10. If you want to connect multiple sites to one Azure environment, you need to configure the Azure **Virtual network gateway** as a **Route-based** VPN and create a **Local network gateway** for each on-premises site. Then you create a connection for each site link. The following diagram illustrates the count of connections that need to be set up:

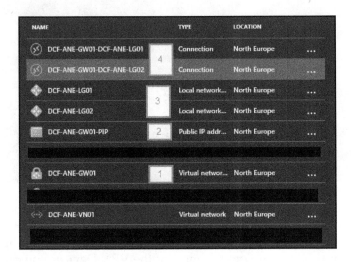

You need at least one route-based **Virtual network** gateway (**1**), one **Public IP address** for the gateway (**2**), two **Local network** gateways (**3**) and two **Connections** between **Virtual network** and **Local network** gateway (**4**).

11. Now you have deployed a site-to-site tunnel to your on-premises environment.

As of September 2016, Microsoft started to support active/active site-to-site VPN tunnels with high performance virtual network gateway. Therefore, you need to configure two local network gateways: VNets and VPN gateways.

Setting up Azure virtual network with MPLS and ExpressRoute

For enterprise customers, a regular VPN connection may not be enough. Most of those customers will want to deploy an ExpressRoute connection. In the next part of the chapter, we will go through an ExpressRoute deployment.

First of all, to deploy ExpressRoute, you need some prerequisites. You need a contract with an ISP who connects your office to an MPLS network. That's a thing Microsoft cannot do for you at the moment.

 The future goal of Microsoft and other Cloud Providers is, that you can deploy and order even ISP connections for your on premises location via Cloud Provider Portals and it's deployed on demand. In most countries that is some kind of science fiction because it requires a full supported and over all available Software Defined WAN in-depended from ISP infrastructures.

After you have signed the contract, you need to evaluate the peering location, the peering partner, and the bandwidth with your ISP. You will need this information during the ExpressRoute deployment.

As soon as you have this information, you can start with the deployment.

Configuring Azure virtual network gateway

We need to configure an Azure virtual network gateway as an ExpressRoute gateway. The following screenshot shows an example:

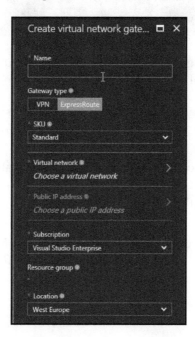

Configuring Azure ExpressRoute circuit

ExpressRoute circuit. To do so:

1. During the installation process of the gateway, you can proceed and install the ExpressRoute circuit. To do so:You need to go back to your Resource group and click Add again. From the marketplace, we select the ExpressRoute:

2. In the next blade, we set up our ExpressRoute circuit. Now we need the information your ISP gave you:

   - **Circuit name**: The name of your ExpressRoute circuit.
   - **Provider**: The provider you or your ISP uses for the peering with Microsoft Azure.
   - **Peering location**: The edge gateway location your provider peers with Microsoft.
   - **Bandwidth**: The bandwidth you ordered from your ISP.
   - **SKU**: Select the service level for your ExpressRoute.
   - **Billing model**: Select your billing. With **Metered** you will pay per download. With **Unlimited** you have a flat rate for your network traffic.

- **Allow classic operations**: Enables your Azure Service Manager deployment model environment to use the ExpressRoute too.

Please be aware that the billing for your Azure ExpressRoute will start as soon as you click Create. To reduce unnecessary deployment costs, you should do that together with your service provider during a live activation session for both sites of the service.

3. After you have created the ExpressRoute circuit, you need to provide the **Service key** to your provider. The **Service key** will identify your Azure **Subscription** against its deployment and it can then create the connection to your environment.

4. You can find the **Service key** within the settings of the ExpressRoute circuit after it is completely deployed:

5. After the **Provider** status has changed to **Provisioned,** you can configure the Azure peering's:

6. To configure the peering's in Azure, you need additional information from your ISP. You need the **Peer ASN**, **Primary subnet**, **Secondary subnet**, **VLAN ID**, and for Microsoft peering, the **Advertised public prefixes**:

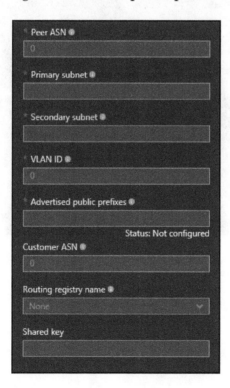

7. To configure the peering, click on the peering type you want to configure:

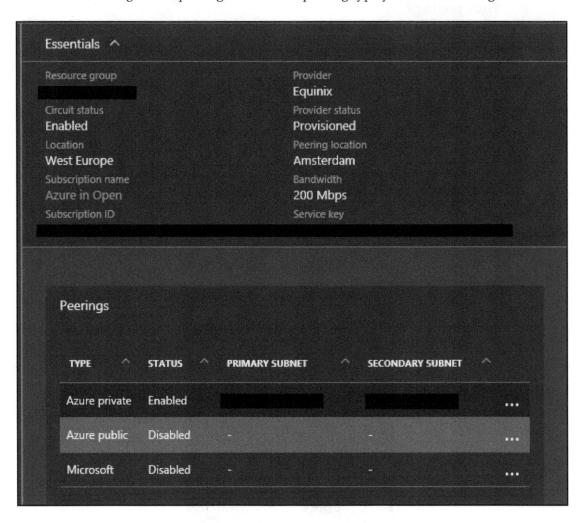

8. Within the upcoming blade, you configure the information you've got from your ISP:

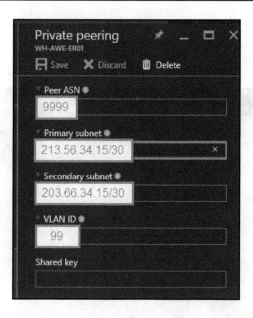

9. In Azure you don't need to do additional routing. As soon as you establish the connection, Azure will directly configure the BGP settings.

10. After you have configured the peering's, you need to create a connection between the ExpressRoute circuit and the Azure virtual network gateway.

Configuring connection between ExpressRoute circuit and Azure virtual gateway

Now we need to establish a connection between the gateway and the ExpressRoute circuit and enable the routing:

1. Please go back to your **Resource group** and click **Add** again. Now we look for `Connection` in the marketplace. Then select **Connection**:

2. In the upcoming blade, you need to configure the connection to be an
    ExpressRoute connection. Therefore, you need to select **ExpressRoute** in the
    Configure basic settings blade:

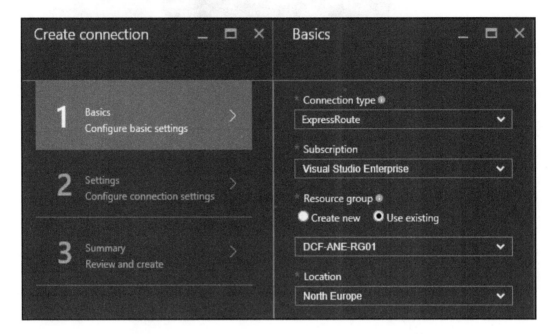

3. Afterwards you need to connect the **Virtual network gateway** and the
    ExpressRoute circuit. You can only select a circuit if private peering is enabled:

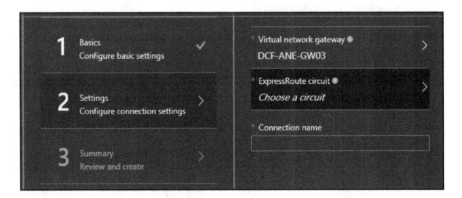

4. After the review and creation of the gateway and all routes on the MPLS site are set, you should be able to reach your services. You can also check them when you open the peering configuration in the ExpressRoute **Settings** again. There you should see some bits of traffic listed in the **Summary**. The following screenshot shows an example:

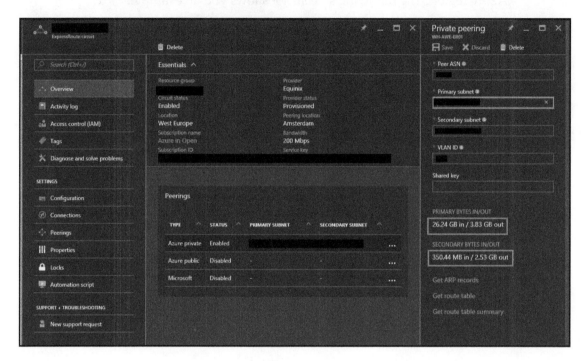

Setting up Azure VNet peering

Now let's look at how you implement the new VNet peering. As already mentioned, you can use VNet peering to configure a connection between VNets in the same Azure region via the Azure backbone.

We will look at the configuration for VNet peering of VNets with different subscriptions. That's the most difficult scenario and you normally would use it to pair networks within different company subscriptions or with subscriptions from other companies.

Preparing the deployment

The following are the steps to prepare the deployment:

1. First you need two subscriptions and both subscriptions need a VNet in the same Azure region. The following screenshot shows you an example:

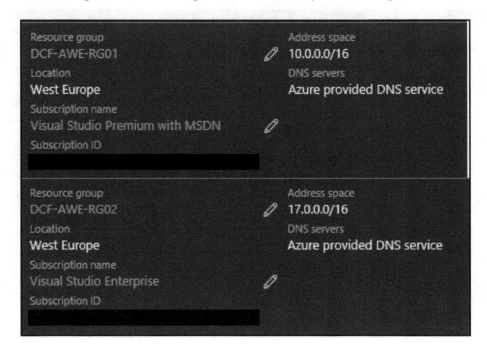

2. Both need to use different IP subnetwork address ranges. In my case, I use 10.0.0.0/16 for **subnet A** and 17.0.0.0/16 for **subnet B**.

3. Before we start, we need to get the **Resource ID** of our partner VNet. You can find your resource IDs by navigating to the settings of your resource. You need to open the **Properties** to find the ID:

4. In the **Properties** blade, you will see the ID in the upper-right corner:

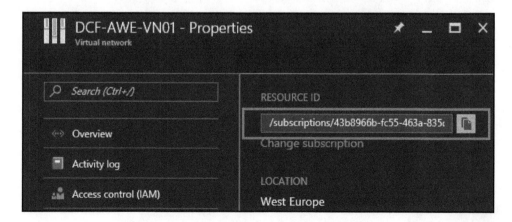

Configuring VNet peering

For configuring the VNet peering, perform the following steps:

1. After the VNets in both subscriptions are prepared, navigate to one of the **Virtual network** and in the **SETTINGS** you need to click on **Peerings**:

2. In the **Peerings** blade, click on **Add**:

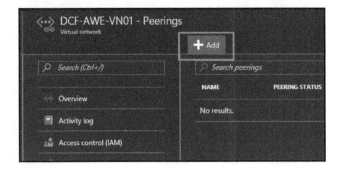

3. In the upcoming blade, you have the opportunity to create a new peering subnet in the existing **Subscription** and **Resource group**. In our current scenario, we need to select **I know my resource ID** to connect a VNet in another subscription:

4. Now you need the resource ID. You need to fill in the ID in the context field after the checkbox:

5. Now you can do some more settings if you need them for your scenario:

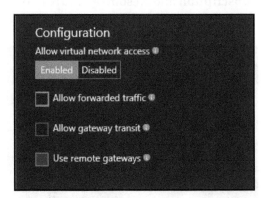

- **Allow virtual network access**: Allows the address space of the peer VNet to be included as part of the Virtual_network. In general the peered networks are linked to each other and become one big network.
- **Allow forwarded traffic**: Allows traffic not originated from the peered VNet to be accepted or dropped.
- **Allow gateway transit**: Allows the peer VNet to use your VNet gateway.
- **Use remote Gateways**: Uses your peer's VNet gateway. The peer VNet must have a gateway configured and a AllowGatewayTransit selected. You cannot use this option if you have a gateway configured.

6. After clicking **OK**, it will take a few minutes until the connection is established. After you have deployed the peering in the first subscription, you should see the status of the connection in the peering blade as **Initiated**:

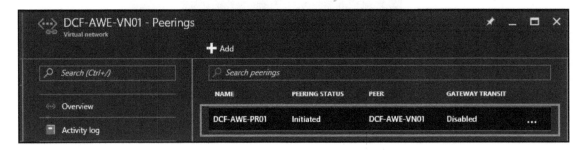

7. To set the **PEERING STATUS** of both networks as **Connected**, you need to repeat the steps mentioned previously in the other subscription too. Afterwards, you change the status in both subscriptions to **Connected** like shown in the following diagram for `DCF-AWE-PR02`:

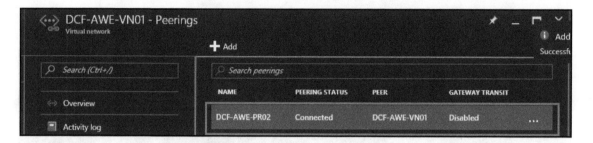

8. The same should happen for `DCF-AWE-PR01`:

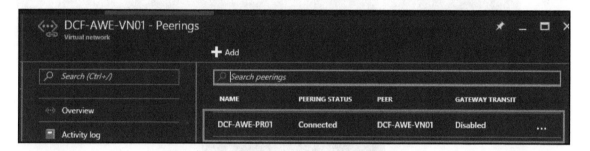

Currently VNet peering is still in preview and under development. Microsoft will extend this service in the near future to support VNet peering with Microsoft Azure public services such as Storage or Azure SQL too.

Configuring custom routes

As you already know, Azure by default routes every traffic to its virtual network gateways. Azure also routes any traffic in any direction. If you want to change those default behaviors, you need to create custom routes:

1. First you need to look for the `Route table` within the Azure marketplace:

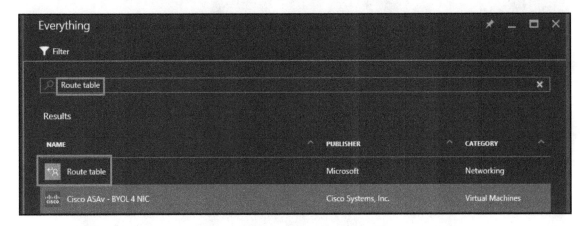

2. The only option in the enrolment process to give your route table a name. The rest will be done through **Route table** settings in the **Resource group**:

3. After you created the **Route table**, you need to go back to your **Resource** group and select the route table you created:

4. The **Settings** blade opens. Here you click first on **Subnets** to open the detail blade to associate subnets to that routing table:

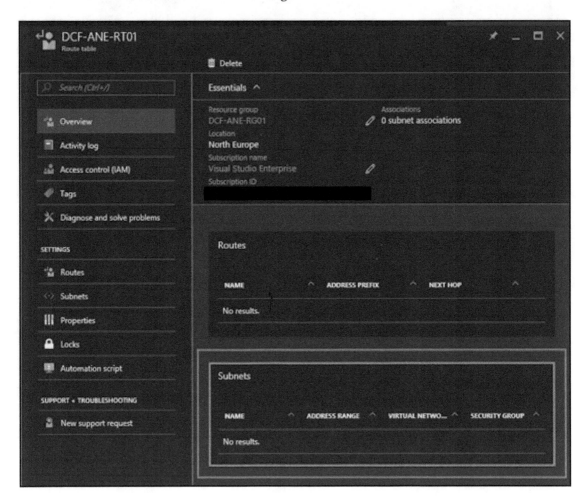

5. In the details blade, you click on **Associate** and add the Azure VNet where the route table should be applied to:

6. Then choose the subnet where you want to apply the table to and click **OK** to commit:

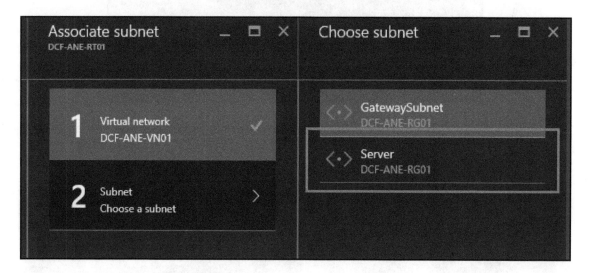

7. As soon as the subnet association is created, you need to configure the route. Click on **Routes** to open the detail blade:

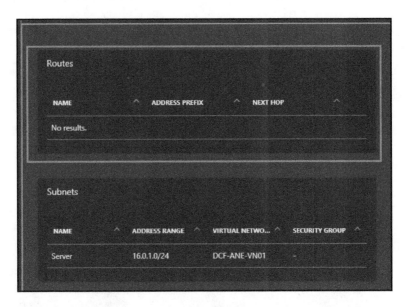

8. In the detail blade, click **Add** to configure the new route. In the upcoming blade, you select a name for your router, the **Address prefix**, the **Next Hop type,** and the address of the next hop:

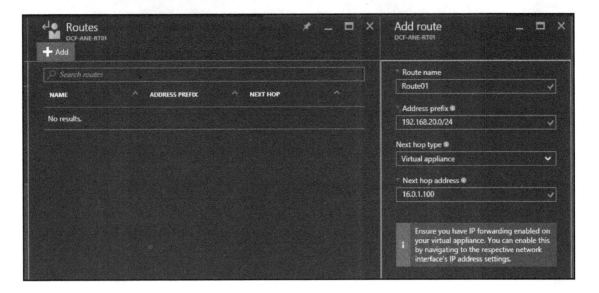

9. It will take a moment until the route will be applied to the subnet.

Configuring third-party network appliances

Basically, third-party networking appliances are Azure VMs running the software of the network vendor. To deploy these machines, you need to:

Set up the click Add in your Resource group:vendor. To deploy these machines, you need to: Basically, third-party networking appliances are Azure VMs running the software of the network vendor. To deploy these machines, you need to: Set up the click Add in your Resource group:

1. Then you need to look for the device you want to deploy:

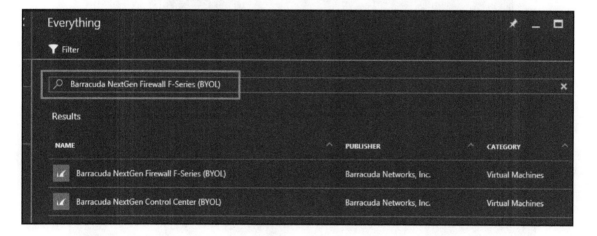

2. Please be aware that for most of these devices, the license is not covered by Azure. So you need to buy an additional license:

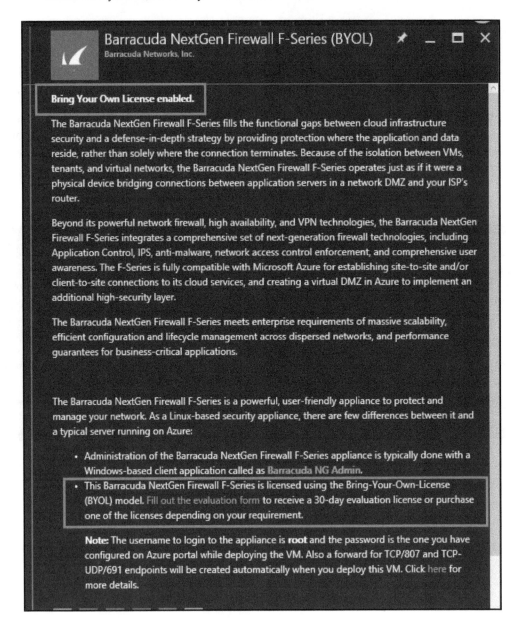

3. In the deployment blade, you go through the different options for deploying a virtual machine.

> We will cover virtual machine deployments deeper in the upcoming chapters.

4. Depending on the operating system of the appliance, the interface may defer. For the used barracuda firewall example you have to give a name to the appliance, add the user account, and set a password or SSH key for connection later:

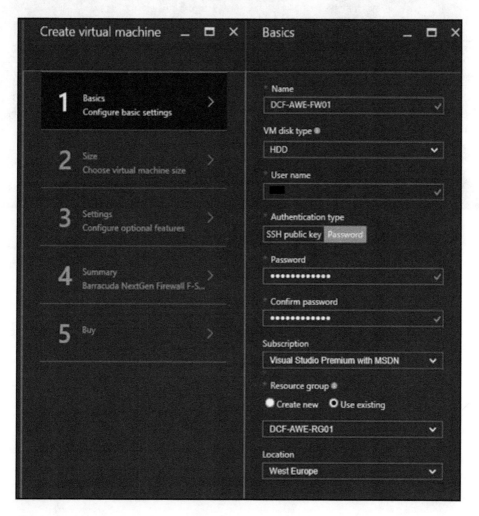

5. Now you need to select the VM size. The vendor already proposes some VM types but you should get in contact with the vendor to get the perfect sizing for your infrastructure:

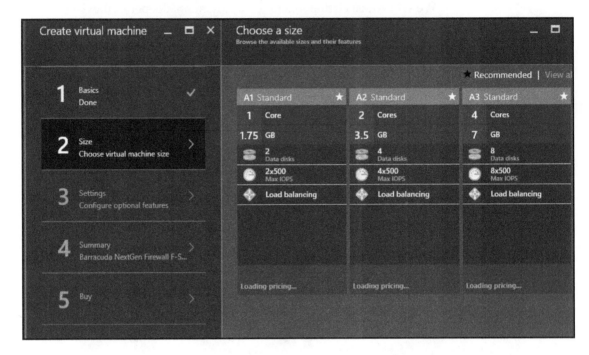

6. After you choose the size, you need to do some optional settings such as setting the **Storage account**, **Network**, IPs, the VM **Extensions**, or **High availability** partners you want to use. For now, go with the defaults; we will explain these deeper in `Chapter 6`, *Planning and Deploying Virtual Machines in Azure*:

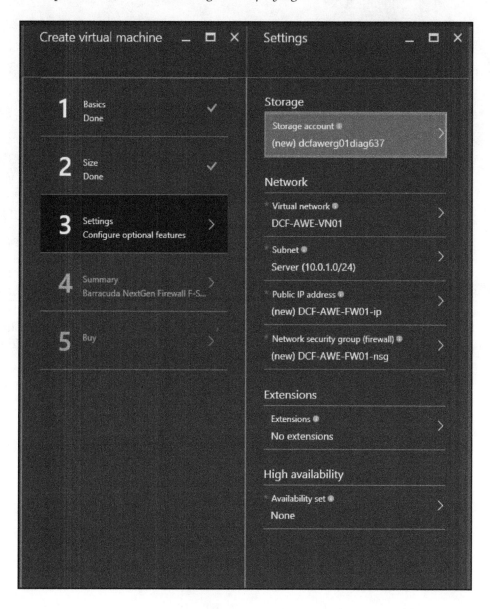

7. Microsoft will show you a **Summary** and validate the settings against the support and configuration matrix:

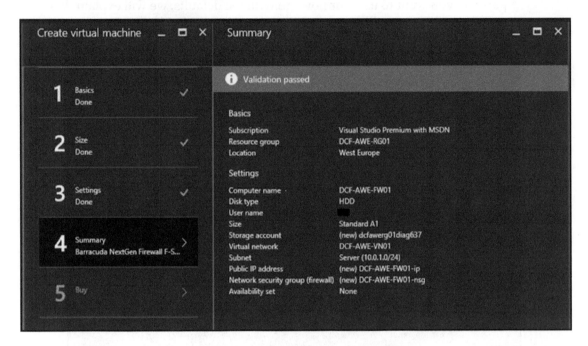

8. For a regular VM, the deployment would be finished at that point, for appliances running on Azure, you need to agree the third-party purchase before deploying:

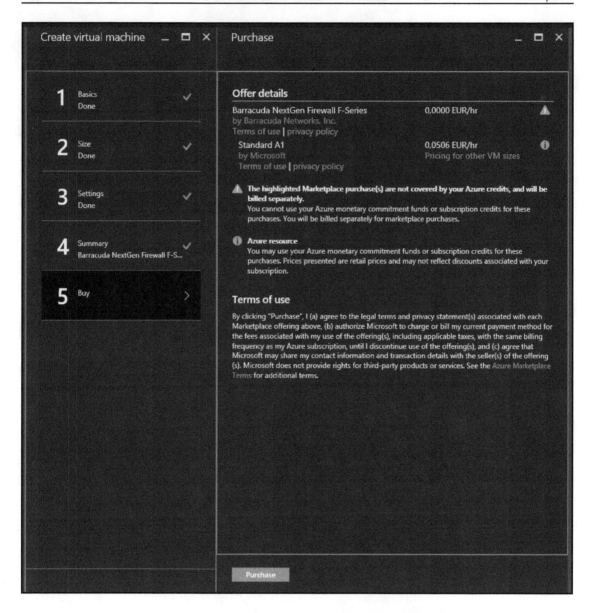

9. After the deployment is finished, you should see the virtual machine in your resource group and also be able to access the device.

10. To connect to the device, you need to look for the IP first. You can find the IP given by Azure in the settings of the device:

 To connect to the device, the vendor normally provides a short How To on its websites. Most providers prefer the connection via SSH, HTTP, HTTPs, or remote desktop.

Common Azure network architectures

Looking at the networking scenarios, the most common one is to integrate Azure and Office 365 directly into your MPLS. Every connection from any location is transmitted via the MPLS network.

The following diagram shows a short abstract of such an environment:

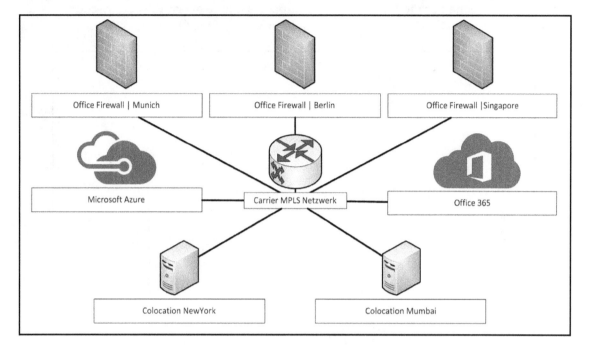

There are also options to use Azure as colocation and connect offices via a VPN. This option is often used by small or medium business companies. There every VPN connection terminates in Azure. Office 365 is reached via Internet from the Office directly:

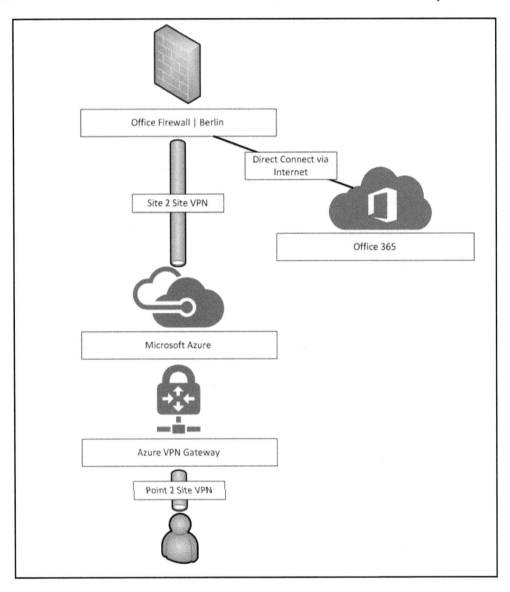

Another very common form of setting up WAN links to offices or other data centers is to have a primary link via ExpressRoute and a secondary link via a **Site 2 Site VPN** with BGP enabled. So your services stay available for your users even if your MPLS fails. You only have a performance impact but stay in production. The rerouting will happen automatically because of the enabled BGP:

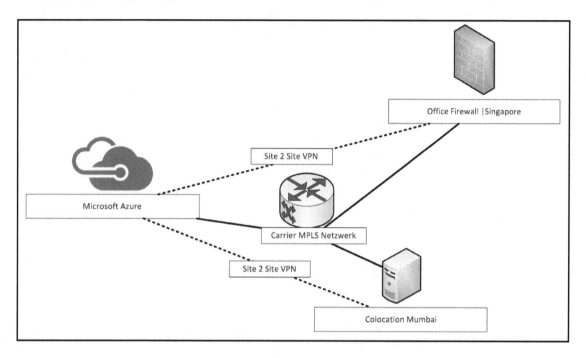

There are also common scenarios where Azure is used only for online services without any on-premises connection or where resources are resold to other customers or end users:

Summary

So let us summarize this chapter. Now you should have learned how networking in and with Azure works. You now know what basics need to be deployed and how to deploy external connections with VPN or MPLS. You also learned about common scenarios and how to change implemented Azure behaviors such as routing.

In the next chapter, we will take a deeper look into Microsoft Azure Storage.

5

Implementing and Securing Azure Storage Accounts

Like you plan the network in your data center or company, you need to do it in Azure also. Many services in Azure are based on storage. Therefore, it has to be planned well.

You should consider scalability, durability, and high availability depending on the scenario and target you try to achieve.

Within this chapter, Azure Storage management is discussed. The key takeaways are how and when to implement and integrate the different Azure Storage types. The following topics and their various options are touched:

- Storage accounts
- Replication and redundancy
- Azure Storage services:
  - Blob
  - Table
  - Queue
  - File
- Exploring Azure Storage with Microsoft Azure Storage explorer
- Premium Storage accounts
- Pricing

This chapter does not handle deep backup, Azure site recovery, or StorSimple topics. We will set up some basic storage configurations in this chapter.

Storage accounts

Azure Storage implements four services: Blob storage, Table storage, Queue storage, and File storage.

Blob storage stores unstructured object data, which can be text or binary data.

Structured datasets are stored in Table storage. Table storage is a NoSQL key attribute data store, enabling rapid development and fast access to data.

In addition to providing reliable messaging for workflow processing, Queue storage makes communication between segments of cloud services available.

Using the standard SMB protocol, File storage offers shared storage for legacy applications. Azure virtual machines and cloud services can share file data over application components using mounted shares. Utilizing the file service REST API, on-premises applications can obtain file data:

1. For creating a Storage account, first search for `Storage` in the gallery and select **Storage account**:

Figure 5.1: Azure Storage account in the gallery

2. After clicking on **Create** button, there is a form with diverse options to fill in:

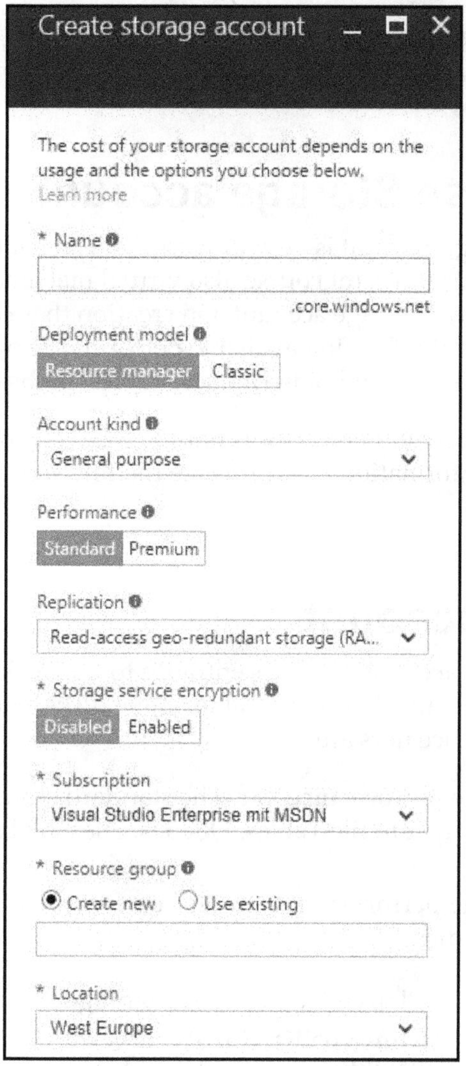

Create storage account _ ☐ ✕

The cost of your storage account depends on the
usage and the options you choose below.
Learn more

* Name ❶

[   ]
.core.windows.net

Deployment model ❶

[Resource manager][Classic]

Account kind ❶

[General purpose   ⌄]

Performance ❶

[Standard][Premium]

Replication ❶

[Read-access geo-redundant storage (RA... ⌄]

* Storage service encryption ❶

[Disabled][Enabled]

* Subscription

[Visual Studio Enterprise mit MSDN   ⌄]

* Resource group ❶
◉ Create new   ○ Use existing

[   ]

* Location

[West Europe   ⌄]

Figure 5.2: Available options at creation

3. The first step is to choose a **Name**. The important thing about Storage account
   names is that they can only consist of lowercase letters and number. No spaces
   here! The example Storage account is named `implementingazuredemo`.

To understand the options in *Figure 5.2*, it is important to understand the different possibilities. There are two separate kinds of Storage account to choose from:

- General purpose Storage account
- Blob Storage account

General purpose Storage account

The general purpose Storage account is very universal. It can contain storage services of any type available. That includes Blobs (of course also virtual machine disks based on Blobs), Files, Queues, and Tables in a Storage account. On creation there are two available performance settings available. The first available performance option is the standard option. This type of Storage account holds Queues, Tables, Blobs, and Files.

The second option is the premium one. This is only capable of storing Azure virtual machine disks. For more information about this see the *Premium Storage* section later in this chapter.

Blob Storage account

A general purpose Storage account provides entrance to Azure Storage services such as Tables, Queues, Files, Blobs, and Azure virtual machine disks, combined under a single account. The two performance tiers are:

- **Standard storage performance tier**: The standard storage performance tier permits the customer to file Tables, Queues, Files, Blobs, and Azure virtual machine disks
- **Premium storage performance tier**: This currently exclusively supports Azure virtual machine disks

To store unstructured data as Blobs (objects), a Blob Storage account is available in Azure Storage. Blob storage shares characteristics with existing general purpose Storage accounts. Similar are the durability, availability, scalability, and performance features. Microsoft recommends using Blob Storage accounts for applications requiring entirely block or append Blob storage.

Blob Storage accounts expose the access tier attribute which can be specified in the process of account creation. It is possible to modify later if needed. Two types of access tiers can be defined based on the data access pattern:

- **Hot access tier**: This tier designates that the objects in the Storage account will be obtained on a frequent basis. This allows data storage at a lower access cost.
- **Cool access tier**: This tier indicates that the objects in the Storage account will be less regularly accessed. This too allows data storage at a lower cost.

It is permitted to switch between these tiers if there is a change in the usage pattern of data. It must be noted that changing the access tier can result in additional costs.

 MSDN subscribers, for example, can get free monthly credits which can be used with Azure services, including Azure Storage.

The requirement to create a Storage account is to have an Azure subscription. The subscription enables the customer access to numerous Azure services. It is possible to create a free Azure account to get started. Once the consumer decides to acquire a subscription plan, it is possible to choose from a variation of purchase alternatives. A single customer can create up to 100 Storage accounts with an individual subscription.

 As there are several differences in pricing for the two account types, in a Blob Storage account, the access tier (hot, cold) also indicates the billing model. The SLAs for both are nonetheless the same.

In the example, we will choose a general purpose Storage account. The next configurable field, besides standard and premium storage, is the replication setting.

To be able to know which one we need, it's important to first understand the different replication redundancy settings.

Replication and redundancy

In order to guarantee stability and high availability, the customer's data in the Azure Storage is replicated constantly. The customer may choose between two replication options: either a storage within the same data center or to a second data center. Replication guards the user's data; in the case of hardware failures, the application is preserved. The use of a second data center provides security for the case of a catastrophic failure in the location of the primary data center.

The process of replication warrants that the customer's Storage account meets the **Service Level Agreement (SLA)** for storage.

There are four replication options between which the user can choose when creating an Azure Storage account.

Locally redundant storage

Locally redundant storage (LRS) means that the data is held three times in a data center in a region. The LRS manages three copies of the customer's data to protect it from hardware failures. LRS does not protect the workloads from the failure of a whole data center.

Zone-redundant storage

Zone-redundant storage (ZRS) stores three copies of the customer's data as well as the LRS. The difference is that the data is guarded in two to three facilities. These facilities can be located in different regions. This concept provides more enhanced durability than LRS. The user profits from durability within a region.

Geo-redundant storage

An even higher durability can be achieved with **Geo-redundant storage** (**GRS**). GRS manages six copies of the user's data. The first three copies are replicated in the primary region. Additionally, another three copies are maintained in a secondary region which is located remotely from the primary region. This concept provides an even higher level of durability. This means that Azure Storage will failover to the secondary region if a failure in the primary region should occur.

Read-access geo-redundant storage

The replication to a secondary geographic location is provided with **Read-access geo-redundant storage** (**RA-GRS**). The customer holds read access to the data, maintained in the secondary location. Access from the primary and the secondary region is possible. The RA-GRS is the default option for your Storage account on creation.

This is an overview about the redundancy options in Azure Storage.

Replication strategy	LRS	ZRS	GRS	RA-GRS
Data is replicated across multiple data centers	No	Yes	Yes	Yes
Data can be read from the secondary location as well as from the primary location	No	No	No	Yes
Number of copies of data maintained on separate nodes	3	3	6	6

Source: https://docs.microsoft.com/en-us/azure/storage/storage-redundancy

For our example, we select **Locally-redundant storage (LRS)**, as high durability is not necessary in our example.

Let's look at the current settings:

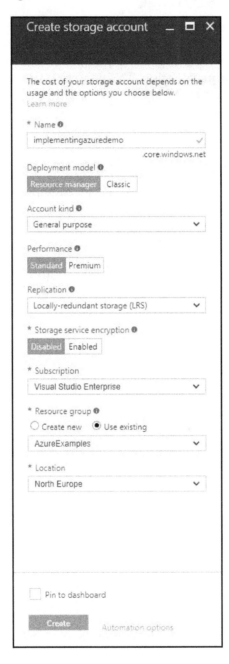

Figure 5.3: Storage account settings

In the example, an existing **resource group** is used to store the Storage account resource. **North Europe** is used as deployment **Location** as it's the nearest location and will probably have the least latency.

To achieve the same using PowerShell with the Azure PowerShell module, the following commands can be used:

```
New-AzureRmStorageAccount `
-ResourceGroupName 'AzureExamples' `
-Name 'implementingazuredemo' `
-Location 'northeurope' `
-SkuName 'Standard_LRS' `
-Kind 'Storage'
```

In the previous command, `ResourceGroupName` is the resource group, that the Storage account should be deployed to. `Name` is the planned name for the Storage account, location is the deployment Azure region, and `SkuName` is a mix of the performance and replication setting from the Azure portal. This parameter can take the following values:

- `'Standard_LRS'`: Locally redundant storage
- `'Standard_ZRS'`: Zone-redundant storage
- `'Standard_GRS'`: Geo-redundant storage
- `'Standard_RAGRS'`: Read-access geo-redundant storage
- `'Premium_LRS'`: Premium locally redundant storage

For more information visit
`https://docs.microsoft.com/en-us/powershell/resourcemanager/azur erm.storage/v2.3.0/new-azurermstorageaccount`.

Azure Storage services

As previously mentioned, the difference between the Blob storage and the general purpose storage is to be found in the purpose of usage. While the Blob storage stores unstructured data, the general purpose account stores structured data. Azure differentiates between four types of storage: Blob, Queue, Table, and File storage. It's important to understand the scopes, in order to be able to decide for a certain type of storage.

Blob Storage services

For customers needing to store large sets of unstructured data, Blob storage offers an attractive and scalable answer. The types of data may be retained in Blob storage are: documents, photos, music, videos, blogs, file backup, databases, images and text for web applications, big data, or configuration data for cloud applications.

Containers offer a useful way to assign security policies to sets of objects; each Blob is assigned a container. A Storage account can hold indefinite containers; a container may contain an indefinite number of Blobs. The only restriction is the 500 TB capacity limit of the Storage account.

There are three types of Blobs: block blobs, append blobs, and page blobs (disks).

Block blobs are utilized for streaming and storing cloud objects. They are a best used for storing documents, media files, backups, and so on.

Whereas block blobs are used for streaming and storing, append blobs fulfill the same task with the addition that they are optimized for append operations. Updating an append blob can only be done by adding a new block to the end. Append blob's field of application consists of logging, in which data has to be written to the end of the blob.

The third type of Blob is the page blob. In most cases, page blobs are used to store IaaS disks. They support random writes. This means that an Azure IaaS VM VHD is stored as a page blob.

In the cases where downloading data over the wire to Blob storage is unrealistic, for example for large datasets, the customer is able to send a hard drive directly to Microsoft, where the data gets directly imported or exported from the data center. In Azure, Blobs are stored in containers. These containers are the upper-most element that needs to be used, to store files as Blobs.

In Azure IaaS there will be a VHDs container created when you deploy an image from the gallery. These containers hold the VHD files for the VMs as page Blobs and also hold status Blobs as block blobs.

Let's look at Azure Blob storage:

1. Navigate to the earlier created Storage account, named **implementingazuredemo**:

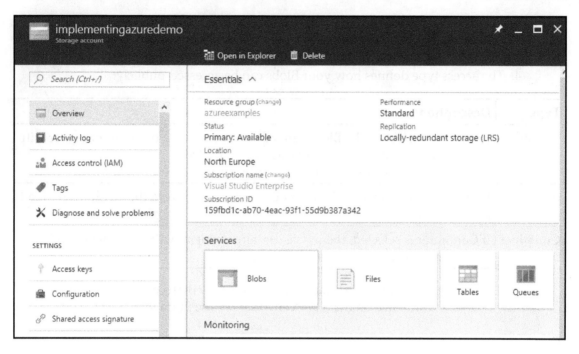

Figure 5.4: Storage account overview

2. In *Figure 5.4*, are all the types of storage that can be used in the Storage account. For managing Blobs, the tile named **Blobs** needs to be clicked:

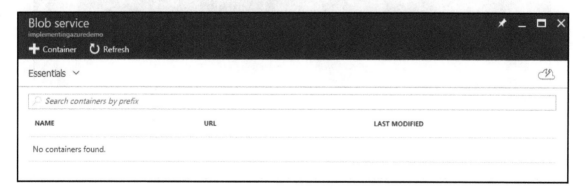

Figure 5.5: Blob service overview

3. There is an empty window, showing, that there are no containers. To create a container, click on **Container**. This will ask for a **Name** and **Access type**. The **Name** has a common Azure policy, so lowercase only.

4. The access type defines how your Blobs can be accessed publicly:

Type	Description
Private	If **Private** is selected, the Blobs can only be accessed by the account owner with the access key and no anonymous access is granted. In PowerShell, this option is referred to as off.
Blob	When **Blob** is selected, only the Blobs can be access from the outside with read permissions.
Container	If **Container** is selected, the whole container content will be publicly available with read rights.

 Remember that these are access policies for the Blob container only and have no influence on the other containers or the Storage account.

5. In the **New container** window, type testcontainer as **Name** and select **Private** as **Access type**:

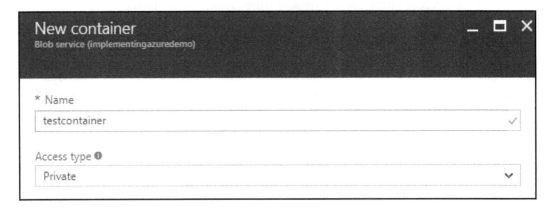

Figure 5.6: New container dialogue

6. After checking all the provided details are correct, click on **Create** button to create new container:

7. The new container is named testcontainer. After clicking on **Create** button the deployment process will start:

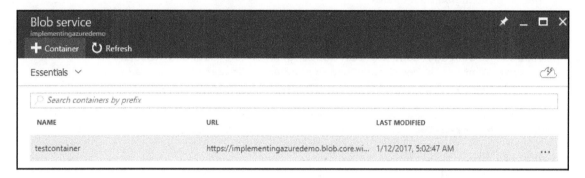

Figure 5.7: Blob services overview

8. After the creation, the newly created resource is listed, and when clicked a new window appears. In this window, it's possible to upload files, view the **Properties** of the container, and manage the **Access policy**:

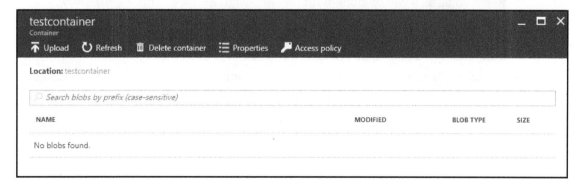

Figure 5.8: Overview of testcontainer's Blobs

9. To achieve the same with PowerShell, the following cmdlets have to be executed. The cmdlets require that Azure PowerShell is already connected to an account and an active subscription is selected:

```
#Define required variables
$storageAccountName = 'implementingazuredemo'
$resourceGroupName =  'AzureExamples'

#Get the Storage account keys
$storageAccountKey = Get-AzureRmStorageAccount `
-name $storageAccountName `
-ResourceGroupName $resourceGroupName `
| Get-AzureRmStorageAccountKey

#Create a Storage context for working with the Storage account
$storageContext = New-AzureStorageContext -StorageAccountName
$storageAccountName -StorageAccountKey $storageAccountKey[0].Value

#Create a blob container named testcontainer
New-AzureStorageContainer -Name 'testcontainer' -Context $storageContext

#Verify the creation
Get-AzureStorageContainer -Context $storageContext
```

10. In the example, we first need to get a so-called Azure Storage context. In this context, we can execute common storage tasks such as creating containers, uploading and downloading files, and so on.

11. To create a remote context, one option is to use a Storage account key. This is the easiest one, as it can be done with the `Get-AzureRmStorageAccountKey` cmdlet.

12. After creating the context based on the Storage account name and the first of both account keys, a container called `testcontainer` is created.

13. For more information on Azure Storage account keys, see the section Access keys.

Blob storage can also be managed via Azure REST API.

Table storage services

Table storage in Azure can be described as a NoSQL database. This basically means that the database has no schema and each value in a table has a typed property name. This property name can be used for filtering, sorting, and as selection criteria. There are multiple entities in a table that each consist of a collection of values and their property names.

NoSQL thus also Azure Table storage has much higher performance, scalability, and flexibility at a much lower, complexity.

Common usage scenarios for Table storage are databases or datasets for web applications, collections of metadata, or bigger collections, for example, addresses.

As with the other Azure Storage services, the only limiting factor for Table storage is the size of your Storage account, which means, there is no limit for the number of tables or entities in tables.

Since Table storage is fast to set up and access, the next demo will show the creation of a simple table. Often Table (NoSQL) storage is much cheaper than traditional relational databases.

Let's create a Table services table:

1. First, click on **Tables** in the **Storage account** dashboard:

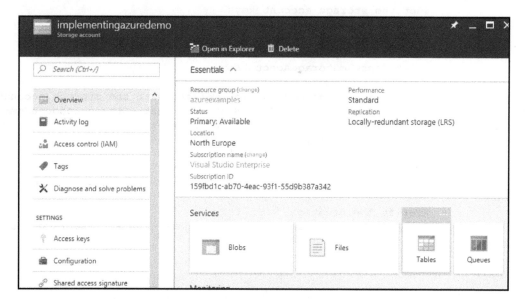

Figure 5.9: Storage account overview

2. After the **Table service** page has loaded, it's recognized that there is no way of creating or interacting with tables in the Azure portal:

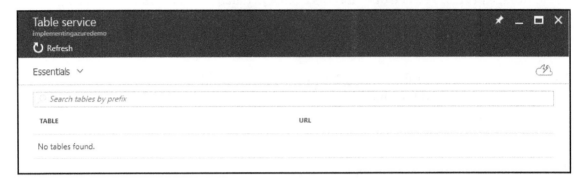

Figure 5.10: Table service overview

3. As there is nothing more to do in the Azure portal, the following PowerShell code is used to create a table:

```
#Define required variables
$storageAccountName = 'implementingazuredemo'
$resourceGroupName =  'AzureExamples'
$tableName = 'testtable'

#Get the storage account keys
$storageAccountKey = Get-AzureRmStorageAccount `
-name $storageAccountName `
-ResourceGroupName $resourceGroupName `
| Get-AzureRmStorageAccountKey

#Create a Storage Context for working with the storage account
$storageContext = New-AzureStorageContext -StorageAccountName
$storageAccountName -StorageAccountKey
$storageAccountKey[0].Value

#Create a table named testtable
New-AzureStorageTable -Name $tableName -Context $storageContext

#Verify the creation
Get-AzureStorageTable -name $tablename -Context $storageContext
```

4. The successful deployment can also be seen in the Azure portal. When navigating back to the **Table service** overview of the Storage account, the newly created table appears under **TABLE** , including its **URL**, on Azure:

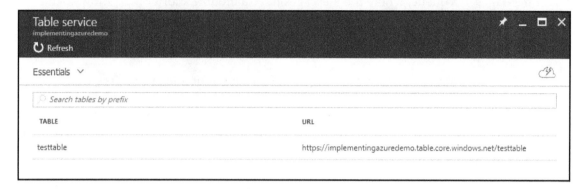

Figure 5.11: Newly created table

5. As there are currently no cmdlets available for managing table entries directly, this has to be done using the SDK in .NET or using the respective library in PowerShell. That is obviously out of scope for this book.

 Table storage can also be managed via Azure REST API.

Queue storage services

Azure Queue enables messaging between different parts of applications. This is used in the development of highly scalable and flexible applications. Components of applications are often decoupled, to enable independent scalability for the single parts.

Queues are also used as an asynchronous method of communication between components that run on different locations (cloud, on-premises, desktop, mobile). It's also possible to build workflows and asynchronous tasks based on Azure Storage Queues.

One Storage account has no limit on the number of queues, as well as the number of messages these contain. A single message can be up to 64 KB in size.

There are two different kinds of queues in Microsoft Azure. The first one is Azure Queues, which is a part of Azure Storage and the one that we are working with in this chapter.

The second is Service Bus queues, which is a feature of Microsoft's Azure messaging infrastructure and has more advanced features for application development. According to Microsoft, Azure Storage queues should be used, when your application must store over 80 GB of messages in a queue, where the messages have a lifetime shorter than 7 days. And Service Bus queues should be used when you need more advanced features such as guaranteed **first in first out** (**FIFO**) ordered delivery, bigger handles, message receiving without polling, and so on.

 For more information on how to choose the right queue solution, visit
https://docs.microsoft.com/en-us/azure/service-bus-messaging/ser
vice-bus-azure-and-service-bus-queues-compared-contrasted.

Let's see how queues look on the Azure portal:

1. First, navigate to the earlier created Storage account:

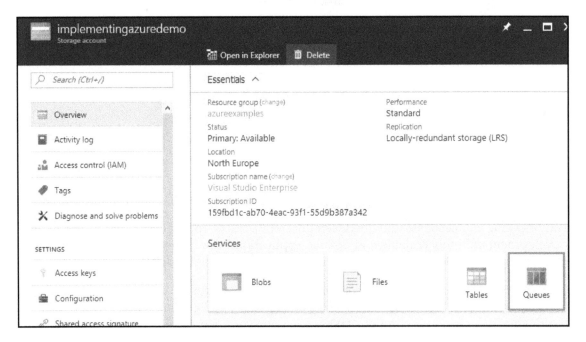

Figure 5.12: Storage account overview

2. Click on **Queues**, to open the **Queue service** overview. There should be no queues in there:

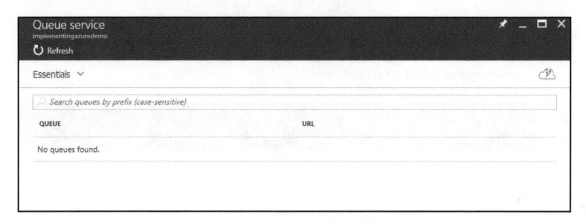

Figure 5.13: Queue service overview

 These are all steps that are possible in the Azure portal. Any creation, polling, or management of queues must happen within PowerShell, Azure CLI or REST API.

3. As all the other things would go too deep into development, we use PowerShell to create a new queue called `testqueue`:

```
#Define required variables
$storageAccountName = 'implementingazuredemo'
$resourceGroupName = 'AzureExamples'
$queueName = 'testqueue'

#Get the storage account keys
$storageAccountKey = Get-AzureRmStorageAccount `
-name $storageAccountName `
-ResourceGroupName $resourceGroupName `
| Get-AzureRmStorageAccountKey

#Create a Storage Context for working with the storage account
$storageContext = New-AzureStorageContext -StorageAccountName
$storageAccountName -
    StorageAccountKey $storageAccountKey[0].Value

#Create a queue named testqueue
$Queue = New-AzureStorageQueue -Name $queueName -Context
$storageContext

#Verify the creation
Get-AzureStorageQueue -name $queueName -Context $storageContext
```

4. As with Table storage, we first need to create a storage context to interact with the queue components. To verify that the deployment was successful, the Azure portal should be opened again. In the **Queue service** overview, there should be a new queue called `testqueue`:

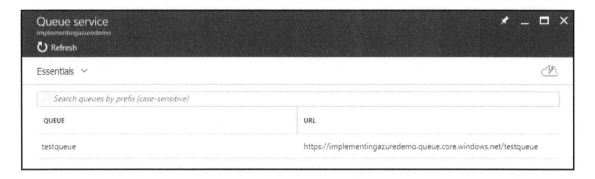

Figure 5.14: Newly created queue service

5. Also, there is no cmdlet available for directly interacting with queues in PowerShell. For interacting with queues the .NET library should be used.

    Queue storage can also be managed via Azure REST API.

File storage services

Currently, the most interesting type of storage for the IT Professional is the File storage.

File storage in Azure refers to cloud-based **Server Message Block (SMB)** or **Common Internet File System (CIFS)** such as that provided by traditional Windows or Samba fileservers.

Like an SMB share, an Azure Storage share can be used from multiple computers and by multiple users simultaneously. The difference is that the users don't have to be connected to the company network anymore.

Azure File shares are commonly used for so called **lift-and-shift** migrations, where the on-premises app is basically copied to the cloud as is. This is often fast and easy, but not always the most cost-efficient solution.

Other scenarios are shares for diagnostics or debugging data, shared application files, or simply temporary storage:

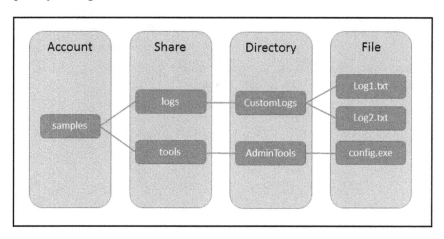

Figure 5.15: Levels of File storage (https://docs.microsoft.com/en-us/azure/storage/storage-dotnet-how-to-use-files)

In *Figure 5.15*, the different logical levels of Azure File storage are shown. Directories and files are optional. Therefore it's enough to create a share and connect to it, to start working with File storage.

Let's create a File share and mount it locally:

1. The first thing is to open the overview of the earlier created Storage account **implementingazuredemo**:

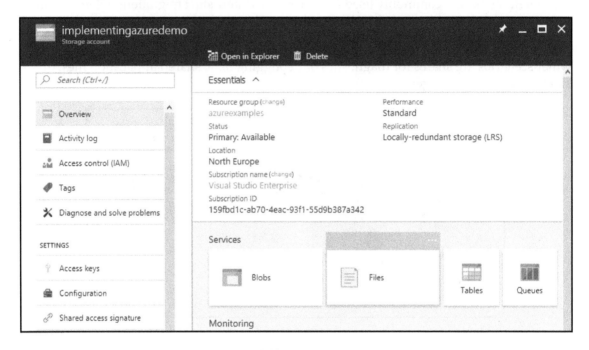

Figure 5.16: Storage account overview

2. After clicking on **Files**, the **File service** overview opens and shows that there are no File shares:

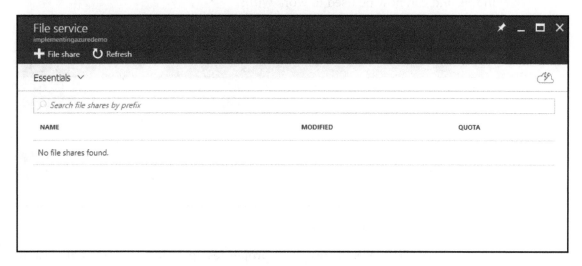

Figure 5.17: File service overview

3. To create a **New file share**, click the **File share** button and fill in a **Name** for the new File share. **Quota** is an optional parameter:

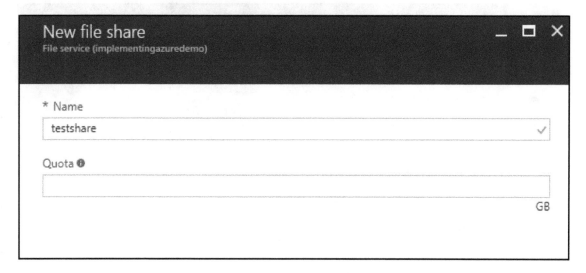

Figure 5.18: New file share dialogue

4. After clicking on the **Create** button, the portal takes us back to the **File service** overview. The new share named `testshare` appears in the **File service** overview window and can now be used to work with:

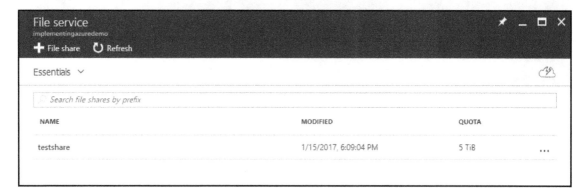

Figure 5.19: Newly created File share in overview

5. When selecting the share, the **testshare** properties open. In contrast to Queue and Table storage, it's possible to interact with the storage in the portal. Creation, directory management, quota setting, as well as uploading and downloading files is supported:

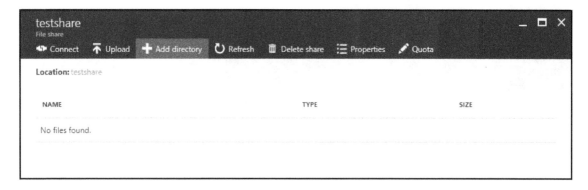

Figure 5.20: File share properties

6. To validate the connection to the test machine, a directory called `testdir` is created:

Figure 5.21: Directory creation dialogue

7. After clicking on the **Create** button, it shows up in the **testshare** contents in a new blade:

Figure 5.22: Directory browser of the testshare

8. Now it's time to connect the share to a desktop computer. For this purpose, the **Connect** button was created. After selecting **Connect**, the instruction to connect to Windows as well as Linux show up:

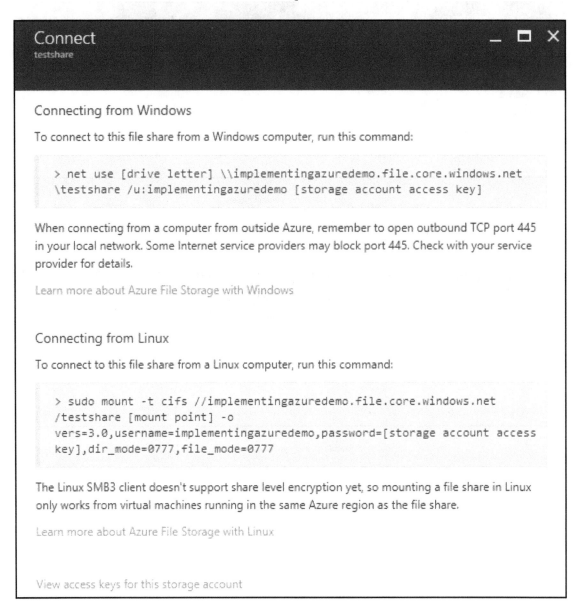

Figure 5.23: Azure File Storage connection commands

9. The Windows instructions are used on a Server 2012 R2 box to connect to the File share. The `net use` command is the traditional command-line tool to connect to network shares. It could also be done via PowerShell with the following line:

```
New-PSDrive -Name Y -PSProvider FileSystem -Root
implementingazuredemo.file.core.windows.nettestshare -Credential (Get-
Credential)
```

10. It's important to use the same credentials as with the `net use` command; the name of the storage account as username and the access key as password. The `net use` command looks like this:

```
net use Y: implementingazuredemo.file.core.windows.nettestshare
/u:implementingazuredemo [AccessKey]
```

11. `[AccessKey]` has to be replaced with one of the Access keys of the Storage account. The output should look similar to this:

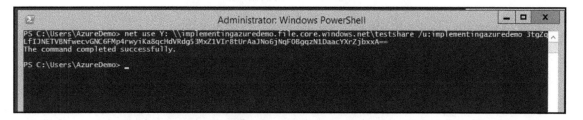

Figure 5.24: Using net use to connect to an SMB share

12. To verify the share connection, just open Windows Explorer and see if there is a new drive under network locations:

Figure 5.25: The connected SMB share in explorer

13. In the following screenshot the network shared drive `testshare` is illustrated:

Figure 5.26: The test directory in explorer

14. Now the File share can be used to store files of any kind.

> To connect a share to a virtual machine, the are some requirements on SMB versions.
> If a VM in the same Azure region as the Storage account is used, SMB 2.1 is supported.
> If a VM in another Azure region as the Storage account is used, only SMB 3.0 or higher is supported.
> If a local machine is used, only SMB 3.0 or higher is supported.

But there are also several downsides of the current File share implementation. Here are some important ones to consider:

- **Storage limit**: Additional to the 500 TB per Storage account and the limit of 200 Storage accounts per subscription, there are also limits on File shares. The maximum size of a File share is 5 TB and the maximum size per file in a File share is 1 TB. On the other hand, there is no limitation on the number of files in total, if you stick to the file and File share size.
- **File access**: Currently, there is nothing like an **Access Control List** (**ACL**) or rights management. Its only possible to allow or deny access to a File share.

The only ways to authenticate for File share access are Access keys and **shared access signatures** (**SAS**). SAS are basically links that can be generated if someone needs limited access to a storage resource. They can be limited by time and storage service type (Queue, Table, Blob, File). Basic permissions such as read, write, delete, and so on can also be defined when generating an SAS. SAS should be used for untrusted external staff, temporary development test, or for customers for tests.

Access keys will be discussed in the next part.

 Microsoft released a tool for working with Blob, File, and Table storage called **AzCopy**. Its main purpose is to transfer data from and to Azure Storage. It can be found at `http://aka.ms/azcopy`.

Access keys

In Azure, storage Access keys are used to authenticate applications that use external or internal interfaces to interact with Azure Storage. Example interactions are a REST API call or a simple net use of an SMB share.

When a Storage account is created, Azure generates two 512 bit Access keys. These keys are very important to the security of the Storage account, for this reason they must be kept safe all the time.

SAS are also created based on the Storage accounts Access keys. That means when the access key that a specific SAS is based on is regenerated, the SAS is invalid and has to be regenerated.

The reason that there are two Access keys in each Storage account is mainly high availability. As it's recommended, to regenerate the Access keys on a regular basis, keys should be rotated to avoid any downtime.

Key regeneration does not influence the access of your VMs to their VHDs.

The current Access keys of a Storage account can be found in the **Access keys** menu in a Storage account:

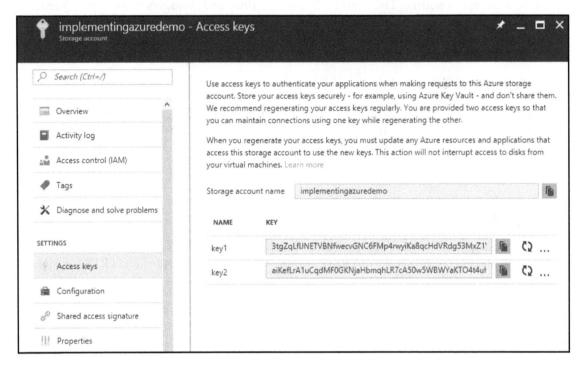

Figure 5.27: Storage account Access key overview

They can also be received with PowerShell:

```
Get-AzureRmStorageAccount `
 -name $storageAccountName `
 -ResourceGroupName $resourceGroupName `
 | Get-AzureRmStorageAccountKey
```

To regenerate a storage key, the regenerate button in the portal is used, as highlighted in the following diagram:

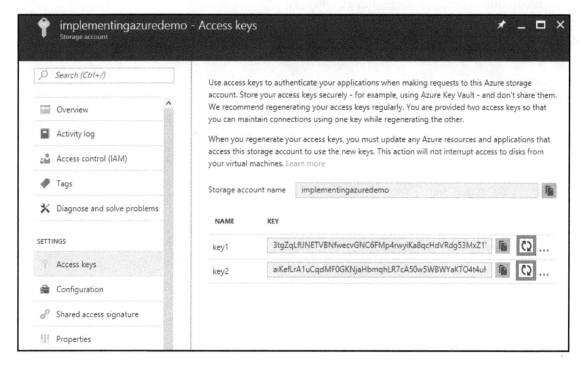

Figure 5:28: Regenerate keys with the marked buttons

To regenerate a key using PowerShell, the following cmdlet is used:

```
New-AzureRmStorageKey -ResourceGroupName "MyResourceGroup" -AccountName
"MyStorageAccount" -KeyName "key1"
```

Exploring Azure Storage with Azure Storage Explorer

Microsoft Azure Storage Explorer is one of the free available graphical tools for managing Azure Storage without the portal or PowerShell.

Storage Explorer is still in preview and could have some bugs in some places. To start working with Azure Storage Explorer, it needs to be downloaded first. The current download link is `http://storageexplorer.com/`.

After downloading and installing, the following screen shows up:

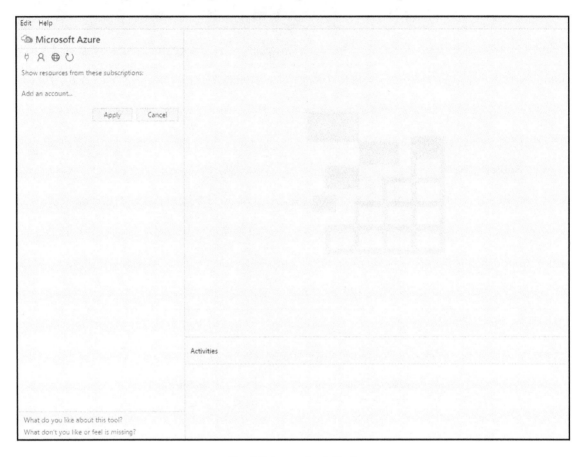

Figure 5.29: Storage explorer dashboard

First, a Storage account needs to be connected. There are two possibilities how one can connect to a Storage account:

1. Add a Microsoft or company account. This is the easiest solution. Azure storage explorer asks for credentials of a Microsoft or company account that has an active subscription. After typing the username and password, Azure explorer has the possibility to select which subscriptions should be managed. By default, all are selected. After clicking on **Apply**, the setup is done, and Azure Storage nodes can be explored:

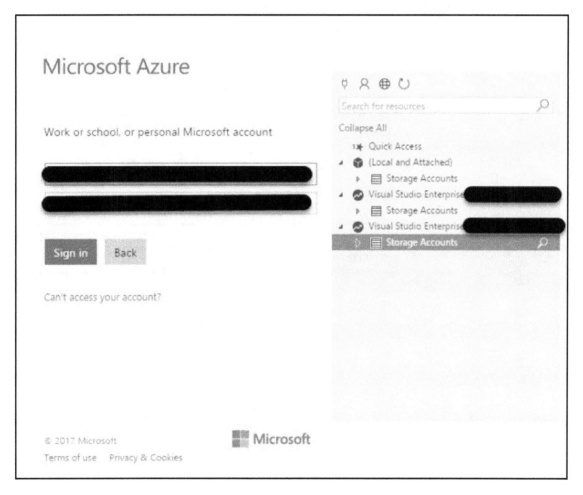

Figure 5.30: Left-Azure login dialogue, Right-Storage Explorer subscriptions overview

2. Add a connection string, SAS URI, or account. It's also possible to connect to your **Storage Accounts** by typing a Storage account key or SAS:

Figure 5.32: Connect with URI, SAS, or key button

The plug symbol opens the dialog, which is used to connect to Azure Storage by SAS, access key, or connection string.

3. After connecting to the Storage account, a node with the name of the added Storage account appears in Storage Explorer. Browsing through the **File Shares**, the earlier created File share can be found:

Figure 5.33: The connected Storage account node

Premium Storage account

In *Figure 5.3* at the beginning of this chapter, there is a performance property at Storage account creation. This property decides whether a standard or a premium Storage account is created. For most workloads, standard accounts are more than suitable but in some cases, more I/O intensive applications need very fast storage. For this case, the premium Storage account was introduced. Premium storage is fully backed by SSD tiers and provides high performance, low latency storage.

Premium storage can currently only be used for virtual disks used in VMs (page blobs). The performance property can't be changed after Storage account creation, but it's possible to migrate VMs from the standard to premium storage tier.

Depending on the machine size, it's possible to attach up to 64 disks to a VM (`Standard_GS5`). A `Standard_GS5`-sized machine supports up to 80,000 uncached IOPS and 2000 MB/s disk throughput.

Microsoft examples for enterprise applications that may need premium storage are Dynamics AX, Dynamics CRM, Exchange Server, SharePoint Farms, SAP Business Suite, SQL Server, Oracle, MongoDB, MySQL, and Redis.

Premium storage requirements

Premium storage supports DS-series, DSv2-series, GS-series, and Fs-series Azure virtual machines. Standard and premium VM disks can be attached to premium storage VMs. Premium storage disks cannot be used if the VM is not premium storage compatible.

Pricing

The billing for Azure Storage usage depends on the used Storage account. Also, storage costs are based on these determinants:

- **Location**: This describes the geographical region in which the account is based.
- **Storage capacity**: This refers to how much of the Storage account is used to store data.

- **Account type**: Based on the usage of either the general purpose Storage account or the Blob Storage account, the account type affects the billing. When using a Blob Storage account, the access tier also defines the billing model for the account.
- **Storage transactions**: Transactions are all read and write operations to Azure Storage.
- **Replication scheme**: This describes the number of copies of your data and where they are stored.
- **Data egress**: This the data that is transported out of an Azure region. This usually happens when the data is obtained by an application that is located in another region or in an on-premises location. If data egresses Azure, charges apply.

 For more information on pricing, please use the Azure pricing calculator, located at `https://azure.microsoft.com/en-us/pricing/calculator/`.

Summary

Now you should have learned about the different types of storage that are available in Azure as well as which replication and availability options they have.

Also, we have created a Storage account and a few storage services in it. You should also know some basic tools and PowerShell cmdlets to interact with Azure Storage.

The next chapter will focus on Azure virtual machines.

6
Planning and Deploying Virtual Machines in Azure

If you want to run your services within Azure and Microsoft has no PaaS or SaaS offering for that specific service, it is necessary to implement virtual machines in your environment.

To identify the right virtual machine for your services, you need to know the virtual machines types that currently exist and how to implement a virtual machine within your Azure environment.

In this chapter, you will learn the basics about Azure virtual machines, how to implement virtual machines, and virtual machine license offerings from the Azure marketplace.

We are going to explore the following topics:

- Virtual machine types and their usage
- License offerings
- How to deploy a virtual machine
- How to change virtual machine settings
- Common virtual machine use cases

We will also setup a virtual machine during this chapter.

Azure virtual machine types

As soon as you start working with virtual machines, you will notice that Microsoft offers lots of different virtual machines and is still expanding its offerings. The reason why Microsoft offers so many virtual machines types is easy to explain. Microsoft needs to support different kinds of workload. virtual machines are always the basement for every Microsoft service offered out of Azure or other Microsoft Cloud services. Virtual machines are also the core component for virtual appliances in Azure such as Hadoop, Microsoft Dynamics Navision, third-party network appliances, or open source appliances.

Microsoft currently offers the following types of virtual machines:

- **Basic A-series**: For testing and development.
- **StandardA-series**: All-round virtual machines for various workloads.
- **Compute intense A-series**: Designed for high performance computing.
- **D and DS-series**: For enterprise applications and applications for higher demand on compute power and temporary disk performance.
- **F and FS-series**: Optimized for network operation. They support workloads for virtualized network devices or applications with a high network demand such as web servers or real-time communication.
- **G and GS-series**: Built for enterprise applications with high compute demand such as databases, SharePoint, and NoSQL or big data calculations.
- **H-series**: Built for high performance computing.
- **N-series**: These virtual machines include an NVIDIA Tesla M60 and K80. They are built for VDI or GPU computing.
- *** LS-series:** Build for low latency storage demands above the offerings of GS-series.

As you can see, there are some virtual machine types which have an *S* within the name. Those types represent the storage. S-series virtual machines use solid state disks or SSDs and Azure premium storage as the primary storage type for data and operating systems. They should be chosen for regular storage performance over 500 IOPS.

Most of the virtual machine types are only made different by certain quality of service standards and priorities against other virtual machine types but there are also connections to their virtualization host. Microsoft mostly uses standard Intel Xeon processors. Microsoft standard is currently based on Intel Haswell architecture and will be upgraded to Skylake processor architecture.

When looking into this you will find an expression for the used CPUs in the Microsoft documentation at `https://azure.microsoft.com/en-us/d ocumentation/articles/virtual-machines-windows-sizes/`.

To get an idea which type of CPU is used by Microsoft to host your virtual machine, you should look up the virtual hardware. For example, the CPU which is used for your virtual machine.

Microsoft updates the virtual machine series along with their hardware and CPU updates. To track these changes, it is recommended to refer to the Microsoft documentation.

A-series virtual machines

A-series virtual machines are divided into two categories. The first one is **basic** and the second is **standard**, which is also the class of all other virtual machine series.

A-series virtual machines are very common and Microsoft deploys them over a variety of hardware types and CPUs. The performance of an A-series virtual machine is throttled, based upon the hardware, to offer consistent processor performance for the running instance, regardless of the hardware.

The differences between Azure A-series basic and standard are:

- **Availability**: Basic tier VMs are only available in small A0-A4 instances for testing purpose, standard tier VMs are available on all size instances and regions.
- **Disk IOPS**: Data disk IOPS for basic tier VMs is up to 300, lower than standard tier VMs which have up to 500 IOPS for the data disk.
- **Price**: The price of a single tier VMs can be up to 27% less expensive than standard tier VMs.
- **Feature cut**: Basic tier VMs do not include load balancing or auto-scaling options. To achieve those features for a basic tier VMs, you need to add those to the availability set for high availability, and implement your own load-balance mechanisms for example with Azure Load Balancer and on application level.
- **CPU**: Standard tier VMs have better CPU performance than basic VMs.
- **Usage**: Basic tier VMs are used for testing and development while standard tier VMs are used for the production usage.

The standard tier is good for common usage such as Active Directory Domain Services, Federation Services, or other basic network and application services.

For basic tier VMs, the following performance and virtual machine types are available:

Size	CPU	Memory	HDD GB	Max disks	Max disk IOPS	Max NICs/Network bandwidth
A0	1	0.768 GB	20	1	1 x 300	1/low
A1	1	1.75 GB	40	2	2 x 300	1/moderate
A2	2	3.5 GB	60	4	4 x 300	1/moderate
A3	4	7 GB	120	8	8 x 300	2/high
A4	8	14 GB	240	16	16 x 500	4/high

For standard tier VMs, the following performance and virtual machine types are available:

Size	CPU	Memory	HDD GB	Max disks	Max disk IOPS	Max NICs/Network bandwidth
A0	1	0.768 GB	20	1	1 x 500	1/low
A1	1	1.75 GB	70	2	2 x 500	1/moderate
A2	2	3.5 GB	135	4	4 x 500	1/moderate
A3	4	7 GB	285	8	8 x 500	2/high
A4	8	14 GB	605	16	16 x 500	4/high
A5	2	14 GB	135	4	4 X 500	1/moderate
A6	4	28 GB	285	8	8 x 500	2/high
A7	8	56 GB	605	16	16 x 500	4/high

The A0 size is over-subscribed on the physical hardware. For this specific size, other customer deployments may impact the performance of your running workload. The relative performance is the expected baseline, subject to an approximate variability of 15%.

Within the A-series, there are some much bigger virtual machine types. The A8-A11 sizes are also known as compute-intensive instances. The hardware that runs these sizes is designed and optimized for compute-intensive and network-intensive applications such as databases, high performance computer cluster software, or modeling, and simulations such as Autodesk or CATIA. The A8-A11 series uses Intel Xeon E5-2670 clocked at 2.6 GHZ and the H-series uses Intel Xeon E5-2667 v3 clocked at 3.2 GHz.

For standard compute-intensive instances tiers, the following performance and virtual machine types are available:

Size	CPU	Memory	HDD GB	Max disks	Max disk IOPS	Max NICs/Network bandwidth
A8	8	56	382	16	16 x 500	2/high
A9	16	112	382	16	16 x 500	4/very high
A10	8	56	382	16	16 x 500	2/high
A11	16	112	382	16	16 x 500	4/very high

 All A-series from A8 to A11 **are remote direct memory access (RDMA)** capable.

D-series and DS-series virtual machines

D-series VMs are designed to run applications that demand higher compute power and temporary disk performance. To achieve this, a D-series VM provides a better processors performance with higher limits against A-series, a higher memory-to-core ratio, and a solid state drive for the temporary disk.

They are built for more modern operating systems such as Windows Server 2012 R2. These virtual machines can easily handle workloads from fileservers, databases, applications, and web servers.

The following performance levels are available with D-series VMs:

Size	CPU	Memory	HDD GB	Max disks	Max disk IOPS	Max NICs/Network bandwidth
D1	1	3.5	50	2	2 x 500	1/moderate
D2	2	7	100	4	4 x 500	2/high
D3	4	14	200	8	8 x 500	4/high
D4	8	28	400	16	16 x 500	8/high
D11	2	14	100	4	4 x 500	2/high
D12	4	28	200	8	8 x 500	4/high
D13	8	56	400	16	16 x 500	8/high
D14	16	112	800	32	32 x 500	8/very high

The following performance levels are available with DS-series VMs:

Size	CPU	Memory	HDD GB	Max disks	Max disk IOPS	Max NICs/Network bandwidth
DS1	1	3.5	7	2	4000	1/moderate
DS2	2	7	14	4	8000	2/high
DS3	4	14	28	8	16000	4/high
DS4	8	28	56	16	32000	8/high
DS11	2	14	28	4	8000	2/high
DS12	4	28	56	8	16000	4/high
DS13	8	56	112	16	32000	8/high
DS14	16	112	224	32	64000	8/very high

Microsoft has already updated the D and DS-series to version 2 which are represented by Dv2 or DSv2. They feature more CPUs. The Dv2-series CPU is about 35% faster than the D-series CPU. It is based on the 2.4 GHz Intel Xeon® E5-2673 V3 (Haswell) processor, and with the Intel® Turbo Boost Technology 2.0, can go up to 3.1 GHz. The Dv2-series has the same memory and disk configurations as the D-series.

F-series and FS-series virtual machines

F-series is based on the 2.4 GHz Intel Xeon® E5-2673 v3 (Haswell) processor, which can achieve clock speeds as high as 3.1 GHz. This is the same CPU performance as the Dv2-series of VMs.

The F-series VMs are an excellent choice for workloads that demand faster CPUs but do not need as much memory or local SSD per CPU core. Workloads such as analytics, gaming servers, web servers, and batch processing will benefit from the value of the F-series.

Beginning with F2 or FS2 you will have two network cards within the virtual machine.

The following performance levels are available with F-series VMs:

Size	CPU	Memory	HDD GB	Max disks	Max disk IOPS	Max NICs/Network bandwidth
F1	1	2	16	2	2 x 500	1/moderate
F2	2	4	32	4	4 x 500	2/high
F4	4	8	64	8	8 x 500	4/high
F8	8	16	128	16	16 x 500	8/high
F16	16	32	256	32	32 x 500	8/extremely high

The following performance levels are available with FS-series VMs:

Size	CPU	Memory	HDD GB	Max disks	Max disk IOPS	Max NICs/Network bandwidth
F1s	1	2	16	2	4000	1/moderate
F2s	2	4	32	4	8000	2/high
F4s	4	8	64	8	16000	4/high
F8s	8	16	128	16	32000	8/high
F16s	16	32	256	32	64000	8/extremely high

G-series and GS-series virtual machines

G-series sizes are built to provide the most memory, the highest processing power, and the largest amount of local SSD of any virtual machine size offered by Azure. This extraordinary performance will allow to deploy very large scale-up enterprise applications such as large relational database servers (SQL Server, MySQL, and so on) and large NoSQL databases (MongoDB, Cloudera, Cassandra, and so on). G-series offers up to 32 vCPUs using the latest Intel® Xeon® processor E5 V3 family, 448 GB of memory, and 6.59 TB local SSD drives. Partly those VMs are running on dedicated physical hardware.

The following performance levels are available with G-series VMs:

Size	CPU	Memory	HDD GB	Max disks	Max disk IOPS	Max NICs/Network bandwidth
G1	2	28	384	4	4 x 500	1/high
G2	4	56	768	8	8 x 500	2/high
G3	8	112	1,536	16	16 x 500	4/very high
G4	16	224	3,072	32	32 x 500	8/extremely high
G5	32	448	6,144	64	64 x 500	8/extremely high

The following performance levels are available with GS-series VMs:

Size	CPU	Memory	HDD GB	Max disks	Max disk IOPS	Max NICs/Network bandwidth
GS1	2	28	384	4	10000	1/high
GS2	4	56	768	8	20000	2/high
GS3	8	112	1,536	16	40000	4/very high
GS4	16	224	3,072	32	80000	8/extremely high
GS5	32	448	6,144	64	160000	8/extremely high

H-series virtual machines

Azure H-series virtual machines are high performance computing VMs used for high end computational needs, such as molecular modeling, and computational fluid dynamics such as wave calculations. These 8 and 16 core VMs are built on the Intel Haswell E5-2667 V3 processor technology with DDR4 memory and local SSD based storage.

In addition to CPU power, the H-series offers diverse options for low latency RDMA networking using FDR InfiniBand and different memory configurations to support memory intensive computational requirements.

The following performance levels are available with H-series VMs:

Size	CPU	Memory	HDD GB	Max disks	Max disk IOPS	Max NICs/Network bandwidth
H8	8	56	1000	16	16 x 500	2/high
H16	16	112	2000	32	32 x 500	4/very high
H8m	8	112	1000	16	16 x 500	2/high
H16m	16	224	2000	32	32 x 500	4/very high
H16r	16	112	2000	32	32 x 500	4/very high
H16mr	16	224	2000	32	32 x 500	4/very high

 The virtual machines with size H16R and H16RM are RDMA capable.

NV-series and NC-series virtual machines

The NC and NV sizes are GPU-enabled instances. These are specialized virtual machines that include NVIDIA's GPU cards. The NV sizes are optimized and designed for remote visualization, streaming, gaming, encoding and VDI scenarios such as with Citrix utilizing frameworks (for example, OpenGL, and DirectX). The NC sizes are more optimized for compute-intensive and network-intensive applications and algorithms, including CUDA and OpenCL based applications and simulations.

NV virtual machines

The NV instances are built with NVIDIA Tesla M60 GPUs and NVIDIA GRID for desktop accelerated applications and virtual desktops where customers are able to visualize their data or simulations. Users will be able to visualize their graphics-intensive workflows on the NV instances to get superior graphics capability and additionally run single precision workloads such as encoding and rendering. The Tesla M60 delivers 4,096 CUDA cores in a dual-GPU design with up to 36 streams of 1080p H.264.

The following performance levels are available with FS-series VMs:

Size	CPU	Memory	HDD GB	GPU
NV6	6	56	380	1 x NVIDIA M60
NV12	12	112	680	2 x NVIDIA M60
NV24	24	224	1440	4 x NVIDIA M60

NC virtual machines

The NC instances are built with NVIDIA Tesla K80. Users can crunch through data faster by leveraging CUDA for energy exploration applications, crash simulations, ray traced rendering, deep learning, and more. The Tesla K80 delivers 4,992 CUDA cores with a dual-GPU design, up to 2.91 Teraflops of double-precision, and up to 8.93 Teraflops of single-precision performance.

The following performance levels are available with FS-series VMs:

Size	CPU	Memory	HDD GB	GPU
NC6	6	56	380	1 x NVIDIA K80
NC12	12	112	680	2 x NVIDIA K80
NC24	24	224	1440	4 x NVIDIA K80

Ls-series virtual machines

The Ls-series is built for workloads that require low latency local storage with high demand on IOPS, like NoSQL databases or virtualized Windows Server Storage Spaces Direct Servers. The Ls-series offers up to 32 CPU cores, using the Intel® Xeon® processor E5 v3 family. This is the same CPU performance as the G/GS-series and comes with 8 GB of memory per CPU core.

The following performance levels are available with Ls-series VMs:

Size	CPU	Memory	HDD GB	Max disks	Max disk IOPS	Max NICs/Network bandwidth
Standard_L4s	4	32	678	8	5000	2/high
Standard_L8s	8	64	1388	16	10000	4/very high
Standard_L16s	16	128	2807	32	20000	8/extremely high
Standard_L32s	32	256	5630	64	40000	8/extremely high

The virtual machines with size Standard_L32s run on isolated and dedicated hardware.

Virtual machine extensions

Together with partners and out of its own portfolio, Microsoft offers a wide range of extensions for virtual machines. Those extensions range from simple anti-malware solutions, backup, to deployment extension for desired state configuration to open source plugins such as for Chef server or Puppet.

The following screenshot shows some of the **Extensions**:

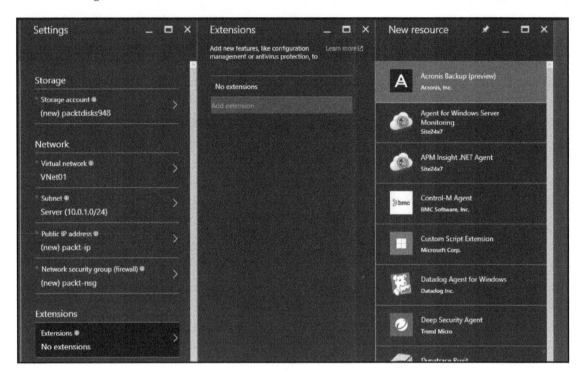

The number of **Extensions** for virtual machines is rapidly growing. To get a full and accurate list, you need to run the following PowerShell command against Microsoft Azure:

```
Get-AzureVMAvailableExtension | Select ExtensionName, Version
```

The virtual machine extensions are already delivered with a license for the product and the cost for that license will be calculated together with your virtual machine costs. Even with the license not purchased by yourself, you can include those extensions into your central management; for example, when it comes to anti malware, and so on.

If you are using, for example, anti-malware software which is also offered in Azure, it could be more cost-effective to use the virtual machine extension license instead of buying a new one.

Managed Disks

With the progress, Microsoft is changing and evolving the Azure environment, Microsoft recently added a new option to virtual machines in Azure.

The option is called **Managed Disks**. These disks are abstracted from the Storage account and Storage account limitations.

You only have to specify the type which can be standard or premium storage and the size of the disk you need, and Azure creates and manages the disk.

Currently Microsoft offers you following types of Managed Disks:

Disk type	Disk name	Disk size
Premium	P10	128 GB
Premium	P20	512 GB
Premium	P30	1024 GB
Standard	S4	32 GB
Standard	S6	64 GB
Standard	S10	128 GB
Standard	S20	512 GB
Standard	S30	1024 GB

To create a virtual machine with Managed Disks, you can do so during the deployment process, we will go through later in the chapter.

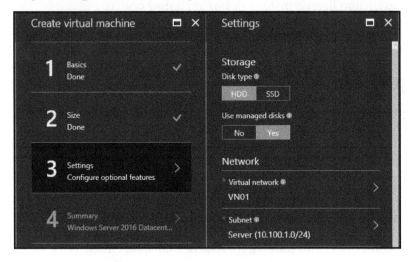

If you want to manage the disks of a virtual machine, you now can find a configuration blade within the virtual machine settings where you can **Edit** or **Add data disk** the managed disks of the VM.

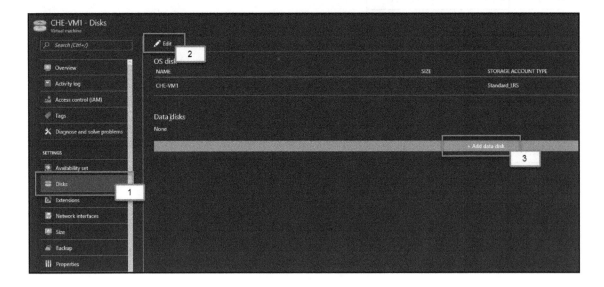

If you are currently working with VM Disks on Storage accounts and want to migrate to Managed Disk, Microsoft offers a detailed guide on the Azure Documentation Website `https://docs.microsoft.com/en-us/azu re/virtual-machines/windows/migrate-to-managed-disks`.

Availability sets

Availability sets are a basic way to let Microsoft Azure know that these two virtual machines belong to a cluster or application group and are now allowed to go down together.

For virtual machines within a availability Azure manages that these machines run within different fault and update domains of an Azure region:

- **Update domain**: Update domain in Azure means, that all physical servers in on update domain will get host updates like firmware, drivers and OS updates at the same time.
- **Fault domain**: Fault domain in Azure means that all servers in these domains run in the same fire sections, with same air condition or electrical source. Which means all physical servers within in those domains, can have an outage at the same time.

The following diagram a schematic view on the distribution of a VM within a availability set:

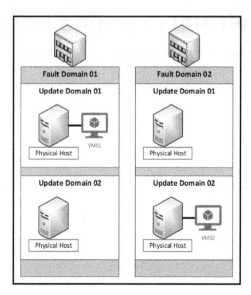

With Azure virtual machine Managed Disks, there is an additional option which comes with availability sets. Azure takes also care that Managed Disks for those VMs within an availability set are placed in different Storage Cluster of the Azure Region.

The following diagram illustrates a simplified how those disks are distributed among the storage clusters:

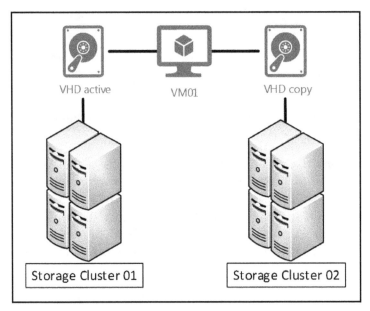

Deploying a virtual machine in Azure

Within this part of the chapter, we will deploy a virtual machine by using the Azure Resource Manager portal. When you followed the guidance in the chapters before, you should have the following things already configured:

- Resource groups
- Virtual networks
- Azure storage

These parts are also the basics for deploying an Azure virtual machine:

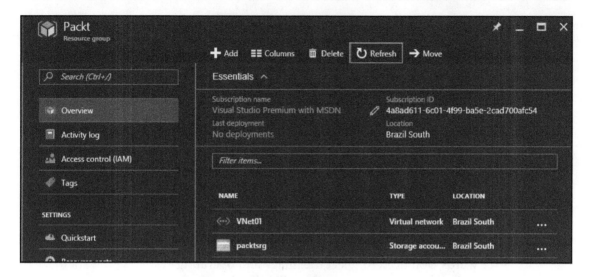

If you have a Resource groups, network and storage ready, you can start to deploy a virtual machine.

1. First you open the side bar and select **Virtual machines**:

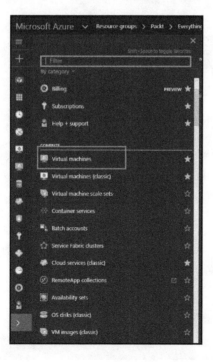

2. Within the new window, click on the **Add** button:

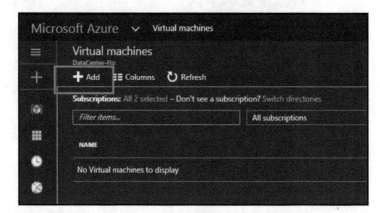

3. Afterwards, you need to select the image and operating system you want to deploy. In the current scenario, we will select **Windows Server**:

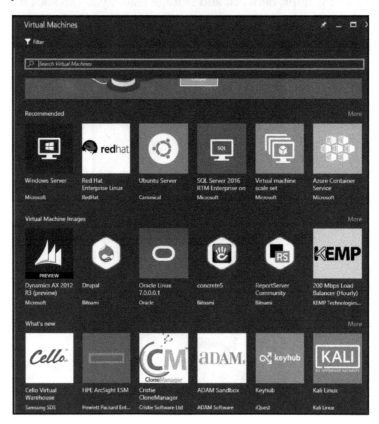

4. Select the version you want to deploy. In this scenario, we will select **Windows Server 2016 Datacenter**:

5. **Select the deployment model** as **Resource Manager** from the drop-down menu. It is not recommended to use **Classic** any more. Click on the **Create** button to start the VM configuration blade:

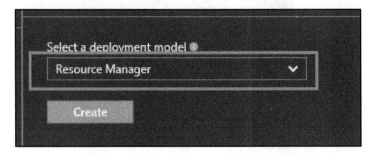

6. Within the basics configuration, you need to set the following things:

- **Name**: The name of your virtual machine.
- **VM disk type**: The disk type you want to use, which is standard storage or premium storage. Depending on this decision, the site and offered VM type will change within the next configuration.
- **User name**: The name of your local administrator. The username can't be *admin* or *administrator*.
- **Password** and **Confirm password**: The password you want to use for the local admin.
- **Subscription**: The subscription you want to use for the VM.
- **Resource group**: The resource group you want to deploy the VM to.
- **Location**: The region you want to deploy to.

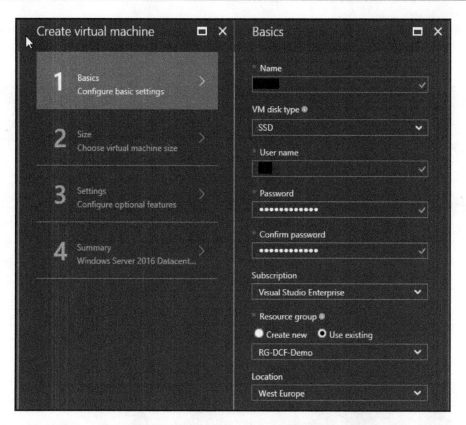

7. Since Microsoft starts support **bring your own license** (**BYOL**) for Windows server VMs in Azure, there came new option available when deploying VM. You now can use your Windows server license with software assurance to active your Azure VM. Afterwards Windows VMs will priced up to 40% less:

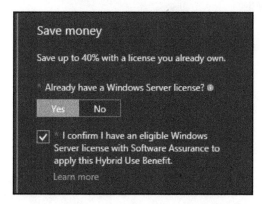

8. After you have configured the basic configuration of the virtual machine, you need to follow up with the sizing. Microsoft shows you recommendations in relation to the operating systems you chose before:

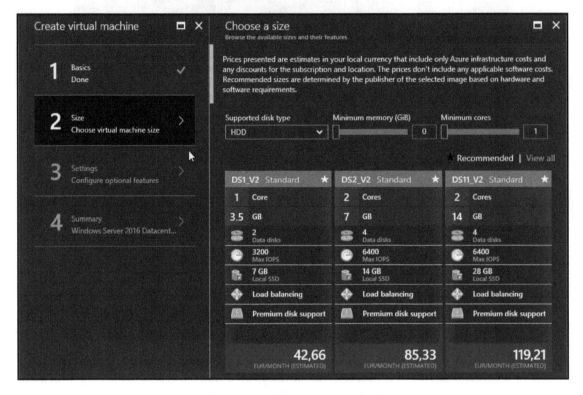

9. Sometimes it is necessary to change the VM type because the application you want to run needs more resources or you have some services running which need less resources. To select other VM types, you need to click **View all** to see all possible VM types:

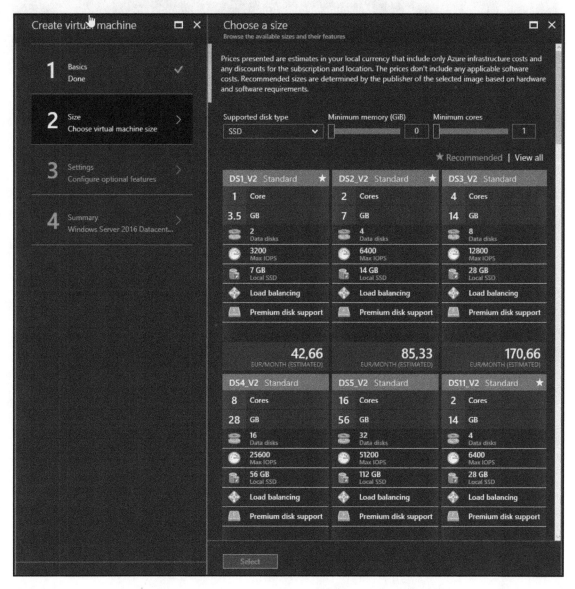

Since the amount of VMs and VM series increased tremendously, Microsoft starts to add filters to support customers to find their right VM series and size. One of the first implemented filter is shown below:

1. After you selected the VM size and type, you need to do the detailed setting. Therefore, we configure the following settings:
    - **Storage account**: Storage of your virtual machine. Here you have the chance to decide if you want to deploy the VM into a Storage account or with Managed Disk
    - **Network**: Private virtual network where you want to deploy your virtual machine
    - **Subnet**: The subnet where you want to deploy your virtual machine
    - **Public IP address**: Here you can configure a public IP for your virtual machine if needed
    - **Network security group (firewall)**: Here you configure the firewall setting of your virtual machine
    - **Extensions**: Here you add the extensions such as antivirus agents or deployment agents to your virtual machines
    - **Availability set**: Here you can add dependencies to other VMs if you need to

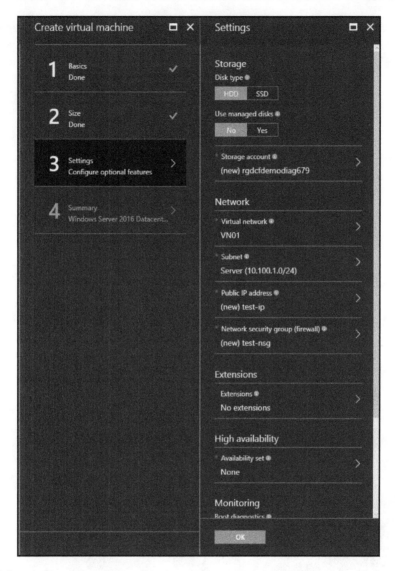

2. Additionally, you can configure monitoring for the virtual machine. The following options can be configured:

- **Boot diagnostics**: Here you give Azure the option to monitor and save the boot of your virtual machine
- **Guest OS diagnostics**: Here you give Azure the option to monitor and save the operating system diagnostic data of your virtual machine

- **Diagnostics storage account**: The storage location of the monitoring log files

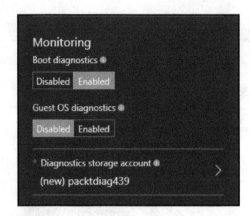

3. Now let us look a bit deeper into the single configuration options.

4. First, we start with the storage. As explained before, now you have the option to configure the storage of our virtual machine. You can decide between Storage account and Manage Disk. In our scenario, we will proceed with deploying a Storage account. Currently Storage account deployments are still the most common and currently the complicate type of VM storage.

5. To deploy the storage, click on the **Storage account** to open the configuration blade for storage:

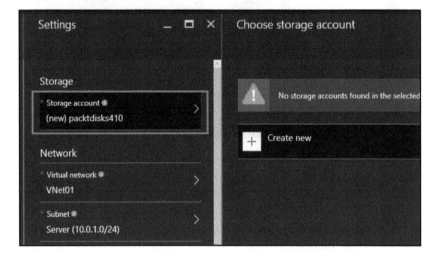

6. If you have already one which fits the type of your virtual machine, you can choose it. Otherwise you need to create a new one:

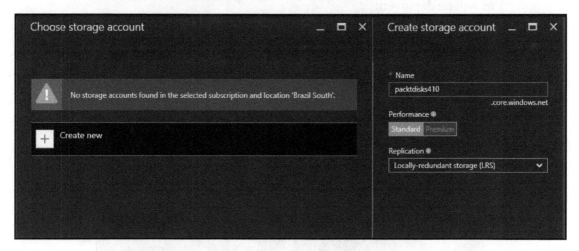

7. After you selected or create the storage disk, you move on and configure the **Network**. Therefore you need to do two options. The first option you configure is the private Azure network and subnet. The second option is only necessary if you do not have any access to your virtual machine via VPN or ExpressRoute. Here you configure the virtual machine with a public IP:

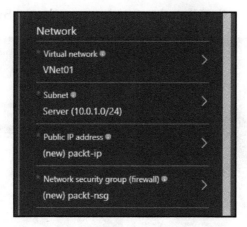

8. If you have already created a virtual network in Azure, it will be listed within the selection. If you have more than one network, you choose in which one the Azure VM will be deployed:

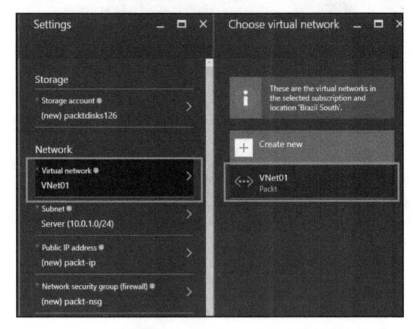

9. After you selected the **Virtual network**, you select the **Subnet**:

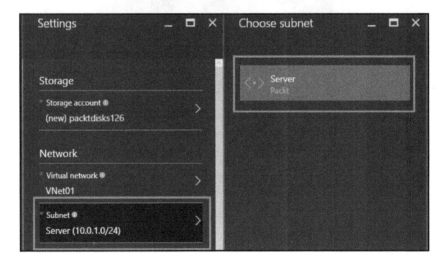

10. Afterwards you create or remove the public IP for the virtual machine:

You should only create a public IP for your virtual machine if it is an Internet facing server or virtual device or you have no other option to access the virtual machine. Otherwise you should click on **None** to remove the public IP.

11. In the next step, you can configure the firewall of your virtual machine. Normally RDP (for Windows VMs) and SSH (for Linux) is already enabled. You shouldn't remove the default settings as soon as you have another way to connect to the virtual machine:

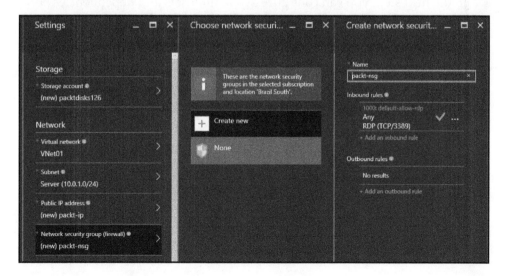

12. After you have configured the firewall, you can add virtual machine **Extensions** such as security software or deployment engines:

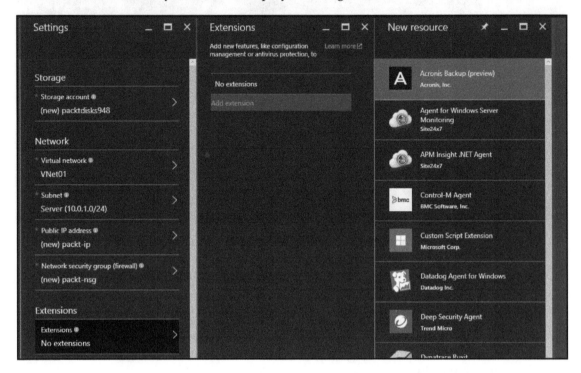

13. In the next step, you can configure availability sets and dependencies between other virtual machines. That supports **High availability** scenarios in Azure, for example when you run clusters or systems which depend on each other:

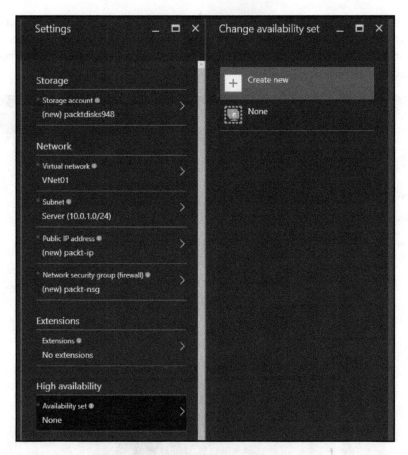

14. Finally, you configure the **Monitoring**. Therefore, you decide what to monitor:

15. As soon as you have **Enabled** or **Disabled** the options you need, you create another Storage account for the diagnostic data. That works the same as the Storage account you already created in the previous chapter or for the virtual machine storage:

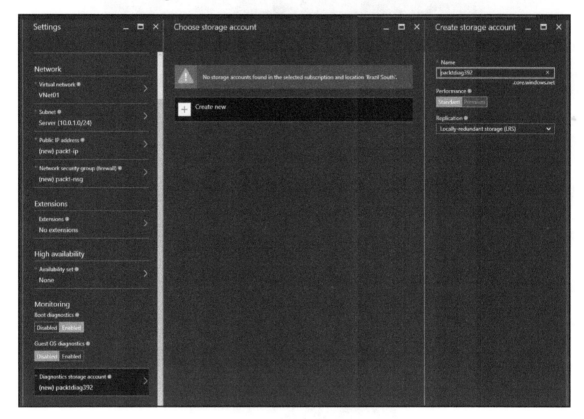

16. At the end, you get a **Summary** for your virtual machine. Click on **Create**:

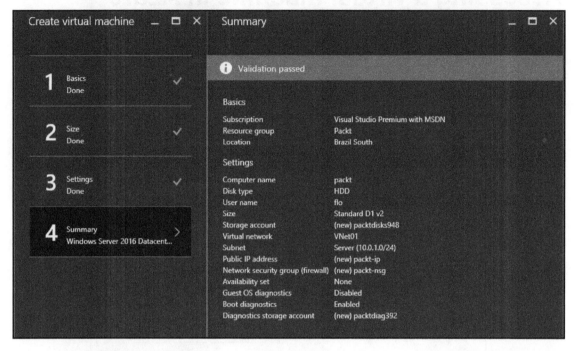

17. Now the creation starts:

 The time needed for deployment depends on your virtual machine size and type. Smaller virtual machines will take longer to be deployed. Every machine in Azure will be installed and configured from scratch. Azure performs no image based deployment such as System Center Virtual Machine Manager.

Accessing a virtual machine in Azure

As soon as your virtual machines are deployed you can access it.

1. Therefore, you can leverage Microsoft **Remote Desktop Connection** for Windows or SSH tools such as PuTTY for Linux:

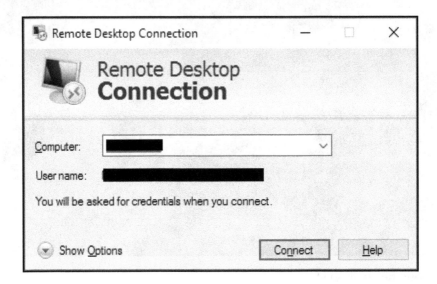

2. To connect to your virtual machine, you need to navigate to your virtual machine within your resource groups. On the **Overview** blade, you will see the **Connect** button:

3. For a virtual machine with a public IP, you can download a **Remote Desktop Connection** file and connect directly to the virtual machine:

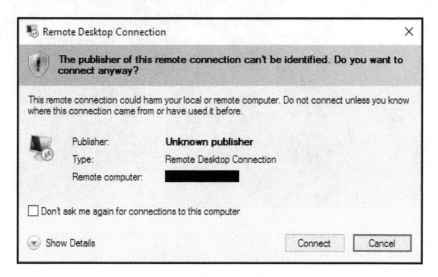

4. If you have a connection to Azure via VPN or ExpressRoute, you can use the private IP given from Microsoft to your virtual machine. This IP can be found on the virtual network adapter of the virtual machine in your resource groups:

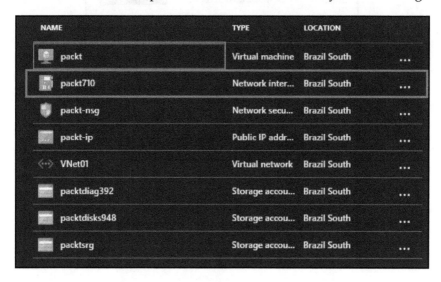

5. There you have also the **Overview** blade and you can see the IP:

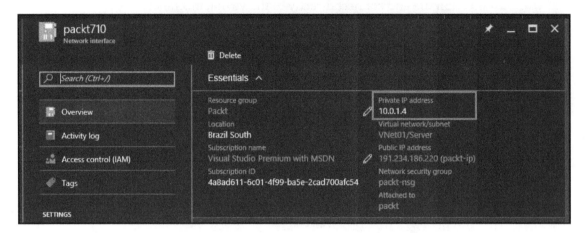

6. After you have started the connection, you will enter the credentials you used for the local administrator:

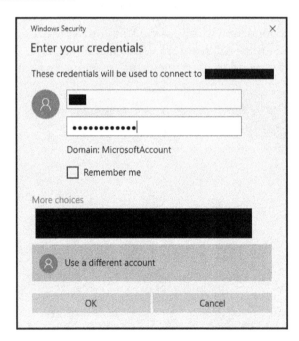

7. Afterwards you should get the desktop of your virtual machine:

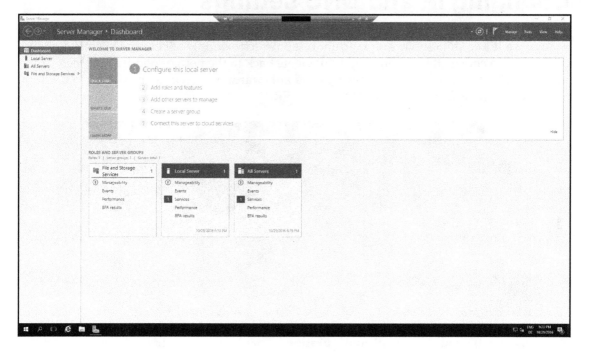

Changing IP and DNS settings

As soon as you are using virtual machines in an enterprise environment, you may want to change the IPs or DNS servers of a virtual machine, for example to connect to your domain controller. To change these, you need to navigate back to the network address of the virtual machine. There you click on **DNS servers** and afterwards you change the option to **Custom** and enter the IP addresses of your **DNS SERVERS**:

To change the IP, you click on **IP configurations**. Then click on the IP configuration. After that you can change the **Assignment** from **Dynamic** to **Static** and change the **IP address** to an IP of your choice within the subnet:

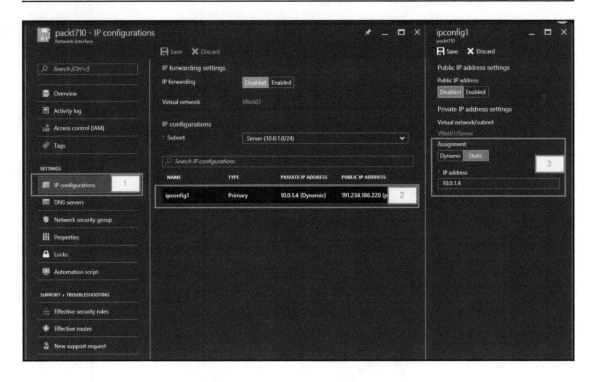

Common scenarios for virtual machines

In the following part of the chapter, you will learn a view common scenarios to start with Azure virtual machines.

Optimization of Azure related communication traffic

As you already learned in Chapter 3, *Deploying and Synchronizing Azure Active Directory*, replication traffic for your hybrid identities normally goes through the Internet. It's only encrypted by using SSL on port 443.

There is an option to optimize security for that traffic by placing the virtual machines in Azure. They will still communicate against the Azure public IP from Azure Active Directory but the traffic is handled on the internal switches and router from Microsoft and the traffic isn't leaving the Azure data center.

To get the Active Directory account from your on-premises, you build up a VPN tunnel or use ExpressRoute to build a secure connection. Afterwards you place an Active Directory domain controller in Azure and replicate from a bridgehead domain controller in your on-premises data center.

The following diagram shows the concept and virtual machine placing:

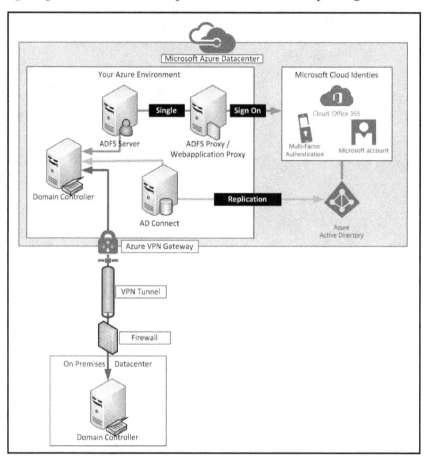

On-demand usage for calculations

Another scenario is to use Azure for workloads which are only temporarily needed; for example, science calculations which need a high amount of calculation capacity and where you have a high investment in the hardware.

So, what do you do? Normally you create a virtual machine Azure Resource Manager template for those machines. Then you create a task which triggers your virtual machine deployment and the transfer of the raw data into Azure. The following diagram shows a draft of the workflow:

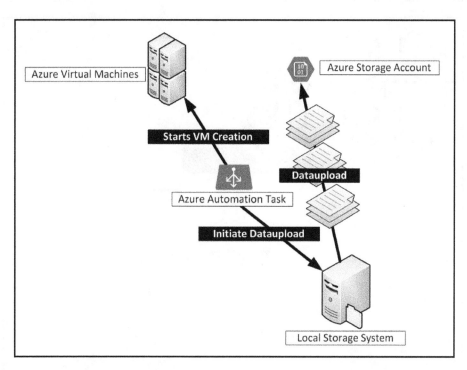

The deployed Azure virtual machines run the necessary calculations and deliver the result into an **Azure Storage Account**. The following diagram shows the process:

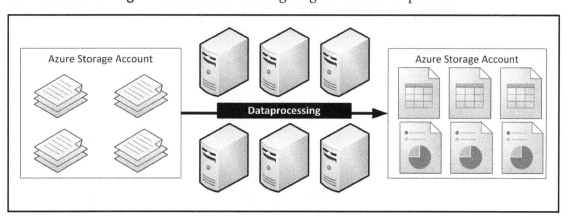

As soon as the calculations are finished, the automation task will shut down and delete the Azure virtual machines. Now the final data can be downloaded or you can use other Azure services such as Power BI Embedded or App Services to present or work further on them. The following diagram shows the workflow:

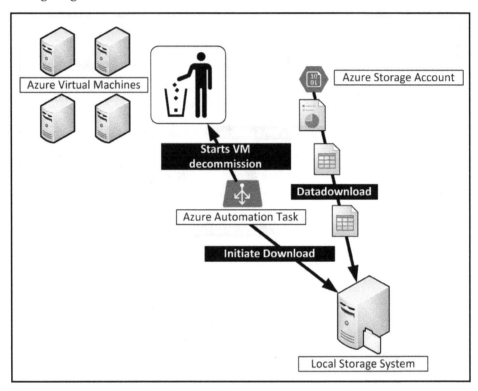

Disaster recovery for on-premises servers

In some cases, it isn't the best choice to place all systems in Azure; for example, when using applications or systems which have a high demand on latency.

In those cases, it is necessary to keep the system on-premises but Azure could still offer support in those situations with disaster recovery or failover options.

For this example, we look at Windows Server 2016 and the new feature storage replication. With storage replication, you can perform an asynchrony storage replication from one Windows Server 2016 to another.

In our case, we place one server on-premises and one server in Azure. The on-premises server is the primary target and replicates to its partner in Azure. That only produces incoming traffic and your clients still connect to the on-premises server. The following diagram shows an abstract of the workflow:

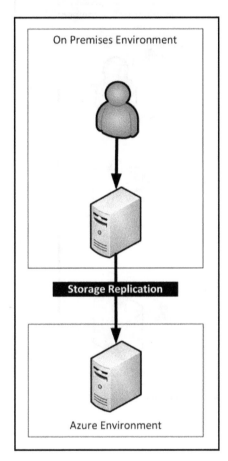

As soon as the on-premises server fails, your users will be redirected to the system within Azure. For most applications, you will have a decreased user experience but your users are still able to work and you get time to get the on-premises server up and running:

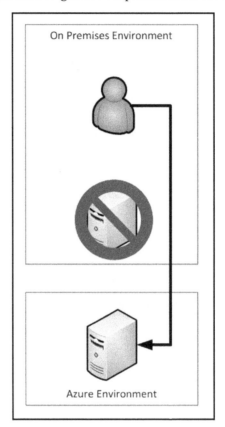

Summary

After this chapter, you should be able to deploy virtual machines and able to decide which VM type and size is the right one for your application. You also know in which scenarios you can benefit from Microsoft virtual machine services and with which scenarios you can start.

In the next chapter, we will take a look into Microsoft Cloud services. Those services are based on Microsoft virtual machines. So, you will recognize some behaviors which are identical to your virtual machines.

7
Implementing Azure Cloud Services

The subject of this chapter is Azure Cloud Services. Azure Cloud Services is the oldest part of the Azure platform and it has been available since its first preview (announced at the Microsoft Professional Developers Conference 2008). Azure Cloud Services is a Pa following screenshot. Otherwise the deployment process would abort with an erroraS offer from Azure and even though there are now some alternatives, it still the leading solution.

What does a service that hasfter a few minutes the project solution will become available. It cons been on offer for so long look like? This question is precisely what I will pursue now and we will ou have already noticed that some instances have additional markings in the form of examine Azure Cloud Services in detail.

In this chapter, we will cover the following topics:

- Azure Cloud Service
- Cloud Service architecture
- Diving deeper into the Cloud Services
- Azure Cloud Services versus Azure App Services
- Creating your first Azure Cloud Service

What is an Azure Cloud Service?

Good question! An Azure Cloud Service is a highly available, scalable, and multi-layered web app hosted on a Windows VM with an installed IIS.

Hosted on a VM? Now you're probably thinking that an Azure Cloud Service is an Azure IaaS solution. Though the idea is obvious, there is a major difference. Cloud Services must be designed to work properly when any parts of the service fail. For this reason, the applications must not store their state in the filesystem of their own virtual machines. Unlike virtual machines created with Azure virtual machines, writes to virtual Cloud Services computers are not persistent because they do not have any virtual machines data disks. OK, enough of the remarks.

Understanding the Cloud Service architecture

We now come to the topic Cloud Service architecture. Look at the following diagram:

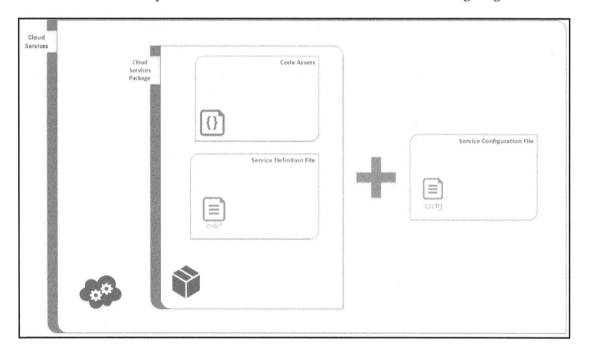

As you can see, an Azure Cloud Service consists of the following two elements:

- **Cloud Services Package**: The service package (`ServicePackage.cspkg`) is a ZIP file and it includes the **Service Definition File** (`ServiceDefinition.csdef`) and the **Code Assets** for the service and the required binary-based dependencies
- **Service Configuration File**: `ServiceConfig.cscfg`

As you also can see, the **Service Configuration File** is outside of the **Cloud Service Package**. This is because changes in the configuration can be made without interruption at runtime (by uploading a new Service Configuration File). However, changes to the service itself require a redeployment of the **Cloud Service Package**.

Roles

Let us continue with the next diagram and the other elements of the Cloud Services architecture. These elements are called **roles** and they are created by the Service Definition File and the code assets.

Each role is an instance of the Cloud Service itself (or at least a part of it). In your planning of the Cloud Service, you should therefore consider which task is associated with a role, how often this task is performed, and, per these findings, determine the number of role instances.

There are currently two options for the roles available:

- WebRoles
- WorkerRoles

The term **WebRoles** is referred to Cloud Service instances that are running on a Windows VM with installed IIS and the term **WorkerRoles** are referred to Cloud Service instances that are running on a Windows VM without installed IIS.

Now we know how the roles are different. The question remains: what are the roles doing?

While instances of the WebRoles serve the actual hosting of your web apps, WorkerRoles are constantly available for the internal processing of business logic and for communicating on the Azure platform (partly using the Azure Service Bus or the Azure Storage Queue Service):

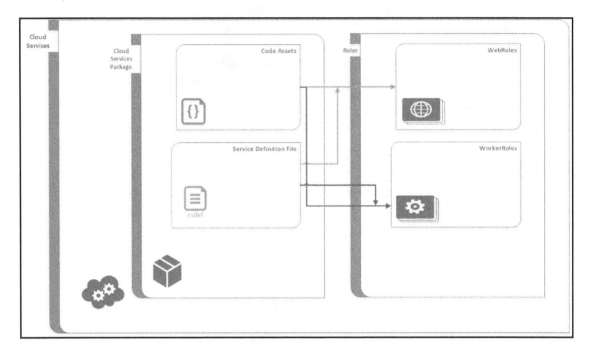

Each Cloud Service has at least one **WebRole** or **WorkerRole**, otherwise the service is not reachable (visible) from outside.

There are limitations for the maximum count of different WebRoles or different WorkerRoles: 25 WebRoles, 25 WorkerRoles, or 25 roles in any combination of both, per provision.

The service endpoint

Let's go to the preceding diagram and thus to the last element of the Cloud Service architecture, the service endpoint.

The service endpoint (an IP address or URL) is provided by a WebRole and it is the public interface to the outside world.

Attention!
Each Cloud Service has only one service endpoint, but this does not mean that additional endpoints cannot be provided.

For example, a **Cloud Service** may have a normal **Service Endpoint** over the HTTP protocol, while a second endpoint may respond to internal calls (for example, from the intranet) over the TCP protocol:

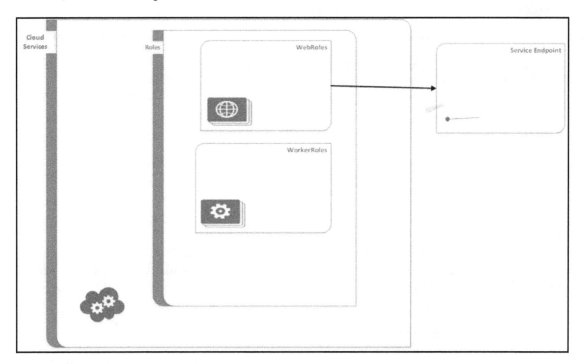

In the first part of this chapter, we learned about the Cloud Services architecture in a rather simple overview and now it is time to discover the finer details of the Cloud Services.

Going deeper into the Cloud Services

For this discovery process, I will explain the blueprints of Cloud Services in more detail. Before the question arises, under blueprints of Cloud Services I understand:

- The Service Definition File (`ServiceDefinition.csdef`)
- The Service Configuration File (`ServiceConfig.cscfg`)

Let's take a look.

Service Definition File

The Service Definition File is an XML file based on the **Azure Service Definition Schema** and it describes the components of the Cloud Service.

A basic template of a Service Definition File looks like this:

```
<ServiceDefinition name="<service-name>" topologyChangeDiscovery="<change-
type>"
xmlns="http://schemas.microsoft.com/ServiceHosting/2008/10/ServiceDefinitio
n" upgradeDomainCount="<number-of-upgrade-domains>" schemaVersion="
<version>">
  <LoadBalancerProbes>
  </LoadBalancerProbes>
  <WebRole ...>
  </WebRole>
  <WorkerRole ...>
  </WorkerRole>
  <NetworkTrafficRules>
  </NetworkTrafficRules>
</ServiceDefinition>
```

Overall, we find five elements in the Azure Services Definition Schema. The root element (that is, top level element) is `<ServiceDefinition>` with the mandatory attribute name and the three optional attributes `topologyChangeDiscovery`, `schemaVersion`, and `upgradeDomainCount`.

The following are additional elements that you will find:

- `<LoadBalancerProbes>`: Defined in the Azure load balancer probe schema
- `<WebRole>`: Defined in the Azure WebRole scheme
- `<WorkerRole>`: Defined in the Azure WorkerRole scheme
- `<NetworkTrafficRules>`: Defined in the Azure network traffic rules scheme

While the use of `LoadBalancerProbes` and `NetworkTrafficRules` is optional, the elements `WebRole` or `WorkerRole` must be filled to at least one of them.

Now we will look at the four elements in detail.

LoadBalancerProbes

Now for the first question: what is a load balancer probe?

The **Azure Load Balancer** (**ALB**) is responsible for routing incoming traffic to your role instances. In order for the traffic to be correctly routed, ALB must first send a query to the respective endpoints and check that the URI returns a HTTP 200 OK code. This process is called **load balancer probe**.

In other words, the load balancer probe is a customer defined health probe of endpoints in your role instances.

A LoadBalancerProbe is not a standalone element, but it exists only in combination with a WebRole or a WorkerRole. A LoadBalancerProbe may be provided for more than one role.

A template of a LoadBalancerProbe element looks like this:

```
<ServiceDefinition ...>
   <LoadBalancerProbes>
      <LoadBalancerProbe name="<load-balancer-probe-name>"
       protocol="[http | tcp]"
       path="<uri-for-checking-health-status-of-vm>"
       port="<port-number>" intervalInSeconds="<interval-in-seconds>"
       timeoutInSeconds="<timeout-in-seconds>"/>
   </LoadBalancerProbes>
</ServiceDefinition>
```

The attribute name and protocol are always required; the attribute path may only be set if you have selected as the attribute protocol value as http. All other attributes are optional.

WebRole

With the WebRole element you define your web application. The only requirement is the ability to run the application on IIS 7 or higher.

Typical examples for this are applications based on ASP.NET (ASP.NET, ASP.NET MVC, and so on), PHP, Windows Communication Foundation, or FastCGI.

A template of a `WebRole` element looks as follows:

```
<ServiceDefinition ...>
  <WebRole name="<web-role-name>" vmsize="<web-role-size>"
   enableNativeCodeExecution="[true | false]">
    <Certificates>
      <Certificate name="<certificate-name>" storeLocation="
       <certificate-store>" storeName="<store-name>" />
    </Certificates>
    <ConfigurationSettings>
      <Setting name="<setting-name>" />
    </ConfigurationSettings>
    <Imports>
      <Import moduleName="<import-module>"/>
    </Imports>
    <Endpoints>
      <InputEndpoint certificate="<certificate-name>"
       ignoreRoleInstanceStatus="[true | false]"
       name="<input-endpoint-name>" protocol="[http| https| tcp| udp]"
       localPort="<port-number>" port="<port-number>"
       loadBalancerProbe="<load-balancer-probe-name>" />
      <InternalEndpoint name="<internal-endpoint-name>"
       protocol="[http | tcp | udp | any]" port="<port-number>">
        <FixedPort port="<port-number>"/>
        <FixedPortRange min="<minium-port-number>"
         max="<maximum-port-number>"/>
      </InternalEndpoint>
      <InstanceInputEndpoint name="<instance-input-endpoint-name>"
       localPort="<port-number>" protocol="[udp | tcp]">
        <AllocatePublicPortFrom>
          <FixedPortRange min="<minium-port-number>"
           max="<maximum-port-number>"/>
        </AllocatePublicPortFrom>
      </InstanceInputEndpoint>
    </Endpoints>
    <LocalResources>
      <LocalStorage name="<local-store-name>"
       cleanOnRoleRecycle="[true | false]"
       sizeInMB="<size-in-megabytes>" />
    </LocalResources>
    <LocalStorage name="<local-store-name>"
     cleanOnRoleRecycle="[true | false]"
     sizeInMB="<size-in-megabytes>" />
    <Runtime executionContext="[limited | elevated]">
      <Environment>
        <Variable name="<variable-name>" value="<variable-value>">
          <RoleInstanceValue
           xpath="<xpath-to-role-environment-settings>"/>
```

```
            </Variable>
        </Environment>
        <EntryPoint>
            <NetFxEntryPoint
              assemblyName="<name-of-assembly-containing-entrypoint>"
              targetFrameworkVersion="<.net-framework-version>"/>
        </EntryPoint>
    </Runtime>
    <Sites>
        <Site name="<web-site-name>">
            <VirtualApplication name="<application-name>"
              physicalDirectory="<directory-path>"/>
            <VirtualDirectory name="<directory-path>"
              physicalDirectory="<directory-path>"/>
            <Bindings>
                <Binding name="<binding-name>"
                  endpointName="<endpoint-name-bound-to>"
                  hostHeader="<url-of-the-site>"/>
            </Bindings>
        </Site>
    </Sites>
    <Startup priority="<for-internal-use-only>">
        <Task commandLine="<command-to-execute>"
          executionContext="[limited | elevated]"
          taskType="[simple | foreground | background]">
            <Environment>
                <Variable name="<variable-name>" value="<variable-value>">
                    <RoleInstanceValue
                      xpath="<xpath-to-role-environment-settings>"/>
                </Variable>
            </Environment>
        </Task>
    </Startup>
    <Contents>
        <Content destination="<destination-folder-name>" >
            <SourceDirectory path="<local-source-directory>" />
        </Content>
    </Contents>
  </WebRole>
</ServiceDefinition>
```

The number of different elements or attributes within the WebRole scheme is, unfortunately, too extensive to be described in detail here. That's why I want just to cover the key elements.

The key elements are:

Key element	Characteristics
Sites	Contains a collection of definitions for websites or web applications that are hosted in IIS. If the no Sites element is specified, you can only have one website or web application hosted.
Site (child of Sites element)	Contains a definition for a website or web application hosted in IIS.
Endpoints	Contains a collection of definitions for input (external), internal, and instance input endpoints for a role.
InputEndpoints (child of Endpoints element)	Contains the definitions for external endpoints that are used to contact the Cloud Service. You can define HTTP, HTTPS, UDP, or TCP endpoints.
InternalEndpoints (Child of Endpoints element)	Contains the definitions for endpoints that are used for the internal communication within the Cloud Service. You can define HTTP, UDP, or TCP endpoints. You can also use Any as a valid value for an endpoint definition.
InstanceInputEndpoint (Child of Endpoints element)	Contains the definitions for instance input endpoints. An instance input endpoint is associated with a specific role instance, and is used for port forwarding in Azure load balancer. You can define UDP or TCP endpoints.
FixedPort	Specifies the port for the internal endpoint, which enables connections to the Azure load balancer.
FixedPortRange	Specifies a range of ports for internal or instance input endpoints, which enables connections to the Azure load balancer.
ConfigurationSettings	Contains the setting definitions for features.
Certificates	Contains the definitions for certificates that are needed for the role.

Imports	Contains the definitions for imported modules.
VirtualApplication	Contains the definition of a virtual application in IIS. When you create a virtual application in IIS, the application's path becomes part of the site's URL.
VirtualDirectory	Contains the definition of a virtual directory in IIS. A virtual directory is a mapping to a physical directory on your IIS.
Startup	Contains tasks that you can use to perform operations before a role starts. Typical operations are: Installing a component (for example, a runtime environment), registering a COM components, setting up windows registry keys, or starting a long running process. The tasks are defined in a `.ps1`, a `.cmd` or executable file.

WorkerRole

With the `WorkerRole` element you define tasks for background processing inside from a `WebRoles` process. `WorkerRoles` run in instances without IIS installed.

A template of a `WorkerRole` element looks as follows:

```
<ServiceDefinition ...>
  <WorkerRole name="<worker-role-name>" vmsize="<worker-role-size>"
   enableNativeCodeExecution="[true | false]">
    <Certificates>
      <Certificate name="<certificate-name>"
       storeLocation="[CurrentUser | LocalMachine]
       storeName="[My|Root|CA|Trust|Disallow|TrustedPeople|
       TrustedPublisher|AuthRoot|AddressBook|<custom-store>]" />
    </Certificates>
    <ConfigurationSettings>
      <Setting name="<setting-name>" />
    </ConfigurationSettings>
    <Endpoints>
      <InputEndpoint name="<input-endpoint-name>"
       protocol="[http | https | tcp | udp]"
       localPort="<local-port-number>" port="<port-number>"
       certificate="<certificate-name>"
       loadBalancerProbe="<load-balancer-probe-name>" />
```

```xml
      <InternalEndpoint name="<internal-endpoint-name"
       protocol="[http | tcp | udp | any]" port="<port-number>">
          <FixedPort port="<port-number>"/>
          <FixedPortRange min="<minium-port-number>"
           max="<maximum-port-number>"/>
      </InternalEndpoint>
      <InstanceInputEndpoint name="<instance-input-endpoint-name>"
       localPort="<port-number>" protocol="[udp | tcp]">
          <AllocatePublicPortFrom>
              <FixedPortRange min="<minium-port-number>"
               max="<maximum-port-number>"/>
          </AllocatePublicPortFrom>
      </InstanceInputEndpoint>
  </Endpoints>
  <Imports>
    <Import moduleName=
      "[RemoteAccess |RemoteForwarder | Diagnostics]"/>
  </Imports>
  <LocalResources>
    <LocalStorage name="<local-store-name>"
     cleanOnRoleRecycle="[true | false]"
     sizeInMB="<size-in-megabytes>" />
  </LocalResources>
  <LocalStorage name="<local-store-name>"
   cleanOnRoleRecycle="[true | false]"
   sizeInMB="<size-in-megabytes>" />
  <Runtime executionContext="[limited | elevated]">
    <Environment>
        <Variable name="<variable-name>" value="<variable-value>">
            <RoleInstanceValue
             xpath="<xpath-to-role-environment-settings>"/>
        </Variable>
    </Environment>
    <EntryPoint>
        <NetFxEntryPoint
         assemblyName="<name-of-assembly-containing-entrypoint>"
         targetFrameworkVersion="<.net-framework-version>"/>
        <ProgramEntryPoint
         commandLine="<application>"
         setReadyOnProcessStart="[true |false]" "/>
    </EntryPoint>
  </Runtime>
  <Startup priority="<for-internal-use-only>">
    <Task commandLine="" executionContext="[limited | elevated]"
     taskType="[simple | foreground | background]">
      <Environment>
        <Variable name="<variable-name>" value="<variable-value>">
            <RoleInstanceValue
```

```
            xpath="<xpath-to-role-environment-settings>"/>
        </Variable>
      </Environment>
    </Task>
  </Startup>
  <Contents>
    <Content destination="<destination-folder-name>" >
      <SourceDirectory path="<local-source-directory>" />
    </Content>
  </Contents>
 </WorkerRole>
</ServiceDefinition>
```

I will dispense with a description of the various elements or attributes within the
`WorkerRole` schema because they are essentially identical to the elements and attributes of
the `WebRole` schema.

NetworkTrafficRules

With the `NetworkTrafficRules` element you can specify how a role communicates with
other roles. Somewhat more specifically, it can limit which roles can access the internal
endpoints of the specific role.

A `NetworkTrafficRules` is not a standalone element, but it exists only in combination
with a `WebRole` or a `WorkerRole`. A `NetworkTrafficRules` may be provided for more
than one role.

A template of a `NetworkTrafficRules` element looks like this:

```
<ServiceDefinition ...>
  <NetworkTrafficRules>
    <OnlyAllowTrafficTo >
      <Destinations>
        <RoleEndpoint endpointName="<name-of-the-endpoint>"
         roleName="<name-of-the-role-containing-the-endpoint>"/>
      </Destinations>
      <AllowAllTraffic/>
      <WhenSource matches="[AnyRule]">
        <FromRole
         roleName="<name-of-the-role-to-allow-traffic-from>"/>
      </WhenSource>
    </OnlyAllowTrafficTo>
  </NetworkTrafficRules>
</ServiceDefinition>
```

The elements of the `NetworkTrafficRules` schema are:

Elements	Characteristics
`OnlyAllowTrafficTo`	Contains a collection of endpoints and the roles that can communicate with them. You can specify multiple nodes of this element.
`Destinations`	Contains a collection of `RoleEndpoint`.
`RoleEndpoint`	Contains a description of an endpoint on a role and allows the communications with this endpoint element. You can specify multiple nodes of this element.
`AllowAllTraffic`	Contains a rule that allows all roles to communicate with the endpoints defined in the `Destinations` node.
`WhenSource`	Contains a collection of roles than can communicate with the endpoints defined in the `Destinations` node.
`FromRole`	Specifies the roles that can communicate with the endpoints defined in the `Destinations` node. You can specify multiple nodes of this element.

Service configuration file

based on the Azure Service Configuration Scheme and it describes how the service is configured.

The Service Configuration File is an XML file based on the Azure Service Configuration Scheme and it describes how the service is configured. A basic template of a Service Configuration File looks as follows:

```
<ServiceConfiguration serviceName="<service-name>" osFamily="<osfamily-
number>" osVersion="<os-version>" schemaVersion="<schema-version>">
  <Role>
  </Role>
  <NetworkConfiguration>
  </NetworkConfiguration>
</ServiceConfiguration>
```

Overall, we find three elements in the Azure Services Configuration Scheme. Root element (that is, top level element) is `<ServiceConfiguration>` with the mandatory attribute `serviceName` and the three optional attributes `osFamily`, `osVersion`, and `schemaVersion`.

The following are additional elements that you will find:

- `<Role>`: Defined in the Azure role scheme
- `<NetworkConfiguration>`: Defined in the Azure network configuration scheme

We will now look at the two additional elements in detail:

Role

The role element specifies the number of role instances, the values of configuration settings, and the thumbprints for certificates associated with a role.

A template of a role element looks as follows:

```
<ServiceConfiguration>
  <Role name="<role-name>" vmName="<vm-name>">
    <Instances count="<number-of-instances>"/>
    <ConfigurationSettings>
      <Setting name="<setting-name>" value="<setting-value>" />
    </ConfigurationSettings>
    <Certificates>
      <Certificate name="<certificate-name>"
        thumbprint="<certificate-thumbprint>"
        thumbprintAlgorithm="<algorithm>"/>
    </Certificates>
  </Role>
</ServiceConfiguration>
```

The components of the role schema are:

Components	Properties
name (attribute)	Specifies the name of the role.
vmName (attribute)	Specifies a DNS name for a VM. This component is optional.

Instances	Specifies the number of instances to deploy for the role. To guarantee a failure-free operation, you need at least two instances but there are no limits to increasing the number of instances according to your needs
Setting	Specifies a setting name and value in a collection of settings. This component is optional.
Certificate	Specifies the name, thumbprint, and algorithm of a service certificate. This component is optional.

NetworkConfiguration

The NetworkConfiguration element specifies virtual network and DNS values. The NetworkConfiguration element is optional for Cloud Services.

A template of a NetworkConfiguration element looks as follows:

```
<ServiceConfiguration>
  <NetworkConfiguration>
    <AccessControls>
      <AccessControl name="aclName1">
        <Rule order="<rule-order>"
         action="<rule-action>" remoteSubnet="<subnet-address>"
         description="rule-description"/>
      </AccessControl>
    </AccessControls>
    <EndpointAcls>
      <EndpointAcl role="<role-name>" endpoint="<endpoint-name>"
       accessControl="<acl-name>"/>
    </EndpointAcls>
    <Dns>
      <DnsServers>
        <DnsServer name="<server-name>" IPAddress="<server-address>" />
      </DnsServers>
    </Dns>
    <VirtualNetworkSite name="<site-name>"/>
    <AddressAssignments>
      <InstanceAddress roleName="<role-name>">
        <Subnets>
          <Subnet name="<subnet-name>"/>
        </Subnets>
      </InstanceAddress>
      <ReservedIPs>
        <ReservedIP name="<reserved-ip-name>"/>
      </ReservedIPs>
```

```
        </AddressAssignments>
      </NetworkConfiguration>
    </ServiceConfiguration>
```

The components of the network configuration schema are:

Components	Characteristics
AccessControl	Specifies the rules for accessing to the endpoints.
Rule	Specifies the action that should be taken for a specified subnet range of IP addresses.
EndpointAcl	Specifies the relations of access control rules to an endpoint.
DnsServer	Specifies the settings for a DNS server.
VirtualNetworkSite	Specifies the name of a virtual network in which you want deploy your service.
InstanceAddress	Specifies the association of a role to a subnet or set of subnets in the virtual network.
Subnet	Specifies a subnet.
ReservedIP	Specifies the reserved IP address that should be associated with the deployment.

 The combination of service definition and Service Configuration Files is denoted as Cloud Service model.

Azure Cloud Services versus other Azure PaaS offerings, such as Azure App Services

Azure Cloud Services and Azure App Services are parts of the PaaS offer from the Azure platform. Both services support applications that are scalable, reliable, and easy to handle. Both services are hosted in a VM. Is everything the same?

Of course not, because Azure Cloud Services also offer more possibilities for influencing the VM. These possibilities of influence are:

- The selection of a Guest OS and an update level
- The selection of an Azure series (that is, VM size)

In Cloud Services it is also possible to build a remote desktop connection to the VM for diagnose and troubleshoot issues. This is not possible in App Services

Let's take a closer look at these selections.

Selection of a Guest OS and an update level

What does this point mean?

The answer is really very simple: you can, if necessary, influence the OS edition (that is, the OS family) and the version (that is, the update level) for the host VM of your Cloud Service.

All you have to do is:

1. In the first line of the Service Configuration File (`ServiceConfiguration.cscfg`), you must add the attributes `osFamily=""` and `osVersion=""` to the `ServiceConfiguration` element.
2. Then fill the attributes with values:

   ```
   <ServiceConfiguration serviceName="<service-name>"
   osFamily="<osfamily-number>" osVersion="<os-version>"
   schemaVersion="<schema-version>">
   </ServiceConfiguration>
   ```

3. Valid values for the `osFamily` attribute can be found in the following table:

OS family	Server OS	Comments
1	Windows Server 2008 SP2	No longer available
2	Windows Server 2008 R2 or Windows Server 2008 R2 SP1	Partially no longer available
3	Windows Server 2012	
4	Windows Server 2012 R2	
5	Windows Server 2016	

With the selection of an OS family, you also have an influence on which .NET framework and which Azure SDK version is supported. Details can be found in the following table:

OS family	.NET framework	Azure SDK
1	No information available	Version 1.0 and higher
2	3.5, 4.0, 4.5, 4.5.1, 4.5.2	Version 1.3 and higher
3	4.0, 4.5, 4.5.1, 4.5.2	Version 1.8 and higher
4	4.0, 4.5, 4.5.1, 4.5.2	Version 2.1 and higher
5	4.0, 4.5, 4.5.1, 4.5.2, 4.6, 4.6.1, 4.6.2	Version 2.9.5.1 and higher

 I cannot publish a list of available values for the `osVersion` attribute, since it is updated every month. The actual valid list can be found at `https://docs.microsoft.com/en-us/azure/cloud-services/cloud-services-guestos-update-matrix`.

In the list of available values for the `osVersion` attribute, you will find three dates:

- **Release date**: From this date, the update level is available
- **Disable date**: Up to this date, the update level is available
- **Expired date**: All instances with this update level are switched off on this date

Between the disable date and expired date are usually 12 months. After this period you must install your instances to a new update level.

Selection of an Azure series

The term Azure series identifies the available performance levels of an IaaS deployment (provision of a Cloud Service and/or a VM). The performance levels (that is, instance) generally differ in the number of CPU cores, the amount of memory, and the maximum size of the data disk.

Some performance levels or even entire Azure series are also defined by special hardware equipment.

Attention! The selection of the performance level also determines the amount of costs incurred for the service.

Let's take a look at the available Azure series.

series A

series A is the classic among the offers and also the only series that is at least partly (in the instances A0 and A4) exists in two versions:

- **Version 1** (basic): This is only intended for workloads in the development and test area
- **Version 2** (standard): This supports the full feature scope of Azure VMs

Instances A8 and A11 are high-end solutions based on an Intel Xeon E5 hardware architecture that is especially suited for data intensive workloads (for example, video encoding, cluster processing, and so on).

Instances A8 and A9 are also network optimized, this means you get a fast network with InfiniBand support.

In detail, each A8 or A9 instance has two network adapters as standard:

- A 10 Gbps Ethernet adapter (to connect to Azure services, such as Azure Storage)
- An InfiniBand 32 GB network adapter and remote direct memory access (RDMA) technology (as a way to communicate with low latency and high throughput between instances in a single Cloud Service or in a single availability group)

The InfiniBand network adapter is reserved for **Message Passing Interface** (**MPI**) traffic only. Typical applications are, for example, high performance clusters, modeling, and simulations.

Instance	Basic	Standard	Cores	RAM	Max. disc size
A0	X		1	0,75 GB	20 GB
A0		X	1	0,75 GB	20 GB
A1	X		1	1,75 GB	40 GB
A1		X	1	1,75 GB	70 GB
A2	X		2	3,5 GB	60 GB
A2		X	2	3,5 GB	135 GB
A3	X		4	7 GB	120 GB

A3		X	4	7 GB	285 GB
A4	X		8	14 GB	240 GB
A4		X	8	14 GB	605 GB
A5		X	2	14 GB	135 GB
A6		X	4	28 GB	285 GB
A7		X	8	56 GB	605 GB
A8		X	8	56 GB	382 GB
A9		X	16	112 GB	382 GB
A10		X	8	56 GB	382 GB
A11		X	16	112 GB	382 GB

series D

Strictly speaking, series D not only one series, but it is divided into series D, Dv2 (version 2), DS, and DSv2.

series D is based on a latest generation CPU (unfortunately not exactly declared) and it reaches a speed of 60% higher than series A (at least for instances A0 to A7).

The Dv2 series is based on a latest generation CPU (Intel Xeon E5-2673 V3 processor (Haswell) with 2.4 GHz) and it achieves a 35% higher speed compared to the D series. In addition, the Dv2 CPU, with the Intel Turbo Boost Technology 2.0, can be overclocked to 3.1 GHz.

The higher CPU performance is only one criterion to describe the series D and its offshoots. Other criteria are as follows:

- The higher ratio of memory to core
- The use of an SSD as a temporary disk

When using the SSD as a temporary data carrier, you should know that this is from the series D local.

The DS and DSv2 series are identical to the D and Dv2 series, but they use Azure premium storage as memory:

Instance	Instance with PS	Cores	RAM	Max. disc size
D1	DS1	1	3.5 GB	50 GB
D2	DS2	2	7 GB	100 GB
D3	DS3	4	14 GB	200 GB
D4	DS4	8	28 GB	400 GB
D11	DS11	2	14 GB	100 GB
D12	DS12	4	28 GB	200 GB
D13	DS13	8	56 GB	400 GB
D14	DS14	16	112 GB	800 GB

The following table shows the available instances of the Dv2 series (version 2):

Instance	Instance with PS	Cores	RAM	Max. disc size
D1v2	DS1v2	1	3.5 GB	50 GB
D2v2	DS2v2	2	7 GB	100 GB
D3v2	DS3v2	4	14 GB	200 GB
D4v2	DS4v2	8	28 GB	400 GB
D5v2	DS5v2	16	56 GB	800 GB
D11v2	DS11v2	2	14 GB	100 GB
D12v2	DS12v2	4	28 GB	200 GB
D13v2	DS13v2	8	56 GB	400 GB
D14v2	DS14v2	16	112 GB	800 GB
D15v2	DS15v2	20	140 GB	1000 GB

series F

series F is based on a state-of-the-art CPU (Intel Xeon E5-2673 V3 (Haswell) at 2.4 GHz), offering 2 GB of RAM per core and a 16 GB temporary disk based on an SSD.

The F series is especially suited for computer-intensive workloads and is used in scenarios such as batch processing, web server operation, analysis, and gaming.

The F CPU can additionally be overclocked with the Intel Turbo Boost Technology 2.0, still up to 3.1 GHz.

The FS series is identical to the F series, but it uses Azure premium storage as its memory.

Instance	Instance with PS	Cores	RAM	Max. disc size
F1	FS1	1	2 GB	16 GB
F2	FS2	2	4 GB	32 GB
F4	FS4	4	8 GB	64 GB
F8	FS8	8	16 GB	128 GB
F16	FS16	16	32 GB	256 GB

series G

series G is also based on a latest generation CPU (Intel Xeon E5-2673 V3) (Haswell with 2.4 GHz) and it is based on the older series D, but the G instances have a twice larger memory and four times larger temporary disks based on an SSD. With exceptional, high-performance VM sizes in the G range, you can easily handle business critical applications such as large relational database servers (SQL Server, MySQL, and so on) or large NoSQL databases (MongoDB, Cloudera Cassandra, and so on).

The G CPU can additionally be overclocked with the Intel Turbo Boost Technology 2.0, still up to 3.1 GHz.

The GS series is identical to the G series, but it uses Azure premium storage as a memory:

Instance	Instance with PS	Cores	RAM	Max. disc size
G1	GS1	2	28 GB	412 GB
G2	GS2	4	56 GB	824 GB
G3	GS3	8	112 GB	1649 GB
G4	GS4	16	224 GB	3298 GB
G5	GS5	32	448 GB	6596 GB

G5 instances are run in isolation on dedicated hardware that is deployed for only one customer.

series N

Now I could report on the type of CPU (it is again an Intel Xeon E5-2690 V3 processor), about memory, or about the size of the temporary disk. But it does not matter, because the series N is not defined by these factors, but by the possibility to use GPUs (the processors of the graphics card) as an additional power factor.

What is the basic idea?

In the form of the GPU, additional computing capacity is provided, whereby the GPU generally operates faster than the CPU in highly parallelizable program sequences (high data parallelism), and therefore, a simple way is sought to supplement the computing performance of CPUs by the computing performance of GPUs. The CUDA and/or OpenCL technologies are used for this purpose.

The use of the GPU performance is particularly suitable for computer- and graphics-intensive workloads and supports you in scenarios such as high-end visualization, deep learning, and predictive analytics.

What is CUDA?
Compute Unified Device Architecture (**CUDA**) is a technology developed by NVidia, which can be used to process program parts through the GPU. In other words, with the help of CUDA, the GPU becomes a coprocessor in the processing process.
What is OpenCL?
Open Computing Language (**OpenCL**) is an interface (or an open standard) for cross-platform computing on CPUs and GPUs. OpenCL was developed by Apple, in cooperation with the companies AMD, IBM, Intel, and NVidia and standardized by the Khronos Group (an industry consortium).

Let us return to series N-all offers includes GPUs from the NVIDIA Tesla accelerated computing platform (this is the NVIDIA high-end data center solution).

All offers with the identification NC (the C stands for Compute) use the GPU NVIDIA Tesla K80 and all offers with the identification NV (the V stands for **visualization**) use the GPU NVIDIA Tesla M60.

For all NV-rated offers the NVIDIA GRID technology (NVIDIA solution for graphics-accelerated virtual desktops) is used in addition.

NC24r is a special case and it offers you a network interface for high throughput (RDMA) and latencies of only a few seconds.

The following table shows the available instances of the N series:

Instance	Cores	GPUs	RAM	Max. disc size
NC6	6	1	56 GB	340 GB
NC12	12	2	112 GB	680 GB
NC24	24	4	224 GB	1440 GB
NC24r	24	4	224 GB	1440 GB
NV6	6	1	56 GB	340 GB
NV12	12	2	112 GB	680 GB
NV24	24	4	224 GB	1440 GB

series H

series H is based on a latest generation CPU (Intel Xeon E5-2667 V3) (Haswell) with 3.2 GHz) and it can be additionally overclocked with the Intel® Turbo Boost Technology 2.0, up to 3.6 GHz (this option is per default active). Furthermore, the H series is characterized by modern DDR4 RAM and an SSD-based data memory.

series H is specifically designed for processing **high performance computing** (**HPC**) workloads. These include, for example, financial risk models, simulations in the field of seismology and deposits, calculation of flow dynamics, and genome research.

Instance	Cores	RAM	Max. disc size
H8	8	56 GB	1000 GB
H16	16	112 GB	2000 GB
H8m	8	112 GB	1000 GB
H16m	16	224 GB	2000 GB
H16r	16	112 GB	2000 GB
H16mr	16	224 GB	2000 GB

You have already noticed that some instances have additional markings in the form of a *lowercase* letter.

Instances with the label m, have a double RAM memory, compared to the normal instance.

Instances with the label r also have a second low latency and high throughput network interface (RDMA) optimized for tightly coupled parallel compute workloads (for example, MPI applications). The second network interface is provided by an FDR InfiniBand network.

 As mentioned previously, there are some Azure series (with the name suffix *S*) that use Azure Premium Storage instead of the normal Azure Storage. Of course, the question arises: Why should I opt for the Azure Premium Storage variant? With Azure Premium Storage, for example, significantly higher costs are involved.

I think we should just clarify what you get, and then you can decide if you need it:

Azure premium storage is a high-performance SSD-based storage that is designed for I/O-intensive workloads with very high throughput and very low latency. The local temporary disk also provides a local SSD disk cache.

In a nutshell

If you don't need the additional control options, it's typically easier to get a web application up and running in Azure app service web apps.

Creating your first Azure cloud service

This workflow is usually divided into two parts. In part 1, we do the necessary preliminary work in the Azure management portal, and then in part 2 we create the process.

Part 1

As mentioned, in the first part we are doing the necessary preliminary work in the Azure management portal. Of course, the question immediately arises: what preliminary work?

Short answer, before we can create an Azure Cloud Service and deploy it to the Azure platform, we still need a so-called hosting container for the service.

We are now going deeper into the hosting of the container. I will show you how to create a hosting container and how you can work with it.

Let's start:

1. Open your Azure management portal at `https://portal.azure.com`.
2. In the portal, click on **New**:

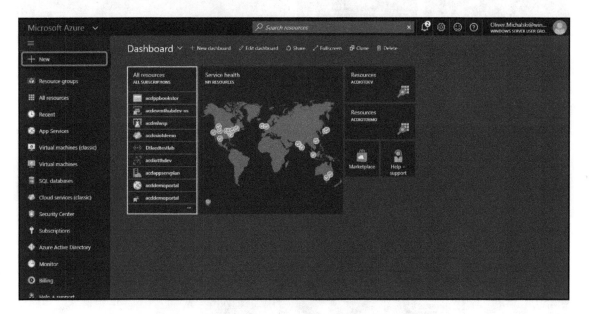

3. Now click on **Compute**, and then click **Cloud Service**:

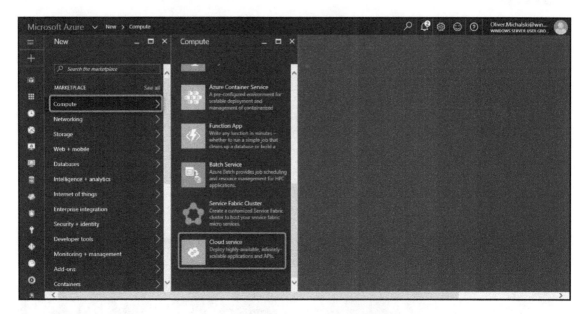

4. Alternatively, you can also click the navigation entry **Cloud Service (classic)**:

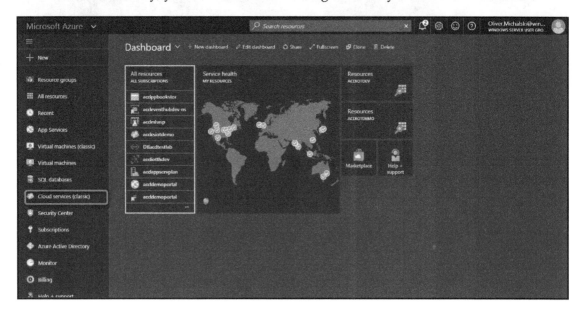

5. Now press the **Add** button in the **Cloud Services (classic)** blade:

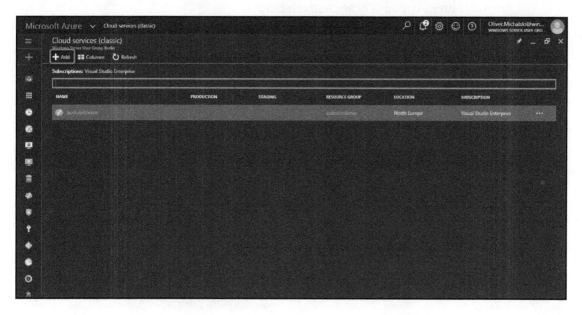

6. Now the **Cloud Services (classic)** window will appear:

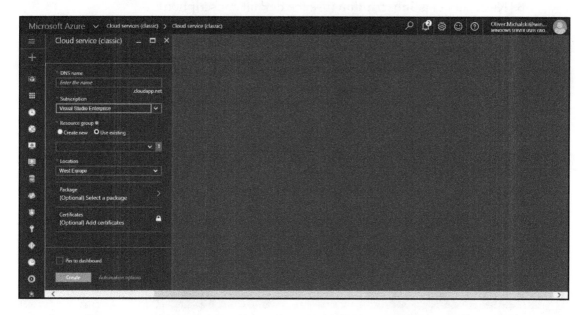

7. Type a unique name for the service you are creating in the **DNS name** box. If the name is unique, you will see a green tick:

8. Next, choose a **Subscription** (use the default subscription):

9. In the **Resource group** section, click the**Use existing** checkbox, and then search and select **acdppbook** (you can find information about creating this resource group,in `Chapter 2`, *Azure Resource Manager and Tools*), in the drop-down list:

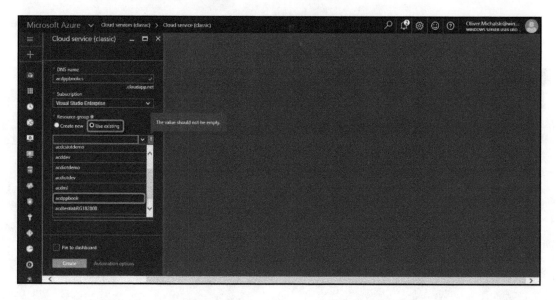

10. In the **Location** list, select the same location you have been using for the Azure resource group:

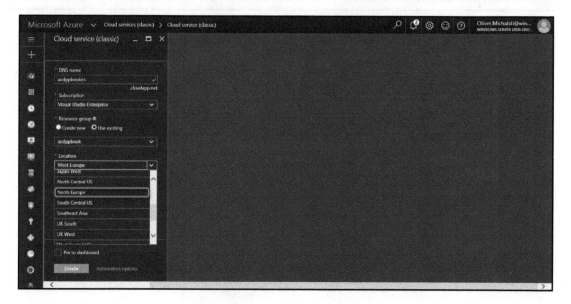

11. In the dialog box two optional settings are available:
    - **Package**: For the deployment of an existing service package file
    - **Certificates**: For the deployment of a certificate

12. Since both settings are not relevant to our description, we will not be using these options for this tutorial:

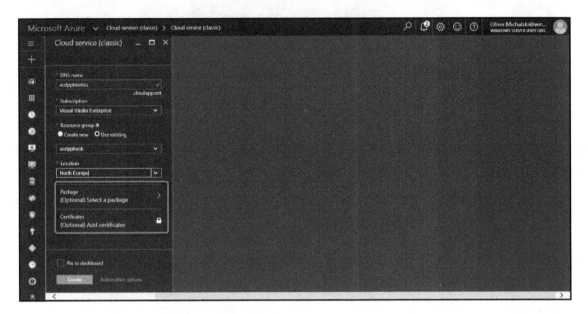

13. Finally, press the **Create** button.

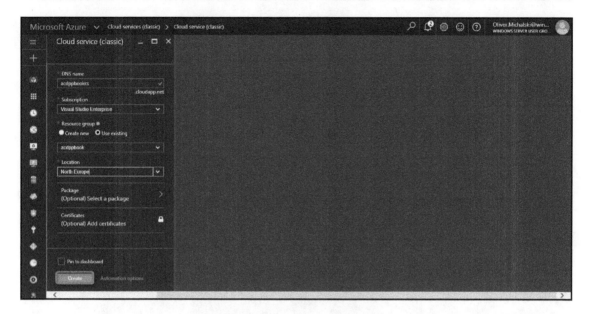

14. A few minutes later you will see the result in the **Cloud Service (classic)** blade. For moving forward, please press the **NAME** field of your new service:

Now the dashboard of your Cloud Services will open. Here we will briefly review the navigation area at the top of the dashboard.

The first part of the considerations concerns the so-called **slots**. Microsoft Azure provides two slots for your later deployments:

- **Production**
- **Staging** (for testing or development)

So you have access to these slots, you will find a fold-out list in the navigation bar:

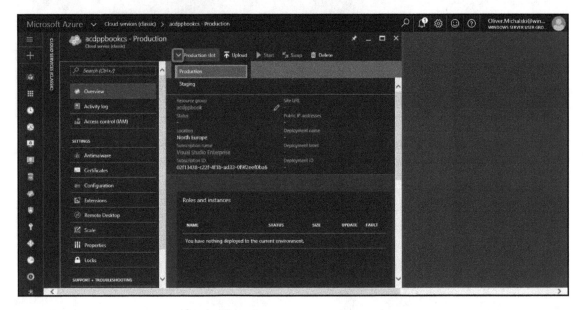

1. A simple click on the list immediately changes the view:

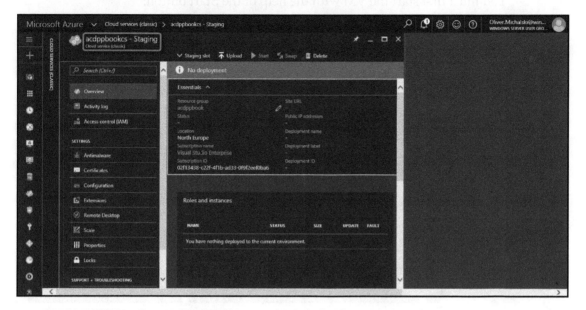

2. As soon as you have completed your tests, and have made the necessary adjustments in the settings, you can use the **Swap** buttons to move the deployment from the **Staging** slot into the **Production** slot:

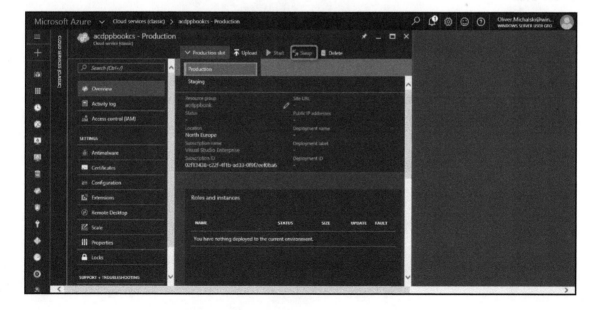

3. Deployment of the service does not mean that the services are already running. You must first start the VM with the help of the **Start** button:

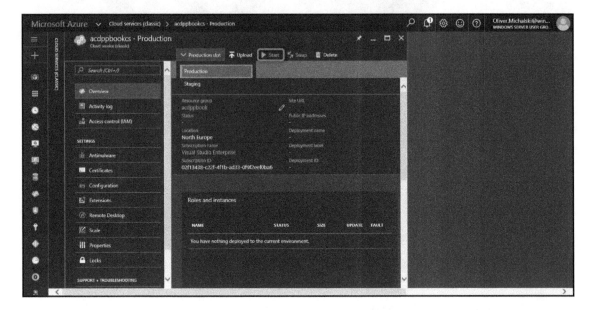

Part 2

Some important notes: We will now create the Cloud Service implementation as an example workflow in Visual Studio, but depending on your desired programming language, you can also use Eclipse or IntelliJ IDE.

I use Visual Studio 2015 Enterprise Edition for my work, but you can also use any other edition of Visual Studio for this. To prevent unnecessary expense, the free Visual Studio Community Edition is sufficient for our purposes completely.

Because we want to work with Microsoft Azure, you must start Visual Studio in the **Run as Administrator** mode:

1. Open **Visual Studio**, and then click the **New Project...** link:

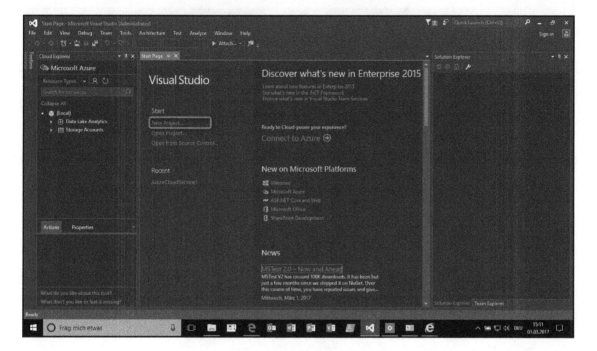

2. Now open the selection dialog with the available project templates. The required template **Azure Cloud Service**, can be found in the **Cloud** area:

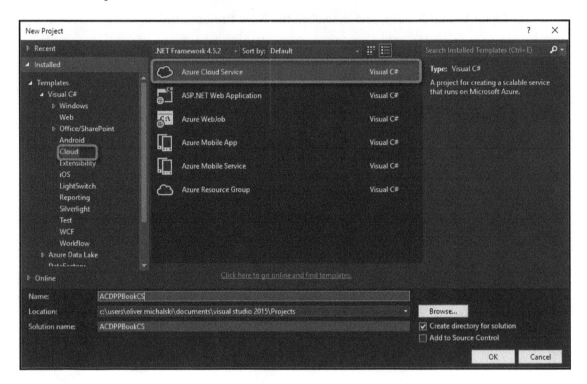

Attention!
If you do not find the entry there, you need to install Azure SDK and Azure VS tooling.

3. If everything is clear, specify a project name (for example, `ACDPPBookCS`) and press the `OK` button:

4. Now open another selection dialog, this time with a list of available role templates:

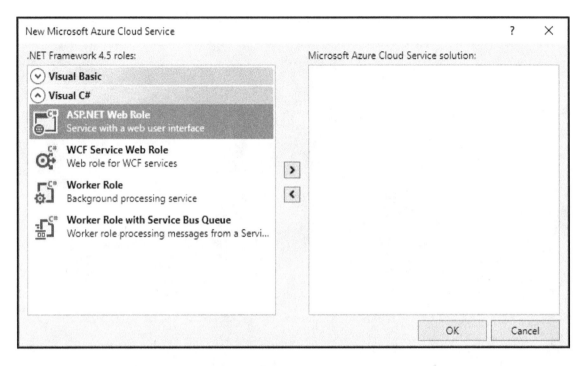

Templates are available for all supported programming languages. Depending on the edition or the chosen installation of Visual Studio, this can also be a more extensive selection.

For example, in the following screenshot, you can also see templates for Node.js, Node.js (Express), and TypeScript:

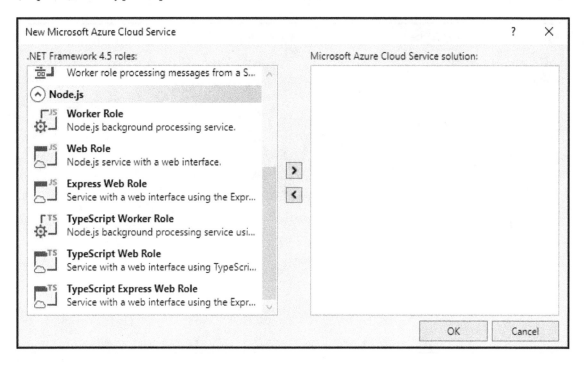

1. For our demo, we will use an **ASP.NET WebRole**. Please select the appropriate role and then press the arrow button:

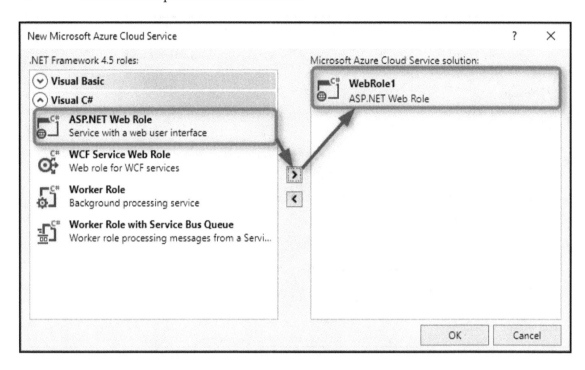

2. **WebRole1** is not a meaningful name. Of course, we want to change that, so please click on the Edit button (button with the pencil icon):

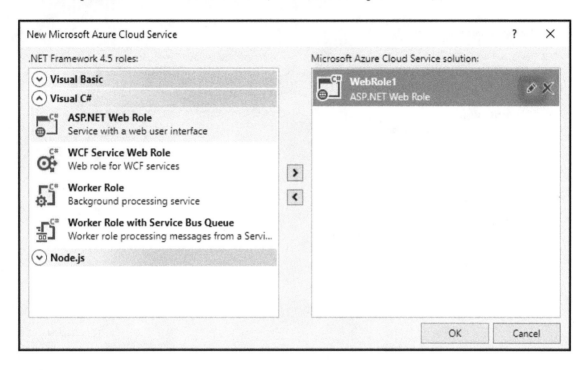

3. Now write the role name of your choice (for example, `ACDCSDemo`) and press the OK button:

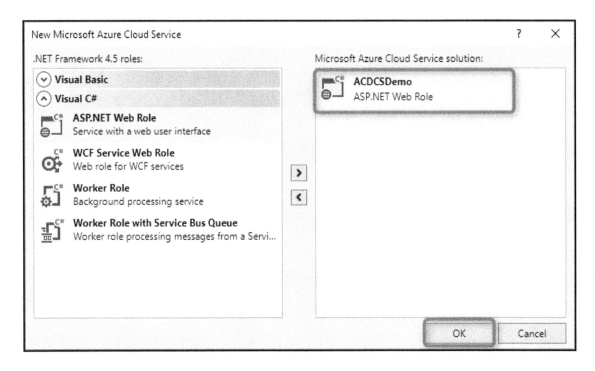

4. We have now created our project and defined the role type. Now it's time to refine the type of our project. For our demo, we will use ASP.NET **MVC**:

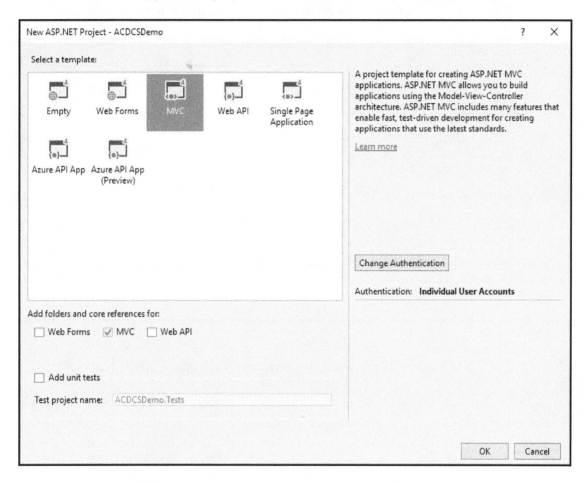

5. If necessary, you can now also change the authentication procedure (simply press the **Change Authentication** button). Since this is not relevant for our demo, I will not pursue it. Changes in the authentication procedure can make individual:

6. Based on Azure AD:

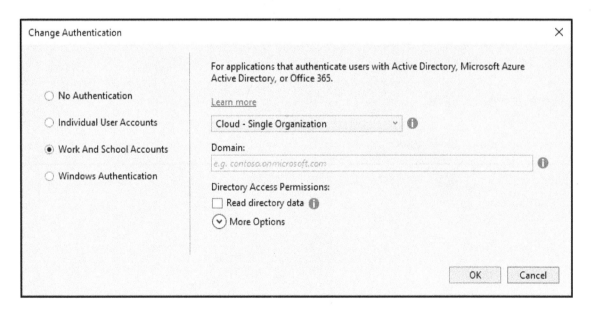

7. To conclude, please press the **OK** button in the project type selection dialog. Then your project solution is created, according to your requirements.

8. After a few minutes the project solution will become available. It consists of the following two projects:
    - The actual web project (website or web application)
    - The role project

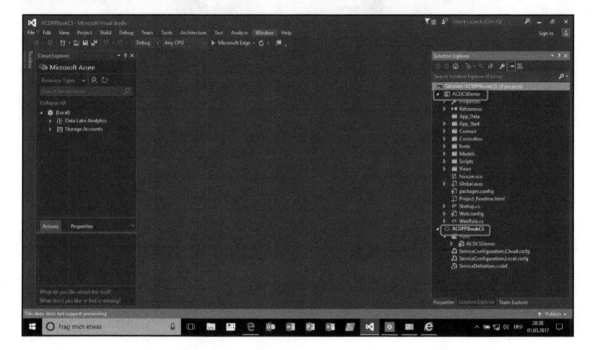

9. Next we will look at the most important components of the solution.

10. In the web project, you will find the file `WebRole.cs`. This is the position where you realize the program logic of your role:

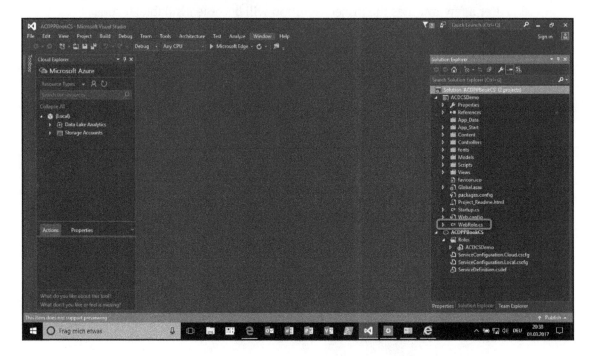

11. A double-click on the filename opens a template, which you can edit according to your ideas:

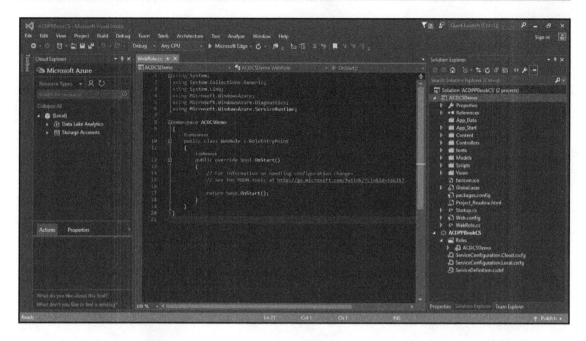

12. In the role project, you will find the templates for the Service Definition File, and the Service Configuration File:

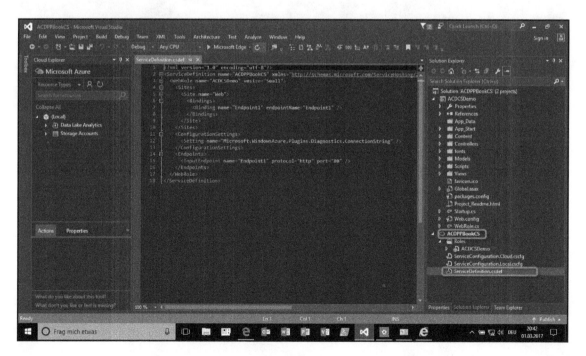

13. The Service Configuration File is available in two variations (*cloud* and *local*). This allows you to separate configuration settings in the local development cycle:

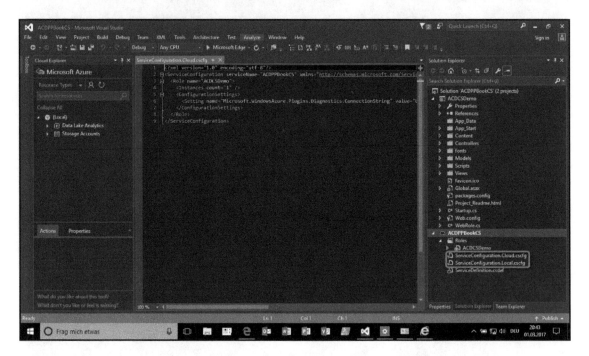

14. What's next? In our demo, we have only defined one role. However, a typical Cloud Service solution usually consists of several roles. How can I define other roles? Very easily! Please right-click on the field marked in the following screenshot:

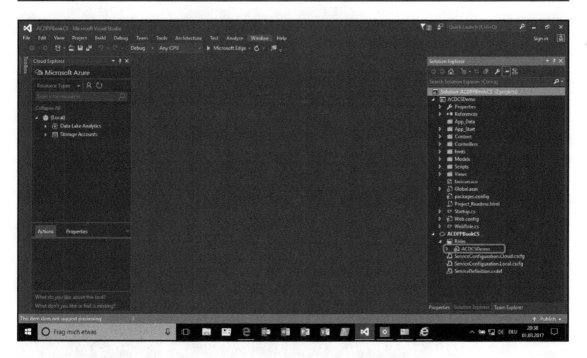

15. Select **Add**:

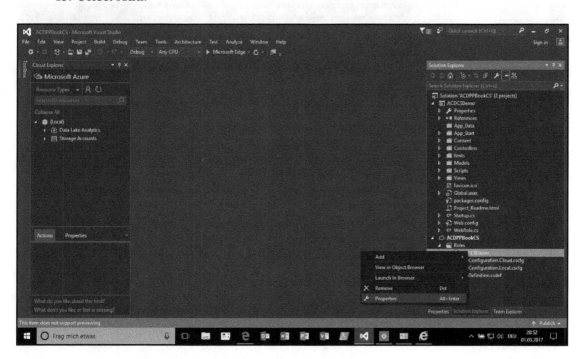

16. Now you can add another role to your solution with the commands **New Web Role Project...** or **New Worker Role Project...**:

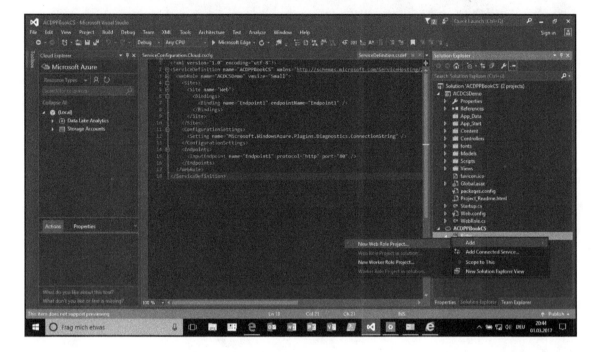

17. And now? The Visual Studio also offers opportunities to edit the Service Definition and the Service Configuration File and not only manually. Please right-click on the field marked in the following screenshot, and then click **Properties**. Now a dialog box with numerous possibilities for individual settings opens. All the settings you define here are immediately applied to the solution:

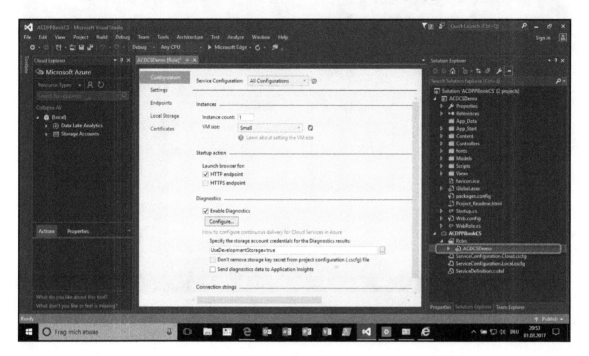

18. For example, please open the **Endpoints** page and then press the **Add Endpoint** button:

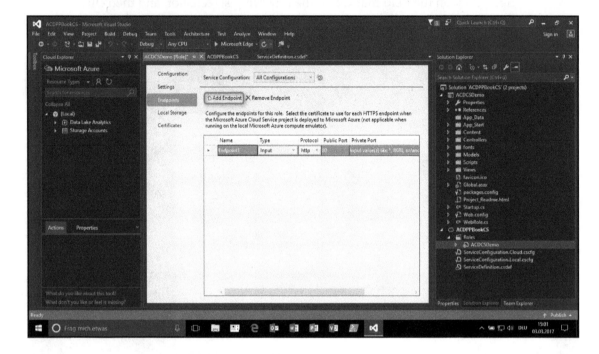

19. Immediately a new endpoint is available:

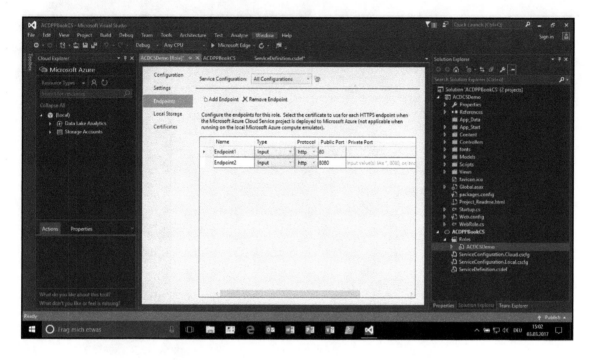

20. Next, select an endpoint **Type**:

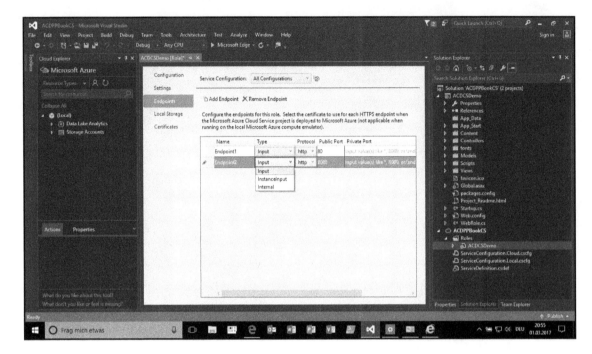

21. And then select a **Protocol**:

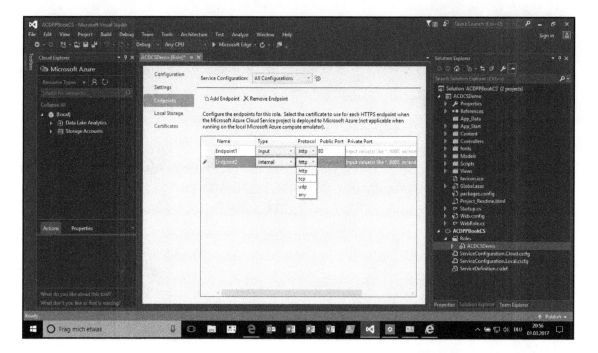

22. The range of protocols varies with the different endpoint types:

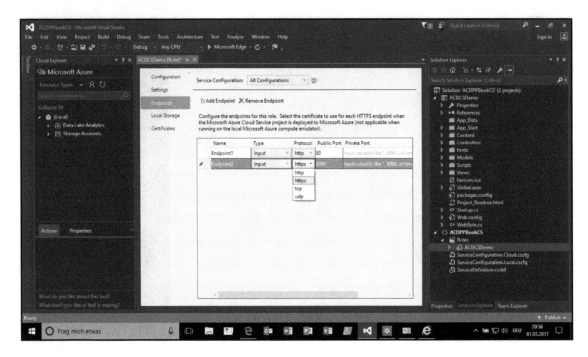

23. Ready, a new endpoint is defined:

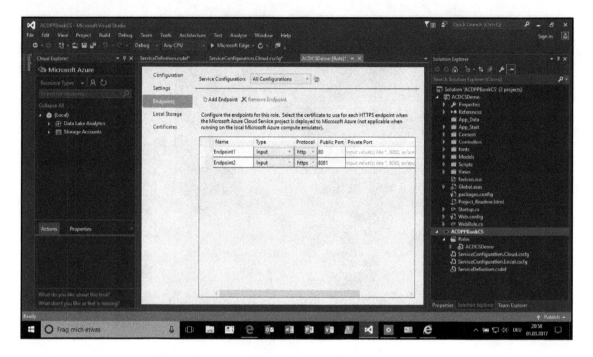

24. The supplements were automatically adopted. Here is the result as evidence:

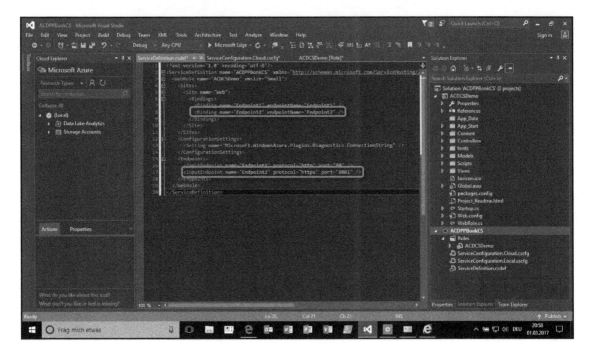

25. The next step is the local test run. Please click on the **Run** button marked in the following screenshot or press the *F5* key:

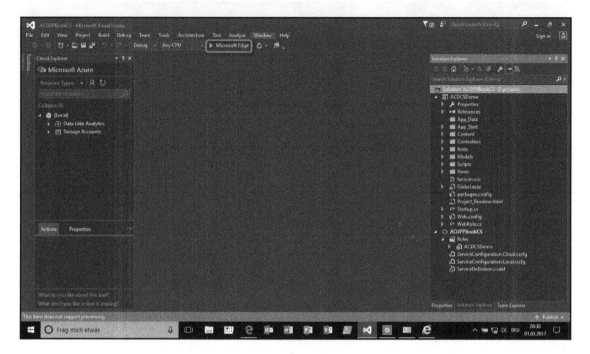

26. Now the **Microsoft Azure Debugging Environment** is starting up:

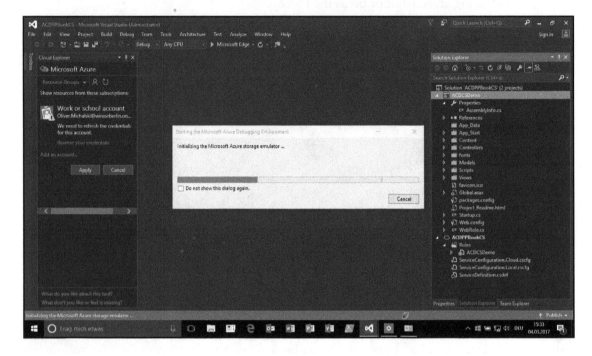

27. You can access the **Microsoft Azure Debugging Environment** over the task bar from your PC. Look for the Azure icon:

28. Please right-click on the icon:

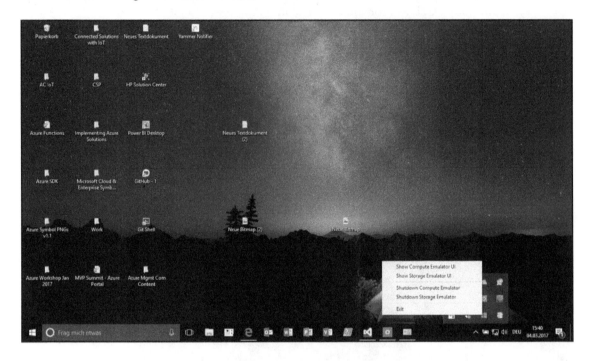

29. Here is the **Microsoft Azure Compute Emulator (Express)**:

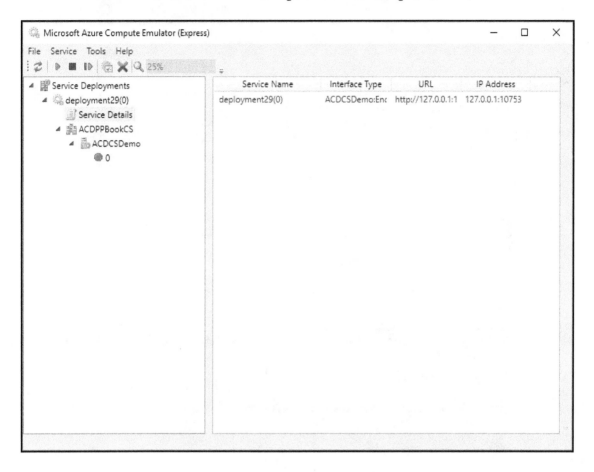

30. And here is the**Storage Emulator**:

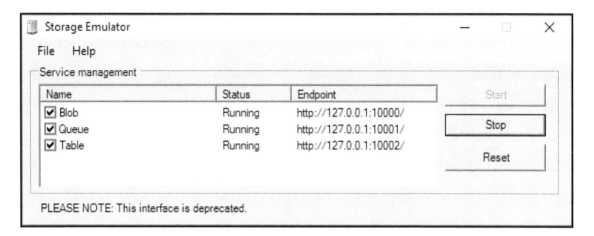

31. At the same time, your web application is loaded into the browser.

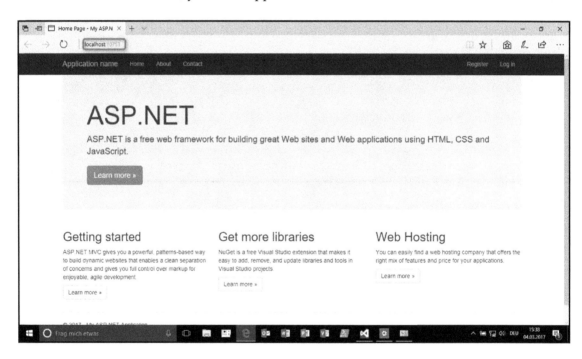

The Microsoft Azure Debugging Environment, with its tools, helps you develop your service, for example, providing you with debugging capabilities. Since the focus of our book is on the implementation of Azure solutions, I will not pursue this further. More information can be found here
`https://docs.microsoft.com/en-us/azure/vs-azure-tools-d`
`ebug-cloud-services-virtual-machines.`

32. The last step is deployment to the Azure platform. There are two possibilities for this. The basis for both ways is a right-click on the role project. For the first option, select the **Publish** command:

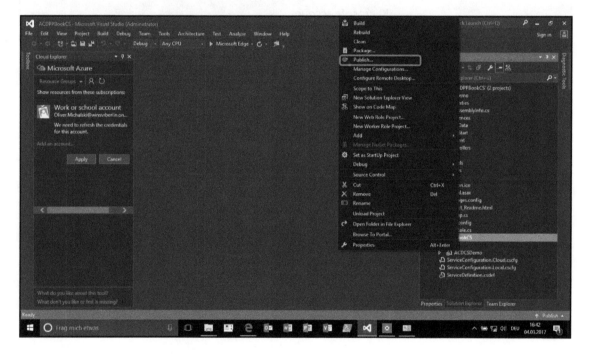

33. Now an extensive dialogue is opened. Numerous inputs are expected here:
    1. On the first page, **Sign in** you must connect with your Azure account. Sign In with the same credentials that you use to login to the Azure Portal:

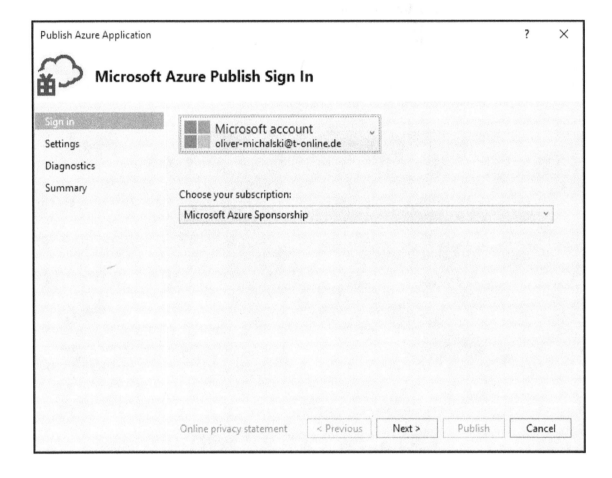

2. On the second page, **Settings | Common Settings**, most of the information are already assigned. However, you should change the **Environment** setting to **Staging** and ensure that **Build Configuration** is set to **Release**:

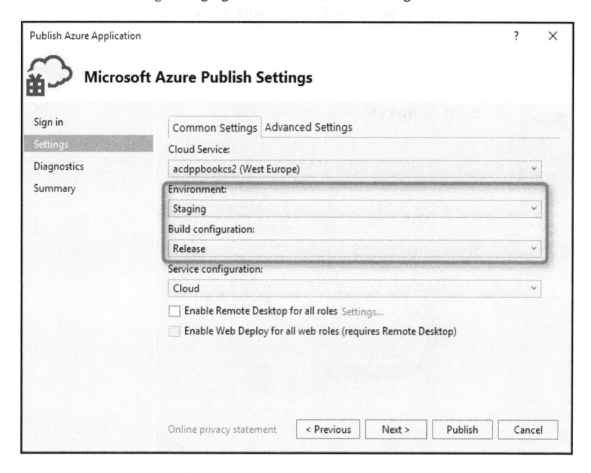

3. On the third page, **Settings** | **Advanced Settings**, the data are also already assigned and can be adopted unchanged. On this page, you have also the possibility to activate remote debugging for later operations. Simple marked the checkboxes **Enable IntelliTrace** and **Enable Remote Debugger** for all roles:

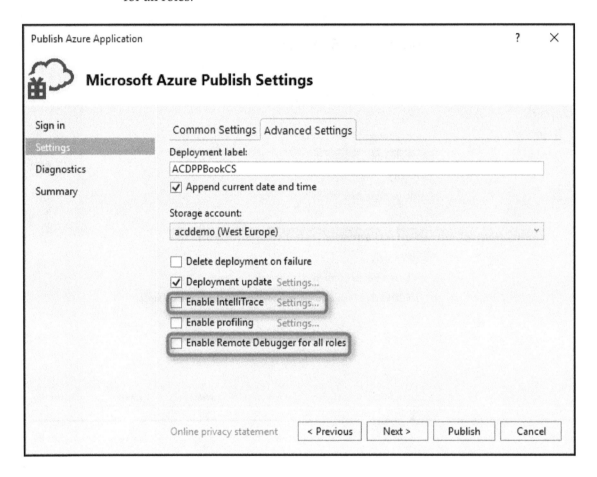

4. The **Diagnostics Settings** page is something special, since you can link your Cloud Services to Application insights:

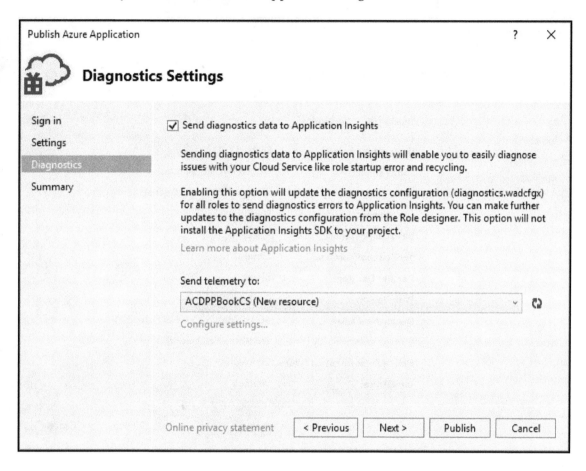

Publish Azure Application   ?   ✕

Diagnostics Settings

Sign in

Settings

Diagnostics

Summary

☑ Send diagnostics data to Application Insights

Sending diagnostics data to Application Insights will enable you to easily diagnose issues with your Cloud Service like role startup error and recycling.

Enabling this option will update the diagnostics configuration (diagnostics.wadcfgx) for all roles to send diagnostics errors to Application Insights. You can make further updates to the diagnostics configuration from the Role designer. This option will not install the Application Insights SDK to your project.

Learn more about Application Insights

Send telemetry to:

ACDPPBookCS (New resource)

Configure settings...

Online privacy statement | < Previous | | Next > | | Publish | | Cancel |

5. Finally, if you are using this path for your deployment, you only need to press the **Publish** button on the **Summary** page:

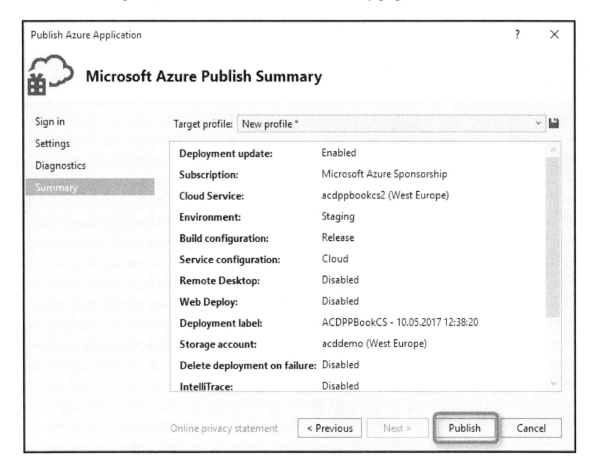

34. Let's now turn to the second option (the classical way). For this option, you must select the **Package...** command:

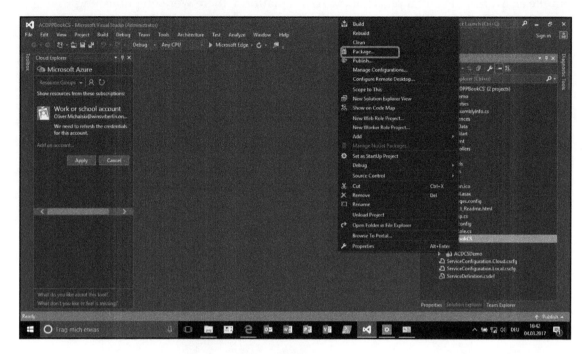

35. This time only a simple window opens, where you must press the **Package** button:

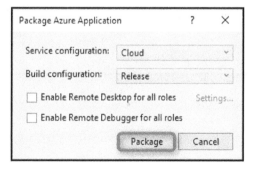

The question arises: what is behind it?

Simple answer-in the initial phase of the Azure platform, there were no publishing procedures. Cloud Services were manually packaged and then uploaded with Azure PowerShell or the Azure management portal.

This process is taken up again, only this time the packing as a background action takes place.

Next question: where can I find the new service package?

1. Go to the `Projects` folders of Visual Studio. There you can open your Cloud Service solution:

2. Now open the role project:

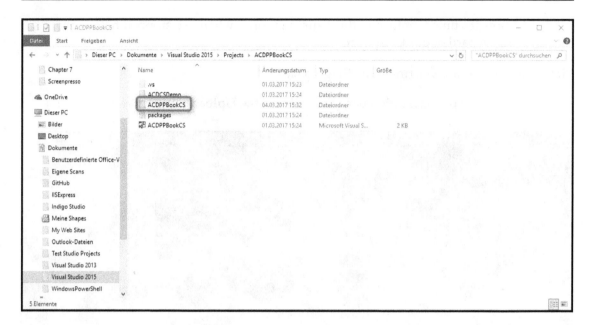

3. Now you must opened the `bin` folder, then the folder that matches to your build (`Release` or `Debug`) There, you can find the service package and also the Service Configuration File in the `app.publish` subfolder :

4. Now it's time to return to the Azure platform, where we stopped before, the dashboard of our Cloud Service.

First please make sure you are in the **Staging** slot:

1. In the upper navigation bar, you will find the **Upload** button. Please click on it:

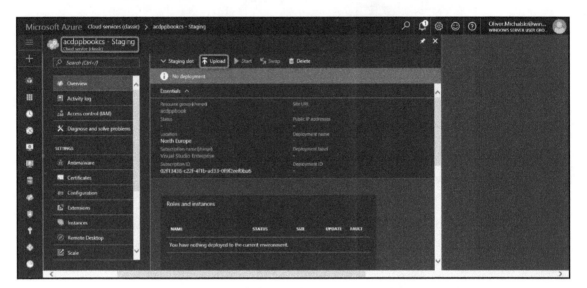

2. Now open the **Upload a package** dialog. Here you must first select an Azure **Storage account** (you can find information about creating a Storage account, in `Chapter 5`, *Implementing and Securing Azure Storage Accounts*), where you want to upload the service package:

3. Then type a name for the **Deployment label**:

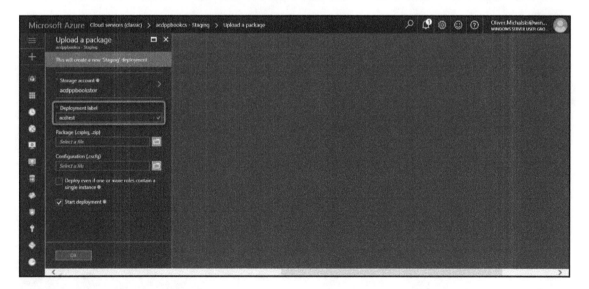

4. First upload the service package and after this the Service Configuration File:

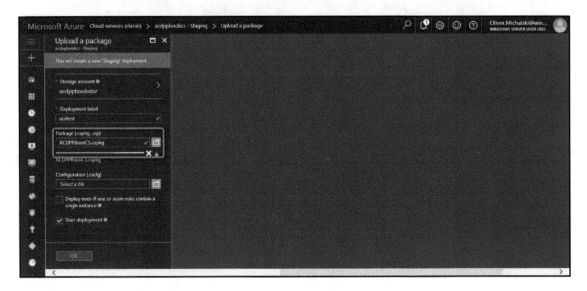

5. The green progress bar gives you information about the status of the upload:

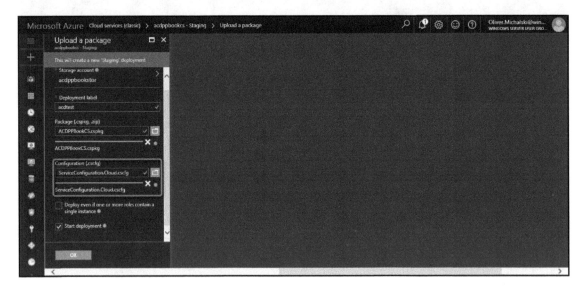

Attention!

Since we use only one role instance in our demo, please ensure that the checkbox has been marked in the following screenshot. Otherwise the deployment process would abort with an error.

6. The last action is to press the **OK** button:

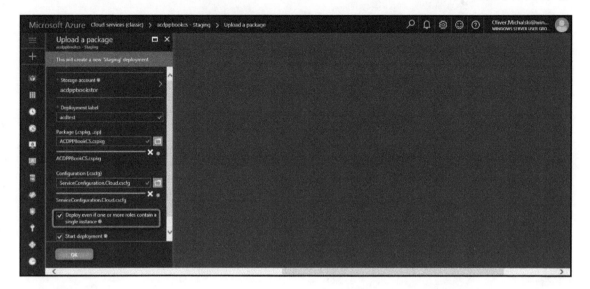

7. Ready! Your Cloud Service is now available on the Azure platform:

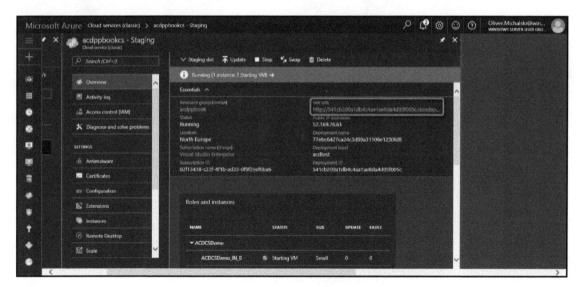

Summary

In this chapter, we learned all about the Azure Cloud Service offer.

In the first part of this chapter, we learned the basic knowledge of the Azure Cloud Service, all about the Cloud architecture and the difference between Azure Cloud Service and Azure App Services.

Then in the second part of this chapter, there followed a detailed description of the create process.

In the next chapter, we will continue with the newest service of the available Azure PaaS offers, the Azure Container Service.

8

Implementing Azure Container Service

Azure Container Services (**ACS**) is the newest part of the Azure platform and at present, at least partially in preview status (for example, in the area Windows container).

Azure Container Services are a new variant of the classical Azure IaaS offer from Azure (described in `chapter 6`, *Planning and Deploying Virtual Machines in Azure*), and use also virtual machines as the technological base.

Two versions of the Azure IaaS are offered, and both are based on virtual machines?

Yes, but Azure Container Services has some advantages over the older solution due to its additional functionality.

I will now take a closer look at these advantages and introduce Azure Container Services in detail.

In this chapter, you will learn:

- The basic knowledge about the Azure Container Services area
- The workflow when creating your first container service and the necessary steps for working with the service afterwards

What is an Azure Container Service?

An Azure Container Service helps you to create, configure, or manage a cluster of VMs. These clusters are preconfigured to run applications in so-called containers.

Ok, this is a complete answer, but we should nevertheless, take a deeper look.

Let's start with a comparison between the two Azure IaaS offers.

The following diagram shows you the classic Azure IaaS offer, or in other words, Windows or Linux VMs on Azure:

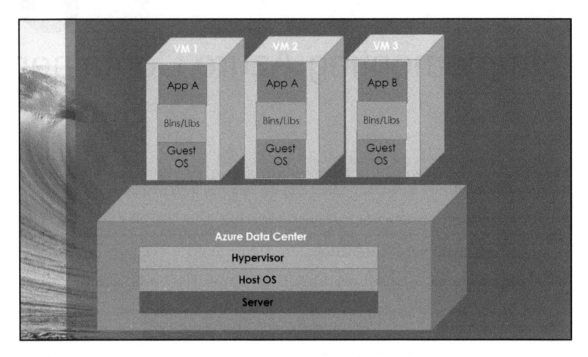

As you can see, the offer consists of the following two layers:

- The infrastructure in the **Azure Data Center**
- The actual VMs

The area infrastructure is easily explained: VMs are an abstraction of physical hardware running on a server and turn one server into many servers. The hypervisor allows you to run several VMs on a single machine.

Now we come to the area VMs-each VM includes one or more apps, the necessary libraries and binaries, and a full guest operating system.

A VM can reach a size in the high GB range and can therefore be very slow when booting.

The next diagram shows you the new Azure IaaS offer, or in other words the IaaS based on container solution:

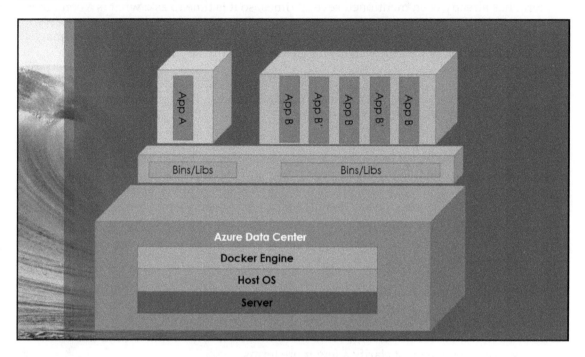

At first glance, this image looks like the first image. But there are some differences.

In the infrastructure layer, for example, you will find a container engine instead of the hypervisor. In ACS, the container engine is a **Docker Engine**. Docker is currently the leading open source project for container solutions.

In good Azure tradition, the ACS Engine is an open source project. If you want to examine the engine internals, or if you need to adjust your needs, you can find the complete source code at `https://github.com/Azure/acs-engine`.

Let's come back to the subject. The container engine is the runtime environment for containers (partially comparable to the Guest OS of the VMs). With their help, multiple containers can run on the same machine and share the OS kernel with other containers that run as isolated processes in their own user space.

The next difference in the new offer, you will find in the provision of the necessary libraries and binaries. They are provided by the container engine in an intermediate layer for individual or as a shared resource for multiple containers.

Understanding containers

The term has already been mentioned several times, so it is time to ask: what is a container?

Simple answer: a container in our mind is an instance of a Docker image. A Docker image is an ordered collection of root filesystem changes and the corresponding execution parameters.

 When you scale your Azure Container Service, you typically run multiple containers from the same image.

A container is defined not only by a Docker image, but also by the following components:

- A so-called Dockerfile is a text file that contains necessary information about the structure of the container
- Something singular like a process, a service, or microservice (for example, an Azure Service Fabric) or an app

Containers take up less space than VMs (typically in a low MB range), and start almost instantly.

Now we have gained our first insights into the container issue. To understand the following, however, we must clarify a few more terms.

Cluster

The first term is cluster or Docker cluster.

A cluster bundles several Docker hosts and represents them as a single virtual host. A cluster is thus able to scale very easily and this with an unlimited number of hosts.

Why do I tell you this?

When I speak later about the creation of your first Azure Container Service, it means the creation of a cluster and not the creation of a container application.

Orchestrator

The next term is orchestrator.

An orchestrator is a management tool for Docker clusters and Docker hosts, and enables users to manage their images, containers, and hosts through a GUI.

The orchestrator allows users to administer container networking, configurations, load balancing, service discovery, high availability, host management, and is responsible for running, distributing, scaling, and healing workloads across a collection of nodes.

When you create your ACS cluster, you also decide about the orchestrator you want to use.

The following orchestrators are currently available:

- DC/OS
- Kubernetes
- Docker swarm

Which orchestrator should I choose?

Microsoft does not recommend a specific orchestrator. If you have experience with one of the orchestrators, you can continue to use this experience in ACS.

However, there are trends that indicate that **Datacenter Operating System (DC/OS)** is good for Big Data and IoT workloads. Kubernetes is suitable for cloud-native workloads and Docker swarm is known for its integration with other Docker tools and for its easy learning curve.

Let's take a deeper look at the three orchestrators.

Mesosphere DC/OS

Mesosphere DC/OS is a distributed operating system based on the Apache Mesos distributed systems kernel.

DC/OS (and Apache Mesos) include the following features:

- Scalability
- Fault-tolerant replicated master and slaves using Apache ZooKeeper
- Support for Docker containers
- Native isolation between tasks with Linux containers
- Scheduling for multiple resources (memory, CPU, disk, and ports)
- Java, Python, and C++ APIs
- A web UI for viewing cluster state (Apache Mesos UI)

By default, DC/OS includes the marathon orchestration platform for scheduling workloads and mesosphere universe, a collection of services that can be added to your service.

The following diagram shows the architecture of an ACS cluster using DC/OS:

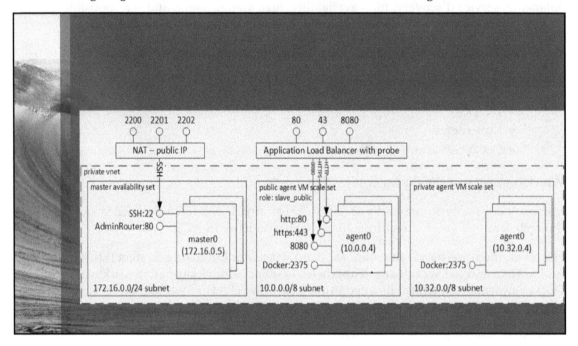

.

 For further information on mesosphere DC/OS please visit `https://dcos.io/`. You can find the complete source code at `https://github.com/dcos`.

Docker swarm

Docker swarm offers a system-specific clustering feature for Docker. Because Docker handles Docker swarm's standard API, any tool that already communicates with a Docker daemon can use swarm.

Supported tools for managing of containers on a swarm cluster are:

- Dokku (an ALM tool)
- Docker CLI
- Docker compose
- Jenkins

The following diagram shows the architecture of an ACS cluster using Docker swarm:

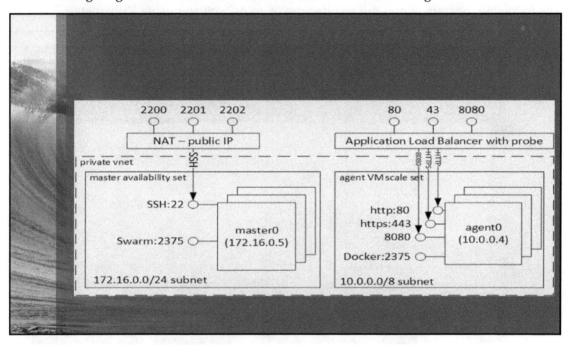

For further information on Docker Swarm please click visit `https://www.docker.com/`. The complete source code you can find at `https://github.com/docker`.

Kubernetes

Kubernetes is a popular production-grade container orchestrator tool. Kubernetes automates deployment, scaling, and management of containerized applications.

Kubernetes includes the following features:

- Horizontal scaling
- Service discovery and load balancing
- Secrets and configuration management
- API-based automated rollouts and rollbacks
- Self-healing

The following diagram shows the architecture of an ACS cluster using Kubernetes:

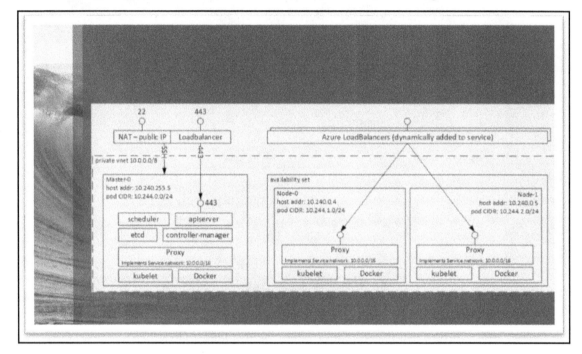

For further information on Kubernetes please visit `https://kubernetes.io/`. The complete source code you can find at `https://github.com/kubernetes`.

All three orchestrators are open source projects with frequent version changes. These version changes are considered by ACS but unfortunately there is currently no possibility to upgrade an existing deployment.

Creating your first Azure Container Service

A preliminary remark: the following description is only an example. However, the described procedure applies in the same way to all supported configurations.

Let's start:

1. Open your Azure management portal at `https://portal.azure.com`.
2. In the portal, click **New**:

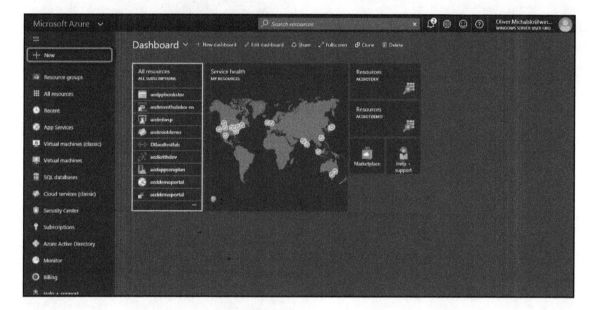

3. Now click **Compute**, scroll down the list, and then click **Azure Container Service**:

4. Alternatively, you can also click **Containers**, and then click **Azure Container Service**:

5. Now open the info page of the offer, press the **Create** button here:

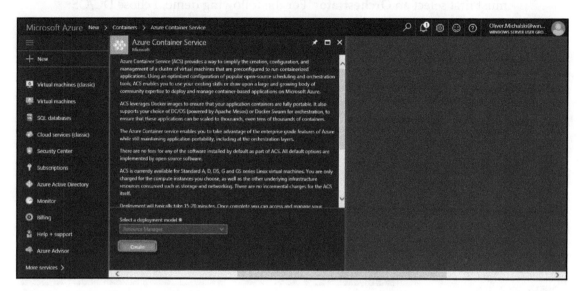

6. Now open the **Create Azure Container Service** dialog:

7. The **Create Azure Container Service** consists of four parts. In part 1 **Basics**, you must first select an **Orchestrator**. For the following demo, I chose DC/OS:

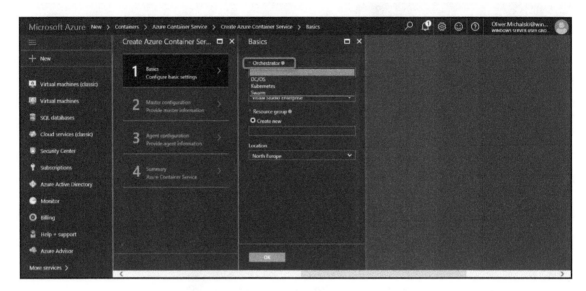

8. Next, choose a **Subscription** (Use the default subscription):

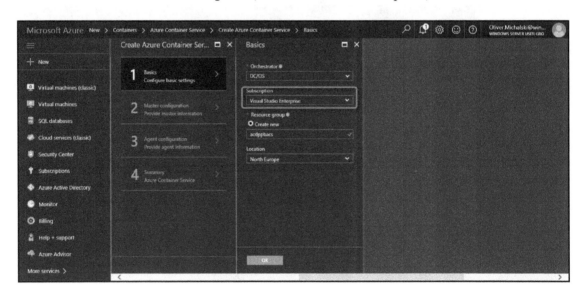

9. In the **Resource group** section, you only have the option to create a new **Resource group** (of course there is a reason, as we shall see later). Type a name of your choice for the **Resource group** in the text field:

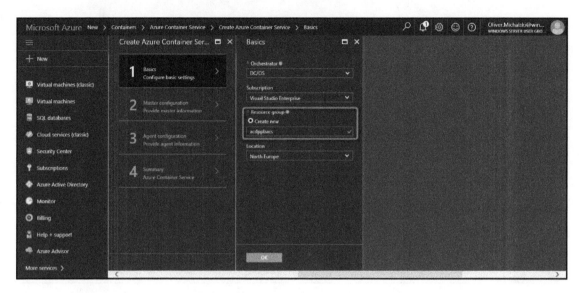

10. In the **Location** list, select the same location you have been using for the Azure Resource groups:

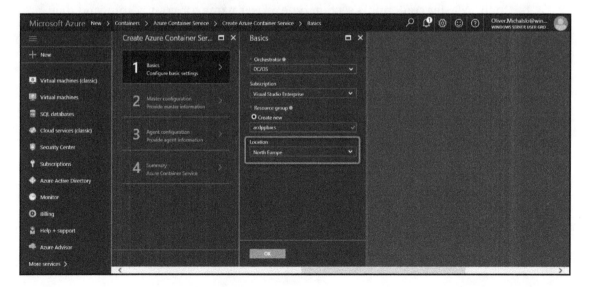

11. Once you have made your settings, press the **OK** button.

12. Now open part 2 **Master configuration** of the **Create Azure Container Service** dialog:

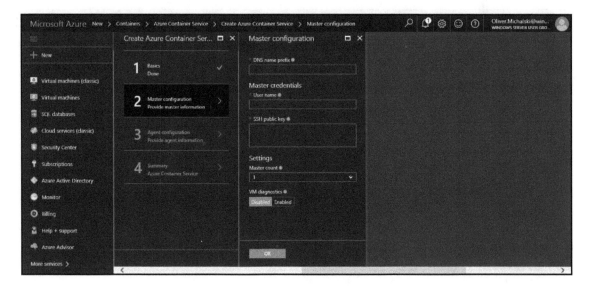

13. Type a unique name for the service you are creating in the **DNS name prefix** box. If the name of the service is unique, you can see the green tick.

14. In the **Master credentials** section type a **User name** for your admin, and then copy and paste a **SSH public key** in the following box. (If you do not already have an SSH key, you should work through the following points. Otherwise, you can go directly to the point 21).

15. For the work with SSH, you need a key pair. The so-called **public key** is stored on the server with which you want to connect. The so-called **private key** then serves as authentication against the server.

16. In principle, there are several possibilities to generate a key pair. These vary depending on your OS and so the following is just one example.

17. Starting out of the premise that you use a PC with a Windows OS, I recommend using PuTTY. You can find an Installer for PuTTY at `http://www.putty.org/`. Download and install PuTTY.

18. Now search for the `PuTTYgen` tool.

19. Open the tool and click the **Generate** button:

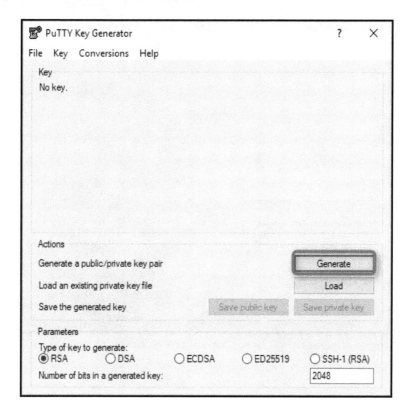

20. The generation process starts. You can speed up the process by hovering over the empty area:

21. Once the key pair has been generated, you must enter a passphrase (a type of password only longer) for the private key and confirm by typing again:

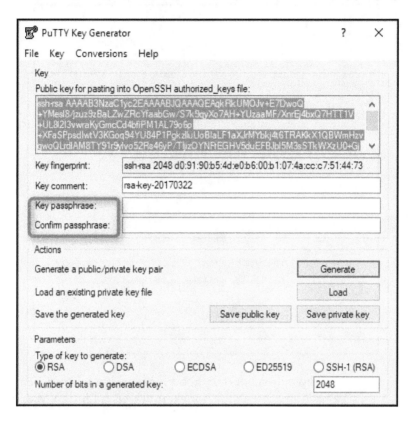

22. Last step, save your SSH keys in the local file system:

The key pair is not only good for working with ACS, but can also be used in other fields, for example, each Linux VM or also GitHub.

23. Now we are back in the **Master configuration** of the **Create Azure Container Service** dialog. In the dialog window, you will also find two optional settings:

- **Master count**: Here you can decide how many master nodes are to be created

- **VM diagnostics**: here you can decide whether the diagnostics feature
  is enabled or not

24. Once you have made your settings, press the **OK** button.
25. Now open part 3, **Agent configuration** of the **Create Azure Container Service**
    dialog.
26. In this dialog window, you will also find two settings:

    - **Agent count**: Here you can decide how many agent nodes are to be
      created
    - **Agent virtual machine size**: Here you can decide which Azure Series
      is used

27. The setting for **Agent virtual machine size** needs a closer look. Once you click on the setting, you will first see the so-called recommendations. Attention: these are usually the most expensive solutions. Therefore, you should now click on the **View all** link:

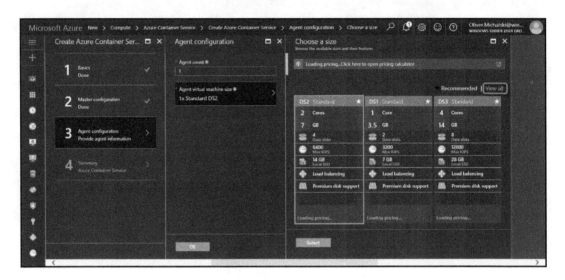

28. Now a much longer list opens. Here you can find a suitable offer. For our small demo, I decided to use the instance A1_V2. This is currently the cheapest deal. Press the corresponding tile once and then press the **Select** button:

29. Once you have made your settings, press the **OK** button:

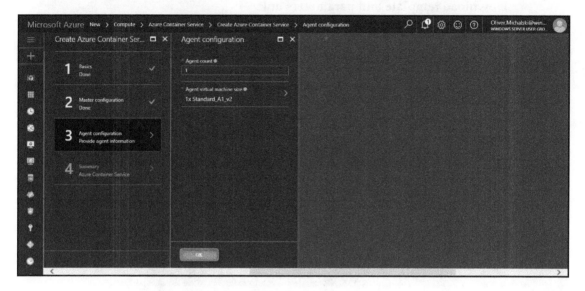

30. Now open part 4, **Summary** of the **Create Azure Container Service** dialog. Here you can now press the **OK** button and the deployment starts:

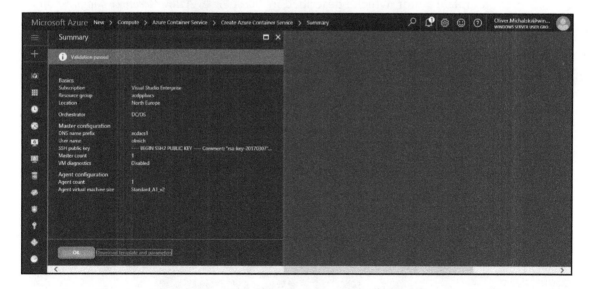

31. You can also download an ARM template for future use. Simple click on the **Download template and parameters** link:

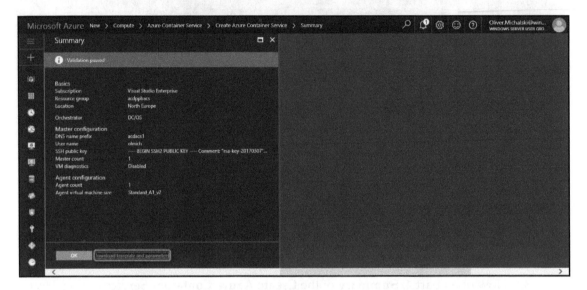

32. Now a **Template** editor window opens. This editor is similar in functionality to the template editor, which I described in Chapter 2, *Azure Resource Manager and Tools*, but does not allow any direct changes to the template:

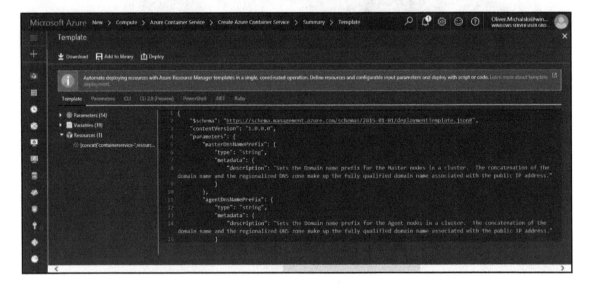

33. Once you have started your deployment, you can take a break:

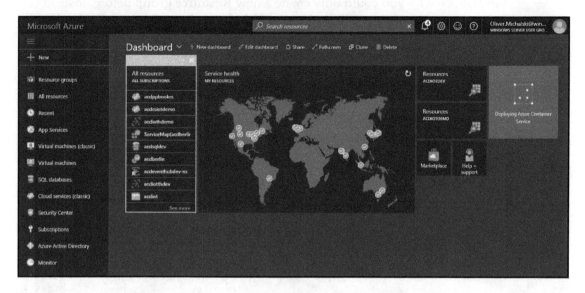

34. Twenty minutes later, you should see a result on the dashboard. Please click the **See more** link in the new tile:

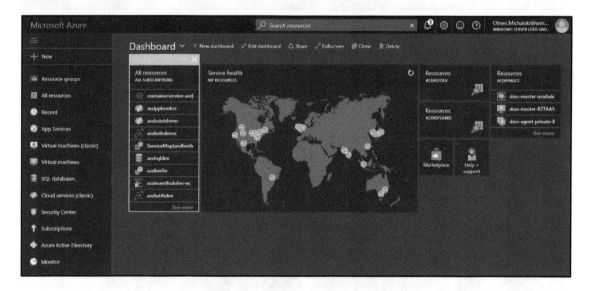

35. This opens the **Resource group** dashboard of your new ACS cluster. Now you can also see why you could only create a new **Resource group** before. Instead of just one new object, you will find a total of **24 items** (container service, load balancer, network interface, network security group, virtual machine, virtual machine scale set, virtual network, and storage accounts):

36. To see all elements of the Resource group, you must scroll down the list

I have important information for you, even if no costs are incurred for the Azure container service, significant costs are incurred for the remaining resources. In my first attempts with ACS, I very quickly consumed the Azure credits of my MSDN subscription. So, keep an eye on cost developments.

How to work with your Azure container service cluster

Now we have created a new ACS cluster. But we also want to work with it. I will now introduce the basic approach.

As important prerequisite, to work with the cluster, you need the Master FQDN (a URL). The Master FQDN can be found in the **Essentials** section of the dashboard of your container service.

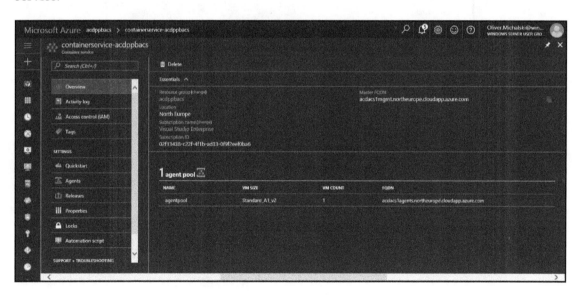

Now that we know the important prerequisites, we can go further.

Each of the three available orchestrators provide you with a work surface. To work with these UIs, you must first create an SSH tunnel.

You don't know how to create an SSH tunnel?

Then I want to bring you closer to the procedure by the way of an example. I assume that you have followed my earlier advice and have installed the PuTTY toolset. I also assume that your SSH key pair is available.

Everything okay? Then let's start:

1. Search for the **PuTTY** tool and then open the tool:

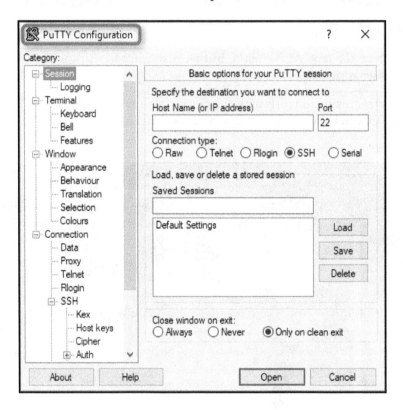

2. On the first page, fill in the **Host Name** field. The hostname is composed of the admin username (from your cluster) and the Master FQDN and has the format `adminusername@masterfqdn`. Change the **Port** to `2200`:

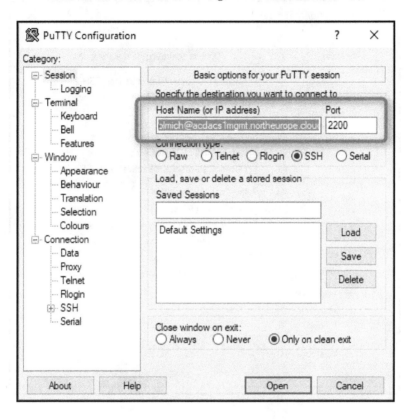

3. Now switch to the **Connection** I **SSH** I **Auth** site. Here you enter the path to your SSH private key:

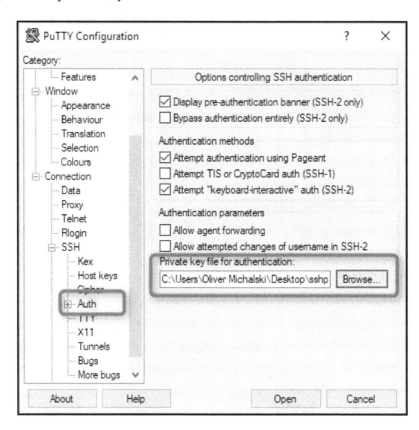

4. Move to the **Connection** | **SSH** | **Tunnels** site. In the **Add** new forwarded port section, type 80 in the **Source port** field and localhost:80 in the **Destination** field. Finally press the **Add** button:

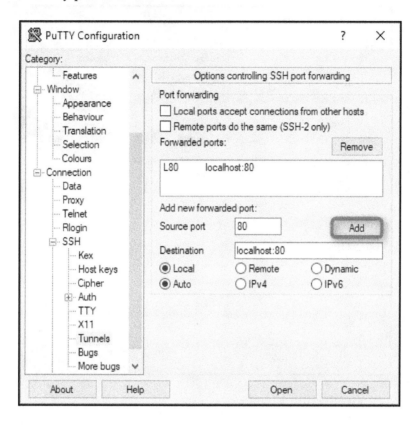

5. Now go back to the first page. Press the **Open** button and the SSH tunnel is built up:

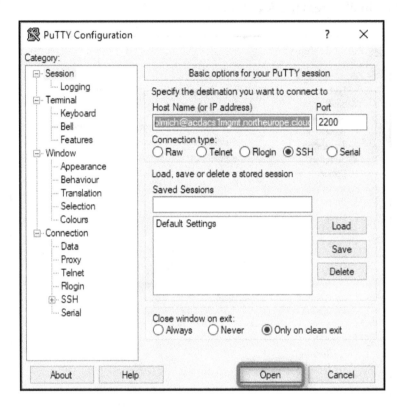

Have you created your SSH tunnel now?

If yes, we will look now at the work surfaces once. Remember, since we have created our cluster based on DC/OS, it is the UIs of DC/OS. The UIs of the other types are very similar.

Let's start with the DC/OS dashboard. To reach this UI, enter the following URL into the browser of your choice:

```
http://localhost:80/
```

With the **DC/OS** dashboard, you can monitor the performance indicators of your cluster or display the health status of individual components:

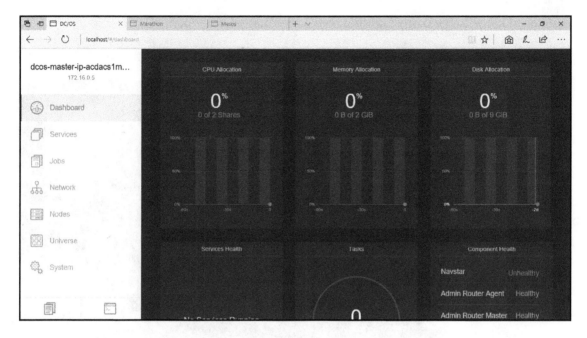

If you want to see the health status of individual components, click the **View all 35 Components** button in the **Component Health** tile:

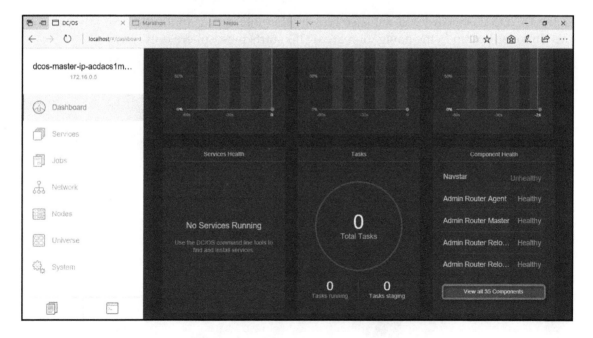

A detailed list with the corresponding status information will open:

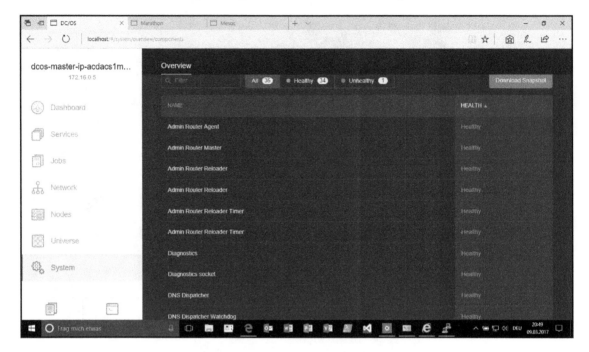

In the **DC/OS** dashboard you will also find another interesting application. Simply press the **Universe** button in the navigation area. This starts mesosphere universe.

Mesosphere universe is a package repository that contains services like Spark, Cassandra, Jenkins, and many others that can be easily deployed onto your cluster:

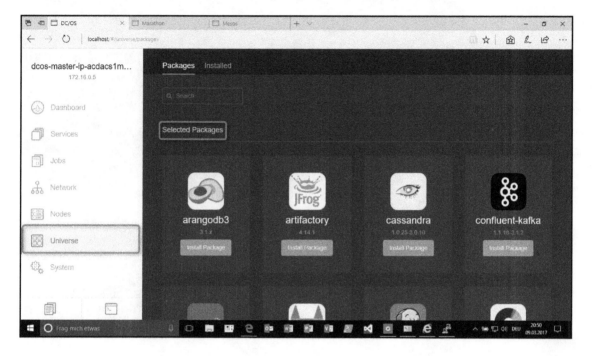

In addition to the solutions provided by mesosphere, there are still solutions from the community. Just scroll the page down:

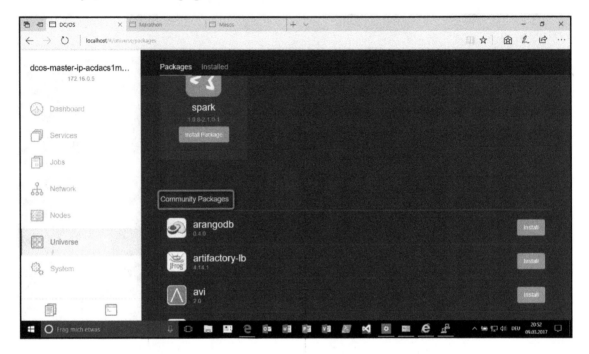

The next area is the **MARATHON** orchestration platform. To reach this UI, enter the following URL into the browser of your choice:

```
http: //localhost:80/marathon/
```

With this UI, you can start a new container and other types of application in the cluster. In addition, the UI also provides information on executed containers and applications and is constantly on-going for planning tasks:

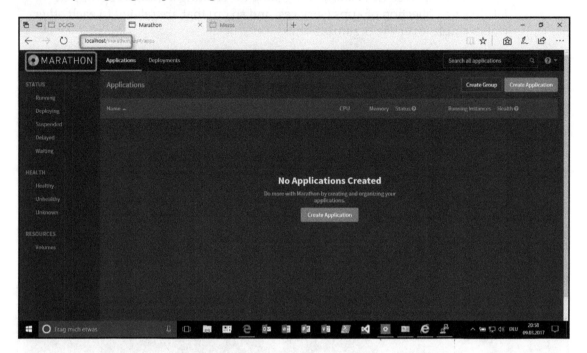

Two short examples:

- The following screenshot shows the dialog for creating a group. A group in DC/OS is a collection of apps (services, and so on) that are related to each other (for example, over the organization):

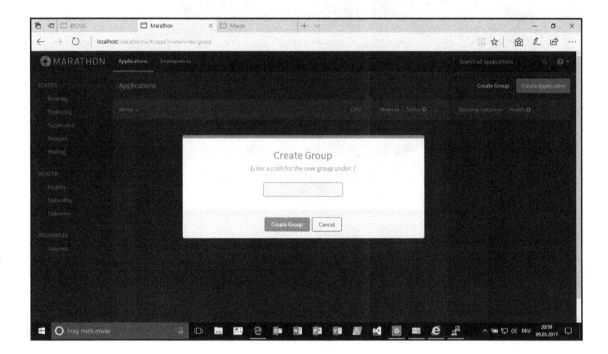

- The next screenshot shows the dialog for creating a **New Application**. An application is a long-running service that may have one or more instances that map one to one with a task:

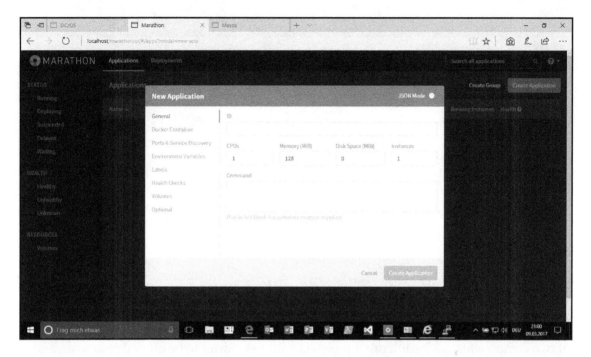

Internally, the user creates an application by providing an application definition (a JSON file). Marathon then schedules one or more application instances as tasks depending on how much the definition is specified.

In the original concept of DC/OS, there is still another part, the pods. A pod is a special case of an application. A pod is also a long-running service that may have one or more instances but map one to many with collocated tasks. Pod instances may include one or more tasks that share resources (for example, IPs, ports, or volumes). Pods are currently not supported by ACS.

The last area is the Mesos. Mesos is a web UI for viewing cluster state, and above all tasks. To reach this UI, enter the following URL into the browser of your choice:

```
http: //localhost:80/mesos/
```

The following screenshot shows the UI for **Tasks**:

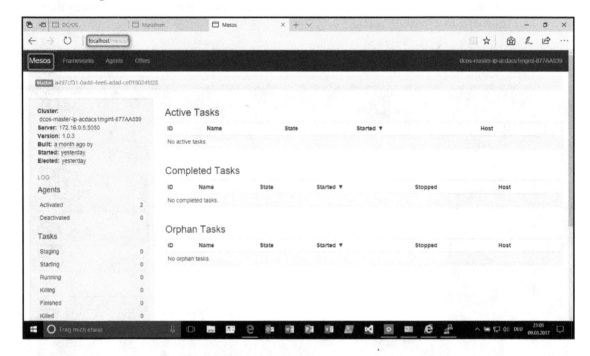

The next screenshot shows the UI for **Frameworks**. A framework running in Mesos consists of two components: a scheduler that registers with the master to be offered resources, and an executor process that is launched on agent nodes to run the tasks:

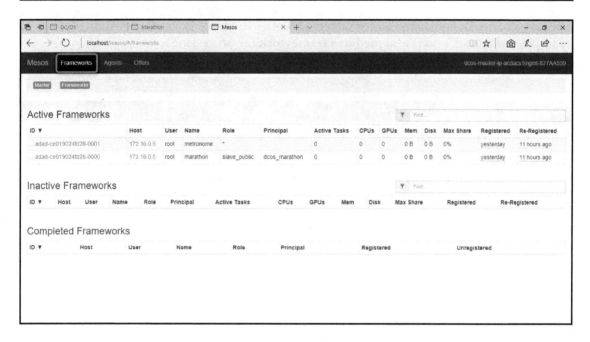

The next screenshot shows the UI for **Agents** and its conditions:

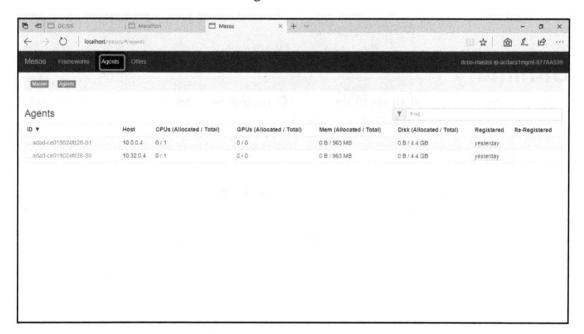

The last screenshot shows the UI for **Offers**. An offer in Mesos is simple a resource (for example, container), and is assigned to a framework for processing:

Summary

In this chapter, we learned all about the Azure Container Services and therefore the basics for implementing a modern Azure IaaS solution.

In the first part of this chapter, we learned the basic knowledge of the Azure container service and the basic terminology.

Then in the second part of this chapter, there followed a description of the create process and a short introduction in working with ACS.

In the next chapter, we will continue with the basics of Azure security (for example Azure AD).

Implementing Azure Security

9

In previous chapters, we learned how to set up and manage Azure infrastructure services. These included Resource groups, Azure Active Directory, virtual networks, and storage accounts.

Security is a very major and important topic and all these services should be created with security in mind. As cloud security is a little different from the classic security we know from our on premise infrastructures, this chapter will provide a brief overview of security.

You should consider scalability, durability, and high availability depending on the scenario and target you try to achieve.

Within this chapter you will learn about most of the basic Azure security offerings. You will learn how and when to implement and integrate security on storage and compute level. We will also take a look at (hybrid) identity security.

First we will take a look at Identity Security in Azure, as it provides the basics for most of the other techniques we will talk about.

After that, Azure Resource (group) security will be discussed. Finally after talking about some Azure networking and storage security, we will delve into the logging and monitoring capabilities of Azure.

This chapter aims to provide an overview of the possibilities of Azure IaaS security. There are some Azure security topics, which are just briefly discussed and others that are not even mentioned. As every security technology in this chapter will probably fill a small book on its own, this chapter is about basic implementations.

We will not talk about any **Operation Management Suite** (**OMS**) or **Enterprise Mobility Suite** (**EMS**) related security techniques in this chapter.

Azure Key Vault should be used whenever possible for key management. It can be leveraged for storage encryption, Azure Active Directory applications and many more. Key Vault is not part of this chapter, because it's a very comprehensive feature that would need a chapter alone.

In this chapter, we will explore most built-in infrastructure and Identity security functions. There will also be a section about Logging.

Azure Identity Security

Security boundaries are often thought of as firewalls, IPS/IDS systems, or routers. Also, logical setups such as DMZs or other network constructs are often referred to as boundaries.

But in the modern world, where many companies support dynamic work models that allow you to **bring your own device** (**BYOD**) or are heavily using online services for their work, the real boundary is the identity.

Identities are often the target of hackers as they resell them or use them to steal information. To make the attacks as hard as possible, it's important to have a well-conceived and centralized identity management. The Azure Active Directory provides that and a lot more to support your security strategy and simplify complex matters such as monitoring of privileged accounts or authentication attacks.

Azure Active Directory

Azure Active Directory (**AAD**) is a very important service that many other services are based on. It's not a directory service like many may think of when they hear the name Active Directory. The AAD is a complex structure without built-in **Organizational Units** (**OUs**) or **Group Policy Objects** (**GPOs**), but with a very high extensibility, open web standards for authorization and authentication, and a modern, (hybrid) cloud focused approach to identity management.

Azure Active Directory editions

Chapter 3, *Deploying and Synchronizing Azure Active Directory* already described the synchronization between on-premise and Azure AD very well. As a result, we will not go deeper into AD Connect.

Just to recapture Chapter 3, *Deploying and Synchronizing Azure Active Directory*, here are the major differences between the AAD pricing tiers. This is important to remember, as there are two (in my opinion) very important security features that are only available in premium P2. We will focus on security related features that were not handled in Chapter 3, *Deploying and Synchronizing Azure Active Directory*.

The following table describes the differences between the four Azure Active Directory editions:

Services	Common	Basic	Premium P1	Premium P2
Directory Objects	X	X	X	X
User/Group Management (add/update/delete)/ User-based provisioning, Device registration	X	X	X	X
Single Sign-On (SSO)	X	X	X	X
Self-Service Password Change for cloud users	X	X	X	X
Connect (Sync engine that extends on-premises directories to Azure Active Directory)	X	X	X	X
Security/Usage Reports	X	X	X	X
Group-based access management/ provisioning		X	X	X
Self-Service Password Reset for cloud users		X	X	X
Company Branding (Logon Pages/Access Panel customization)		X	X	X
Application Proxy		X	X	X
SLA 99.9%		X	X	X
Self-Service Group and app Management/Self-Service application additions/Dynamic Groups			X	X
Self-Service Password Reset/Change/Unlock with on-premises write-back			X	X
Multi-factor authentication (Cloud and On-premises (MFA Server))			X	X
MIM CAL + MIM Server			X	X

Cloud App Discovery			X	X
Connect Health			X	X
Automatic password rollover for group accounts			X	X
Identity Protection				X
Privileged Identity Management				X

Overview of Azure Active Directory editions

Privileged Identity Management

With the help of Azure AD **Privileged Identity Management** (**PIM**), the user can access various capabilities. These include the ability to view which users are Azure AD administrators and the possibility to enable administrative services on demand such as Office 365 or Intune. Furthermore, the user is able to receive reports about changes in administrator assignments or administrator access history.

The AAD PIM allows the user to monitor the access in the organization. Additionally, it is possible to manage and control the access. Resources in Azure AD and services such as Office 365 or Microsoft Intune can be accessed.

Lastly, the user can get alerts, if accesses to privileged roles are granted. Let's take a look at the PIM dashboard. To use Azure PIM, it needs to be activated first:

1. Azure AD PIM should be found in the search easily:

Azure AD PIM in the marketplace

2. After clicking on Azure AD PIM in the marketplace, PIM will probably ask you to re-verify MFA for security reasons. To do this, the MFA token needs to be typed in, after clicking on **Verify my identity**:

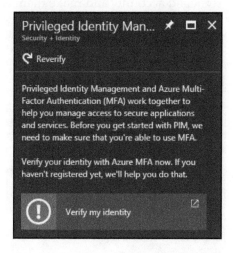

Re-verify identity for Azure AD PIM setup

3. After a successful verification you will get an output as illustrated here:

Successful re-verification

Now the initial setup will start. The setup guides the user through the task of choosing all accounts in the tenant that have privileged rights. It is also possible to select them if they are eligible for requesting privileged role rights.

4. If the wizard is completed without choosing any roles or user as eligible, it will by default assign the security administrator and privileged role administrator roles to the first user that does the PIM setup. Only with these roles it is possible to manage other privileged accounts and make them eligible or grant them rights:

Setup wizard for Azure AD PIM

5. In the following screenshot the tasks related to **Privileged Identity Management** are illustrated:

Azure AD PIM main tasks

6. As my subscription looks very boring after enabling Azure AD PIM I chose to show a demo picture from Microsoft that shows how Azure AD PIM could look in a real-world subscription:

Azure AD PIM dashboard (https://docs.microsoft.com/en-us/azure/active-directory/media/active-directory-privileged-identity-management-configure/pim_dash.png)

7. It's now possible to manage all chosen eligible privileged accounts and roles through Azure AD PIM. Besides removing and adding eligible users to Azure AD PIM, there is also a management of privileged roles, where the role activation setting is available. This setting is used to make privileged roles more transparent, trackable, and to implement the **just-in-time** (**JIT**) administration model. This is the activation setting blade for the **Security Administrator**:

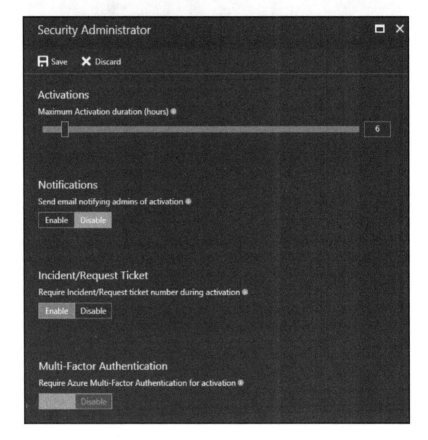

Role activation settings for the role Security Administrator

It's also possible to use the rich monitoring and auditing capabilities of Azure AD PIM and never to lose track of the use of privileged accounts and to track misuse easily.

Azure AD PIM is a very useful security feature and it is even more useful in combination with Azure AD Identity Protection.

Identity protection

Azure AD identity is a service that provides a central dashboard that informs administrators about potential threats to the organizations identities. It is based on behavioral analysis and it provides an overview of risks levels and vulnerabilities.

The Azure AD anomaly detection capabilities are used by Azure AD Identity Protection to report suspicious activities. These enables one to identify anomalies of the organization's identity in real time, making it more powerful than the regular reporting capabilities. This system will calculate a user's risk level for each account, giving you the ability to configure risk-based policies in order to automatically protect the identities of your organization. Employing these risk-based policies among other conditional access controls provided by AAD and EMS enables an organization to provide remediation actions or block access to certain accounts.

The key capabilities of Azure Identity Protection can be grouped into two phases.

Detection of vulnerabilities and potential risky accounts

This phase is basically about automatically classifying suspicious sign-in or user activity. It uses user defined sign-in risk and user risk policies. These policies are described later.

Another feature of this part is the automatic security recommendations (vulnerabilities) based on Azure provided rules.

Investigation of potential suspicious events

This part is all about investigating the alerts and events that are triggered by the risk policies. So basically, a security related person needs to review all users that got flagged based on policies and take a look at the particular risk events that triggered this alert and so contributed to the higher risk level. It's also important to define a workflow that is used to take the corresponding actions.

It also needs someone who regularly investigates the vulnerability warnings and recommendations and estimates the real risk level for the organization.

It's important to take a closer look at the risk policies that can be configured in Azure AD Identity Protection.

We will skip the **Multi-factor authentication registration** configurations here. For more details on MFA, read the next paragraph. Just because it can't be said often enough, *I highly recommend enforcing MFA for all accounts*!

The two policies we can configure are user risk policy and sign-in risk policy. The options look quite similar, but the real differentiation happens in the background:

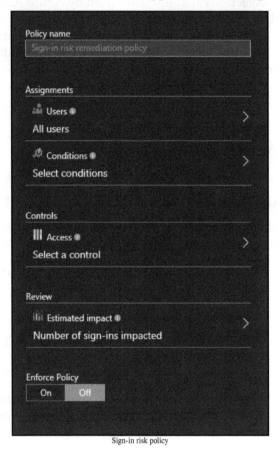

Sign-in risk policy

In the following diagram, user risk policy view is illustrated:

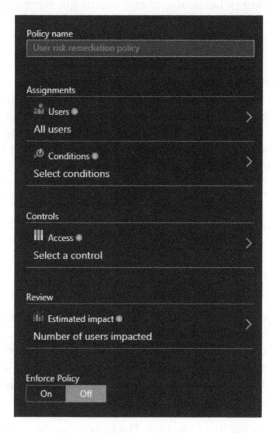

User risk policy

The main differentiation between Sign-in and User risk policies is where the risk events are captured. The Sign-in policy defines what happens when a certain account appears to have a high number of suspicious sign-in events. This includes sign-in from an anonymous IP address, logins from different countries in a time frame where it would not be possible to travel to the other location, and a lot more.

On the other hand, User risk policies trigger a certain amount of events that happen after the user was already logged in. Leaked credential or abnormal behavior are example risk events.

Microsoft provides a guide to simulating some risks to verify that the corresponding policies trigger and events got recorded. This guide is provided at this address `https://docs.microsoft.com/en-us/azure/active-directory/active-directory-identityprotection-playbook`.

The interesting thing after choosing users is the **Conditions** setting. This setting defines the threshold of risk events that is required to trigger the policy. The different option for the threshold are **Low and above**, **Medium and above**, and **High**. When **High** is chosen, it needs much more risk events to trigger the policy, but it also has the lowest impact on users. When **Low and above** is chosen, the policy will trigger much more often, but the likelihood of false positives is much higher, too.

Finding the right balance between security and usability is one more time the real challenge.

The last option provides a preview of how many users will be affected by the new policy. This helps to review and identify possible misconfigurations of earlier steps.

Multi-factor authentication

Authentications that require more than a single type of verification method are defined as two-step verifications. This second layer of sign-in routine can critically improve the security of user transactions and sign-ins. This method can be described as employing two or more of the typical authentication factors, defined as either one, something you know (password), two, something you have (a trusted device such as a phone or a security token) or three, something you are (biometrics).

Microsoft uses Azure MFA for this objective. The user's sign-in routine is kept simple, but Azure MFA improves safe access to data and applications. Several verification methods such as phone call, text message, or mobile app verification can help you to strengthen the authentication process.

 There are two pricing models for Azure MFA. One is based on users, the other is based on usage. Take your time and consider both models. Just go to the pricing calculator and calculate both to compare them.

Now we will see how easy it is to activate MFA in Azure:

1. First sign in to the old Azure portal (`https://manage.windowsazure.com`). After choosing the right Azure Active Directory, click on **USERS**:

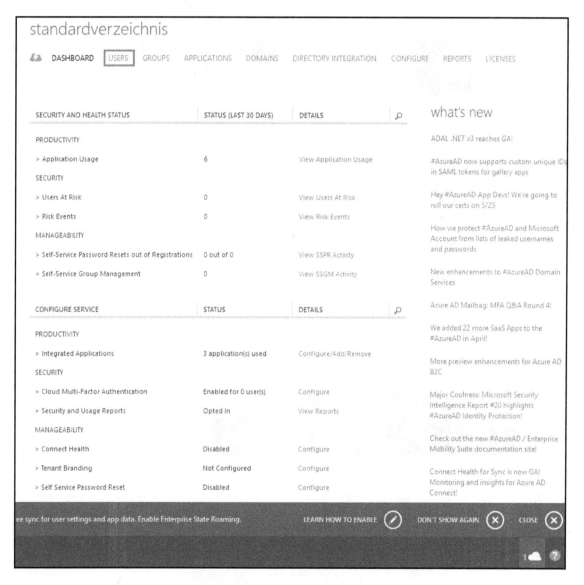

Azure Active Directory in the old Azure portal

2. At the **USERS** page click on **MANAGE MULTI-FACTOR AUTH** at the very bottom:

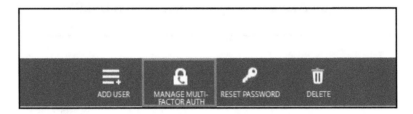

Multi-factor authentication settings

3. Now a redirection to the MFA portal should take place. In this portal, the MFA management takes place. I will use my demo user **Frederik** to show the process of activating MFA:

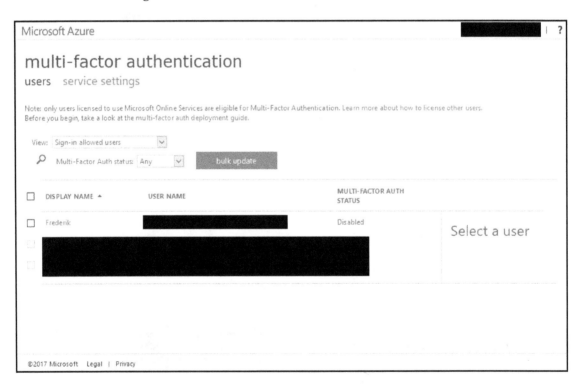

MFA portal

4. Just choose the user that needs to be enabled for MFA and press **Enable**:

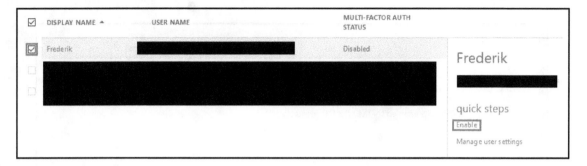

Choosing users for MFA and enabling them is enabled for MFA.

5. After confirming the change, it takes a few seconds and the user is enabled for MFA.

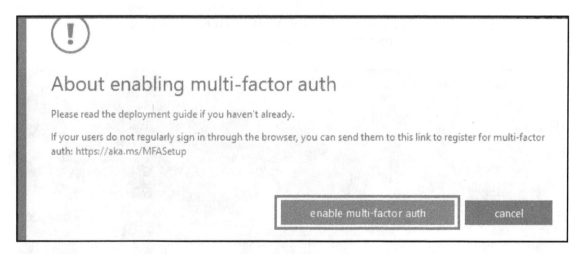

Do you really want to enable MFA?

6. Search for the `Multi-Factor Authentication` in the search box and then click on it:

Confirmation for enabling MFA

7. To change the billing model for MFA, a new MFA provider needs to be created to replace the existing one. For this, the **Multi-Factor Authentication** resource should be created from the marketplace:

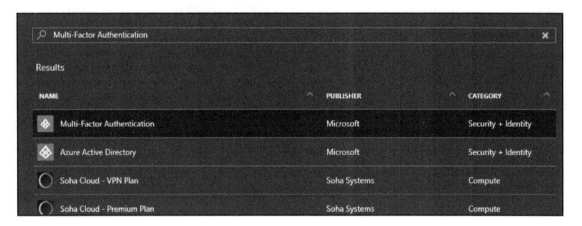

MFA provider in the marketplace

8. Click on Create button to proceed:

Redirection at creation

9. The little arrow in the box indicates a redirection to the old portal. In the old portal, the MFA provider page directly opens up. There is an exclamation mark next to the usage model. This and the text at the bottom warns that it's not possible to change the usage model afterwards:

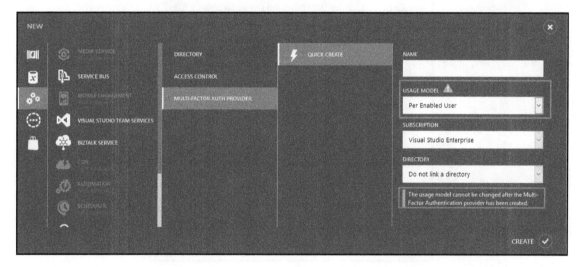

New MFA provider

There are many more features related to Azure Active Directory and Identity Security that we are not able to discuss in this book. I encourage you to take a look at Azure AD Connect Health, Azure AD Cloud App Discovery, and Azure Information Protection (as part of EMS). It's important to know what services are offered and what advantages they could offer your company.

This is an example dialogue that will be shown after typing the password, when MFA is enabled and the Authenticator-App was chosen as main method:

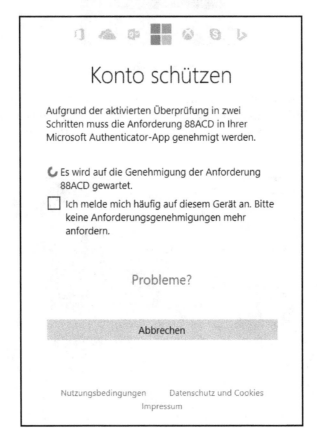

MFA with authenticator-app

Conditional access

Another important security feature that is based on Azure Active Directory is conditional access. Although it's much more important when working with Office 365 it is also used to authenticate against Azure AD applications.

A conditional access rule grants or denies access to a certain resource based on location, group membership, device state, and the application the user tries to access.

After creating access rules that apply to all users who use the corresponding application, it's also possible to apply a rule to a security group or the other way around, and exclude a group from applying. There are scenarios with MFA, where this could make sense.

> Currently Conditional access is completely managed in the old Azure portal (`https://manage.windowsazure.com`). There is a conditional access feature in the new Azure portal, but it is still in preview and not supported for production.

The administrator is also able to combine conditional access policies with Azure AD **Multi-factor authentication (MFA)**.

This will combine the MFA policies with those of other services such as Identity Protection or the basic MFA policy. This means that even if a user is per group excepted from authenticating with MFA to an application, all the other rules still apply. So if there is a MFA policy configured in Identity Protection that enforces MFA, the user still needs to log in using MFA.

In the old portal the conditional access feature is configured on application basis, in the new portal the conditional access rules are configured and managed in the Azure Active Directory resource:

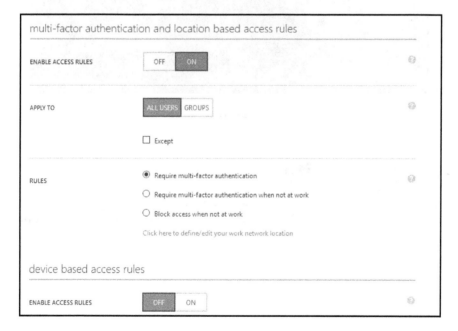

Per application management old Azure Portal

Following screenshot shows view of new Azure AD:

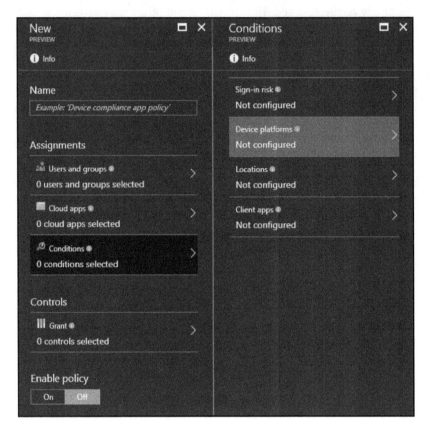

Central management in Azure Active Directory in the new portal

Resource security

The subscription is the lowest level of identity verification (for Global Administrator/Co-Administrator) and the connected Azure AD takes control of all the identities and the assigned roles and rights.

These are the basics for the **Role-Based Access Control** (**RBAC**) on Azure Resources. With the release of the new portal, the concept of an Azure Resource was introduced. Every service you create in Azure is part of a resource group or is itself a resource.

This is the place where access control takes place in Azure.

Role-based Access Control

Azure RBAC enables you to use detailed access management for Azure. Employing RBAC makes it possible to make specific choices about how user access is granted in order to perform their tasks (for example, SQL Administration). Two ways of control are possible when using the fine-grained RBAC:

RBAC role assignments are bound to a specific subscription or resource (group). Giving access to a specific Resource, does not imply access to any other resource in the same subscription.

The role can narrow the access even further within the scope of an assignment. These roles can be on a general level, such as owner, but also specific such as virtual machine reader.

We will take a look at RBAC roles as well as role assignment:

1. First navigate to the **Billing** blade:

Billing button in Azure portal

2. After clicking on the**Billing** option, you will have a new windows named **Billing**:

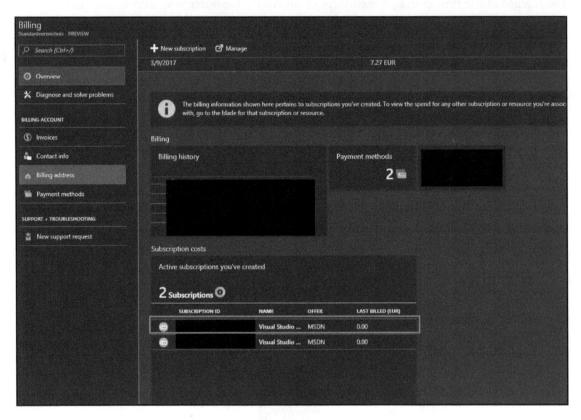

Billing dashboard

3. Now select the subscription that needs to be managed:

Subscription management

4. In the **Subscription** management choose **Access control (IAM)**. You will be presented with an overview of users and groups connected to that subscription and their assigned roles. To see which roles are existent in your subscription, click on **Roles**:

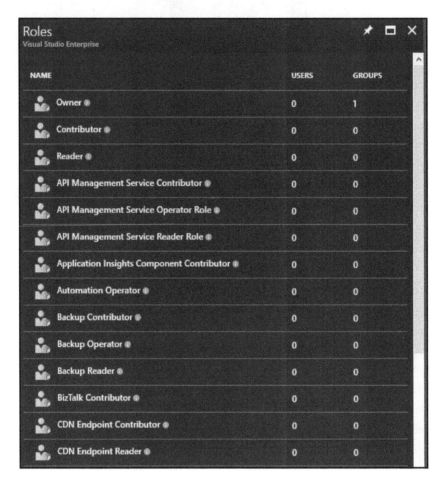

List of existing roles

If you have not yet configured custom roles, a list of all built-in roles and their assigned users and groups will be displayed. To assign users or groups to that role click at the role and use the **Add** button at the top to add new users or groups to the role. This assigns the role and the associated rights to the user or to all users of the group. In the following screenshot, the default role of **Owner** gets assigned to all subscription admins:

Assigned users and groups of the Owner role

Custom roles must be created programmatically through one of the existing interfaces. Azure PowerShell is a good way for beginners to achieve that task. First someone has to define the exact rights that the custom role should provide. These are very granular rights for single resources and they look as follows:

```
"Microsoft.Network/*/read"
"Microsoft.Compute/*/read"
"Microsoft.Compute/virtualMachines/restart/action"
```

Now these are used to create a JSON-based role definition file that will be uploaded to Azure for role creation.To do that, use the following cmdlet:

```
New-AzureRmRoleDefinition -InputFile "C:temproleDefinition.json"
```

To find out how exactly custom role creation works, go to
https://docs.microsoft.com/en-us/azure/active-directory/role-bas
ed-access-control-custom-roles.

Resource tags and policies

a security topic, I should at least explain what tags are and how they are used to improve security.

Although tagging is more a governance than a security topic, I should at least explain what tags are and how they are used to improve security. Tags are used to organize resources in Azure. They can be added to a Resource group as well as to single resources. They provide up to 15 key value fields to add some information to the object. This could be a billing related field such as department or project or just general information. These tags could also be used as a method for filtering events and applying policies to certain resources.

Examples for tags could be `startup-time`, `shutdown-time`, `customer`, `cost-center`, `accountable`. In general tags are mainly used to help organizing/automating and to improve the governance.

Azure resource manager policies are a way to control resource deployment to, for example, meeting compliance rules. This could be for example a rule, that requires resources to be deployed in a specific region. A resource policy is basically a JSON-based `if, then` statement that is checked at resource deployment. Resource policies can be used to:

- Append
- Deny
- Audit

when a specific condition is met. The audit feature is extremely interesting for security investigations. When suspicious activities happen in a Resource group or a resource, audit policies could help with logged events for several actions. It could also help to track actions of suspicious users.

 For more information on Resource manager policies, use this link
`https://docs.microsoft.com/en-us/azure/azure-resource-manager/re`
`source-manager-policy`.

Azure network security

Azure network security is based on classic network security. Just because the hardware underneath is managed and the whole networking is virtualized doesn't mean that all classic network security principles are invalid.

Network security groups

A very basic feature when it comes to network security in Azure is the network security groups. It would be too much to call them firewalls, but they fulfill basic firewall activity. They are best compared to access lists on a Layer 3 network switch. They consist of inbound and outbound network security rules. These rules control the network traffic flow and can be given several parameters at creation.

Priority

The **Priority** of a rule defines the order in which the rules are applied to traffic. The rules are processed in order, what means that a lower number means a higher priority.

Source

There are a few different setting for source traffic. The source traffic needs to be categorized first. An important setting is the **Tag** categorization. This makes it possible to choose from the **Source** from **Internet**, **AzureLoadBalancer**, and **VirtualNetwork**. Where **Internet** means the public IP address space, **VirtualNetwork** the private and virtual address space, and **AzureLoadBalancer** the traffic that originates from deployed load balancers to determine the service health.

The last setting is the **Protocol**. There are many service templates for common services such as RDP, SMTP, or FTP. This makes it easy to quickly create some rules in the portal.

Destination

Destination has the same settings as **Source** besides the**Protocol** setting, as this is already defined by the **Source** setting.

Note that all port and protocol settings get disabled when choosing a service template, because the standard ports are used. When you create a rule for a network service that doesn't use the standard ports, use a custom setting. This is how a new network rule looks:

New inbound security rule

Network security groups can be associated with multiple network interface cards and multiple subnets. That means that all security rules defined in that security group apply to the complete network traffic in all associated subnets.

By default, all subnets are routed. To implement basic security based on NSGs, it's best practice to implement traffic flow control between subnets first. After connecting to an on-premise network via VPN or ExpressRoute (see `Chapter 4`, *Implementing Azure Networks*), it's also very important to ensure that all unnecessary traffic from the Internet is blocked and that all Internet facing services/virtual machines are isolated by, for example, a DMZ.

Network virtual appliances

Although there are already extensive built-in network protection capabilities against threats from the outside, like DDoS and other common attack patterns, these are mainly protecting Azure as a platform. That means, that when one customer is affected by a DDoS attack, no other customer will be influenced by that. But that also means, that you still have to protect yourself against DDoS attacks against your own isntances.

When it comes to advanced network filtering or routing scenarios Azure has *network virtual appliances* in place. These are virtual appliances that are deployable from the marketplace. They are third-party solutions for different scenarios from vendors such as Barracuda, Cisco, or F5. If none of the marketplace appliances meet the requirements, it's possible to create an NVA based on a VM. With that method, a free firewall solution such as pfSense could be used for several scenarios including test environments.

To use appliances in Azure, network traffic needs to be routed through them. This is done with **user defined routes** (**UDRs**). User defined routes can be deployed to control traffic flow in virtual networks.

Common scenarios for network virtual appliances are:

- Separation of corporate and Azure network (for example, additional scanning of traffic that's gone through a VPN)
- VPN to Azure-NVAs can also be used to set up a VPN tunnel instead of using the Azure VPN Gateway
- WAN optimizer architectures
- Specific scanning such as web application filtering, additional DDoS protection, IPS/IDS scenarios, or other detailed traffic analysis

User defined routes are also used to configure forced tunneling. Forced tunneling is used to control outbound Internet traffic and it helps to meet compliance rules.

With the help of UDRs, outbound traffic is routed back to the company network and is then redirected to the Internet. A central internet breakout helps in cases where it's important to apply policies for antivirus scanning, data leakage protection, or other security measures.

 To learn more about user defined routes, use the following link
`https://docs.microsoft.com/en-us/azure/virtual-network/virtual-n`
`etworks-udr-overview`.
For available third-party appliances, check out this marketplace link
`https://azuremarketplace.microsoft.com/de-de/marketplace/apps/ca`
`tegory/networking?page=1&subcategories=appliances`.

Azure Storage security

Azure Storage is the base for nearly all IaaS services. It's a high scalable, available, and fully virtualized cloud storage solution that can be used to provide storage space in many ways.

When talking about storage security it's very important to remember that all earlier discussed security measures such as RBAC or strict identity management should already be deployed.

After that is ensured, it's useful to leverage the special security abilities of Azure Storage. These include:

- Shared access signatures
- Data encryption in transit
- Storage account encryption at rest
- Virtual Hard Disk encryption
- Advanced analytics

Key management

Azure uses 512 bit strings as storage account keys. Paired with the storage account name it enables the user to access the objects in the storage account, for example, blobs, entities within a table, queue messages, and files on an Azure Files share. The access to the data plane of an Storage account is based on the controlling of the access to the Storage account keys.

Two keys, here defined as `Key 1` and `Key 2` in the PowerShell cmdlets and the Azure portal, are assigned to each storage account. By employing the Azure portal, PowerShell, Azure CLI, .NET Storage Client Library, or the REST API these can be manually regenerated if desired.

Regenerating your Storage account keys can have several reasons. One option would be to regenerate them in regular time intervals to improve the security of your organization, especially if someone was able to hack into your account or obtain the keys from hardcoded piece of software. This would give the (evil) person full access to your Storage account. If several different SAS have been compromised, you should replace all of them, especially if they are based on the same Storage account key.

Make sure that you have a list of all your applications and Azure services, which are possibly dependent on the Storage account before you regenerate your keys. For example, if you use an Storage account in combination with Azure Media Services, make sure to re-sync the access keys in your Media Services after regenerating the key. This also applies to other services as well, such as the storage explorer. It is important to notice that the VHD files of your VMs stored in your storage account are not affected by this action. After regenerating your keys in the Azure portal, it will take up to 10 minutes to be synchronized across all storage services.

The following part contains the general process of how to change your keys. It is assumed that currently `Key 1` is in use and the goal is to change to `Key 2`. Just reverse the key names for the process if you are currently employing `Key 2`.

First, you should regenerate `Key 2` in the Azure portal to make sure it is secure.

You can change each application to use the new key and publish it as part of the migration process. After you have completed this, keep in mind to regenerate the old key, so it doesn't work anymore.

Storing the key in Azure Key Vault and making the application retrieve from the service is another possible option. An adavantage of this method is that the applications will not need to be redeployed, because they can get the key from the updated Azure Key Vault automatically. It is also possible to cache the key in your memory and only read it from the Azure Key Vault if it fails when using it.

Another level of security is added by deploying Azure Key Vault, because it avoids the key from being hardcoded in the configuration file, making it vulnerable to several attack vectors.

Using Azure Key Vault also gives you the ability to control access to your keys with the use of Azure Active Directory. applications that require access to keys from Azure Key Vault can be granted the information, while making sure that other applications don't have this privilege without the specific permission of you.

Shared access signatures

It is important to remember that sharing your storage account key grants complete access to that person. Someone could potentially replace your files with virus-infected versions or steal the data. So, granting someone unlimited access to your storage account is a very risky practice. A shared access signature consists of query parameters as a part of the URL, aiming to provide information about the access parameters and the period for which access is granted.

Shared access signatures can only be created programmatically or within the Azure storage explorer.

The storage service uses input query parameters from the received request and creates a signature based on the method of the calling program. The service checks if the two signatures are identical. In case of a positive result the storage then validates other parameters, such as storage service version, correct time and date in the specified window, if the access requested corresponds to the request made, and so on.

There are two types of shared access signatures.

Service-level SAS

A service-level SAS enables the user to access specific resources in an Storage account. In this kind of SAS this could, for example, be retrieving a list of blobs in a container, the download of a blob, the update of an entity in a table, or uploading a file to a file share.

Account-level SAS

An account-level SAS is capable of all service-level SAS plus several additions. Multiple options can be chosen, which are not available in service-level SAS, giving you the ability to create file shares, tables, queues, and containers. It is possible to specify access to several services at once, for example, enabling you to give someone access to blobs and files in your storage account at the same time.

Remember that all SAS that are signed with a specific storage access key are invalidated, as soon as the access key in re-generated.

Storage Encryption

As customer and compliance needs including encryption at every stage, there are several ways to achieve encryption at rest in azure.

Storage account encryption

In order to protect and safeguard your data to meet organizational security and compliance commitments, Azure **Storage Service Encryption** (**SSE**) is used. Prior to persisting to storage and retrieval, Azure Storage encrypts and respectively decrypts your data. Currently SSE only takes care of blobs and files (Preview) that are stored on an Storage account.

> Currently there is a preview feature called SSE for Azure File Storage. This feature uses the same techniques as SSE for blobs to protect the Azure storage file service.

1. The following screenshots provide guidance on how to enable Storage account encryption on any supported storage account:

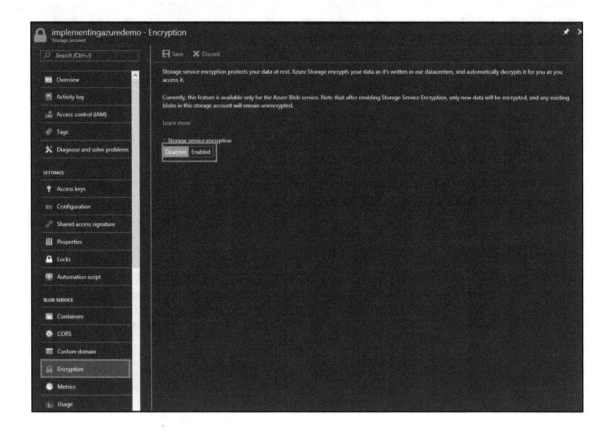

Blob encryption

2. Now click **Enabled** and **Save**:

Enabling storage encryption

That's it. Storage encryption is enabled now.

 It's important to remember that the process of SSE is completely transparent. That means that all keys, as well as encryption and decryption, is managed by Microsoft. Because of that, there is no possibility to receive, back up, or use your own keys for the AES-256 encryption taking place.

Azure disk encryption

It is fully supported to enable and use Azure SSE for **Virtual Hard Disks** (**VHD**) that are used by virtual machines. But as SSE is only used on data that is added after the encryption was turned on, the basic VHD would stay unencrypted.

SSE has full support for marketplace resources, so what basically happens is that new writes from the virtual machine to the storage account will be encrypted, while the vhd used for enrolment stays untouched.

To meet compliance and security requirements, Microsoft introduced a service that explicitly takes care of virtual machines in Azure.

This service is called Azure disk encryption and it uses internal system technologies to encrypt the virtual disks of virtual machines. This software is BitLocker in Windows and DM-Crypt in Linux VMs.

Virtual machine disk encryption can currently only be enabled using PowerShell with the following steps:

1. At first, we need a service principal in the Azure AD. Afterwards an Azure Key Vault is needed to store the key encryption key.
2. After these are set up, the principal needs to be connected to the Key Vault for managing keys.
3. After that is done and the Azure AD application is set up for certificate-based authentication, this PowerShell cmdlet is used to enable disk encryption for a certain VM:

```
Set-AzureRmVMDiskEncryptionExtension -ResourceGroupName $resourceGroup
-VMName $vm -AadClientID $adApplication -AadClientCertThumbprint $certThumb
-DiskEncryptionKeyVaultUrl $encryptionUrl -DiskEncryptionKeyVaultId $kvId
```

Because many technologies involved in this process are changing very fast, I did not mention the whole process here.

 To find the current implementation and learn how to implement disk encryption, please use this link https://docs.microsoft.com/en-us/azure/security/azure-security-disk-encryption.

Logging and monitoring

Logging and monitoring are the most important techniques in today's threat landscape. Logs and monitoring data is the basis for later analysis and behavioral analysis of network traffic, user actions, failed processes, and more. The more data you have, the more likely you are to find an anomaly or a pattern that can be used for automated threat analysis.

But as data is nothing without former analysis, the visualization and analytic tools are as important as the behavioral threat detection tools.

Azure Logs

Azure collects lots of logs for you by default. There is a central dashboard for viewing logs and events called **Monitor**. The Monitor is still in preview, but in my opinion it is the best organized place to manage logs and diagnostics.

There are three main categories of logs that are collected. These are under the **EXPLORE** point in the Azure Monitor.

- **Activity log**: The activity log keeps track of all actions that are happening on Azure. It logs all activities no matter if they were initiated by users or other resources including resource creation, change of resources and resource deletion. Activity logs can be analyzed using different Azure Services. These include PowerBI, Event Hub or just save them to a storage account to handle them otherwise.
- **Metrics**: Metrics are basic telemetry logs for resources like Network traffic, CPU percentage, context switches etc.. It depends on the monitoring settings that are configured for the resources if all metrics are available. The metrics that can be collected from the fabric have the [Host] prefix.

Metrics can also be used as trigger for alerts. These alerts can be used to trigger events like a custom script, an alert mail or a WebHook when a certain threshold is reached.

- **Diagnostic log**: Diagnostic Logs contain very specific logs for individual resources. For example, when diagnostic logging on a network security group is activated, the diagnostic logs contain events connected to NSGs and their rules as well as several counters.

Diagnostic Logs can also be used as a source for analysis by Operation Management Suite Log Analytics.

Azure monitor management blade

In the following screenshot log filter options are shown:

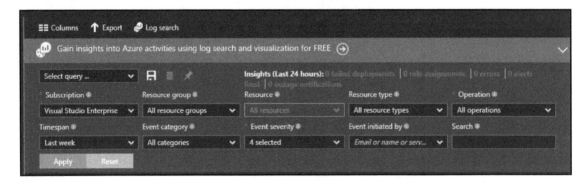

Log filtering options

There is a special kind of logs for storage accounts. These logs are saved directly in the storage account itself. They can be accessed by PowerShell, REST API or by using the Azure Storage Explorer that was introduced in `Chapter 5`, *Implementing and Securing Azure Storage Accounts*.

To view the metrics recorded for the Storage account `implementingazuredemo` you need to login, provide an SAS or Access Key first. Now you should be able to see the content of the storage account. Expand the tables node and there will be the metric tables for several counters.

These are

- Capacity metrics
- Transaction Metrics Blob
- Transaction Metrics Queue
- And Transaction Metrics Table.

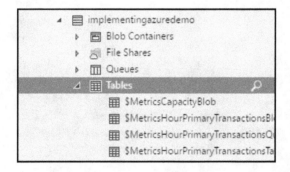

Storage account metrics

Azure Security Center

Azure Security Center is an offering, that helps users to protect their environments and helps detecting suspicious events and vulnerabilities.

It's able to monitor Azure Virtual Machines, Azure SQL Databases, Azure virtual Networks, and many more PaaS and IaaS services.

Based on the collected metrics it's possible to detect threats and increase the transparency of critical actions based on rulesets and threat analytics.

With the help of security center, the Security Operator always has an overview of the current security threats and the state of security measures as well as vulnerabilities across all azure resources.

 All collected data is stored in your own storage account, that is create per region on policy creation.

When opening the Security Center by clicking on the icon at the left, it opens the dashboard. At first time launch, the security center will tell you, that it is working with limited function. This is because just the basic version of the Security Center is free. For evaluating I recommend to use the free test ride, because many of the, in my opinion very valuable, functions are only available in the paid version.

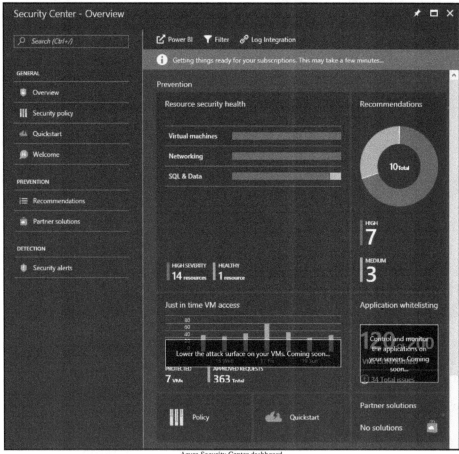

Azure Security Center dashboard

After launching the dashboard, you will realize, that it works on subscription base. What that means is that the Security Center provides recommendations based on policies that are applied to single subscriptions. To change a policy just click on **Security policy** then click on the subscription that you want to change.

In the subscription blade, it's also possible to choose a pricing plan, activate the free trial, configure notification option and, what we are here for, configure the **Prevention policy**:

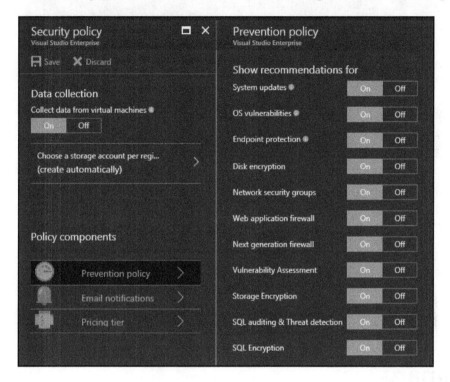

Configure the Prevention policy

After it's configures which resources should be collected data for, recommendations will show up in **Recommendation** as well as potential security alerts, as long as you use the standard pricing:

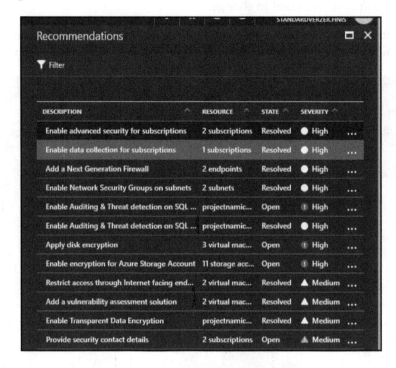

Security Center recommendations

Summary

Let's summarize this chapter. You should have learned the basics of Azure security. This means understanding principles and possibilities of implementation and maintaining secure Azure environments.

It's very important to create your architecture with security in mind and Microsoft Azure does help a lot in taking complexity away and focusing on the important parts of IaaS security.

In the next chapter, we will see some example architecture from real-world examples.

10
Skill Wrap Up and Migration Scenario

In the following chapter, we will use our previously learned skills to migrate a common IT infrastructure to Azure and design a solution that covers most of the required infrastructures.

In the first part of the chapter, we will look at a common on-premises infrastructure that will resemble most of the scenarios you will see on a customer site.

In the second part of the chapter, we will migrate the on-premises services to Azure and you will get an explanation for every architectural decision.

We'll explore the following topics:

- Connection of Microsoft Active Directory Domain Service to Azure Active Directory
- Option to provide Microsoft Exchange Server out of the cloud
- Option to provide SharePoint
- Option to provide Skype for Business
- Common workloads and how they can be integrated into Azure Scenarios

On-premises infrastructure scenario

In our scenario, we are looking for a traditional corporate IT infrastructure with the following components:

- Microsoft Active Directory
- Microsoft Exchange Server
- Microsoft SharePoint Server (general standard)
- Microsoft Skype for Business Server
- Document management system based on SMB shares
- Public website based on TYPO3 CMS
- Backup services
- File servers

The customer has three main offices—one in EMEA, one in the US, and one in Japan. Additionally, he has twenty more offices around the globe and two more offices in China. All these offices are currently supported by three data centers—one data center in EMEA, one in the US, and one in Hong Kong. The customer has around 4,000 users, where 25% are in the Americas, 50% are in EMEA and 25% are in APAC.

The company is also using Salesforce to maintain their customer relationships and opportunities.

Background network infrastructure

Luckily, the customer already has a fully meshed MPLS network from one of the major Internet service providers in place. He also has a different subnetwork with IPv4 in all of his office locations.

The MPLS network looks like the following:

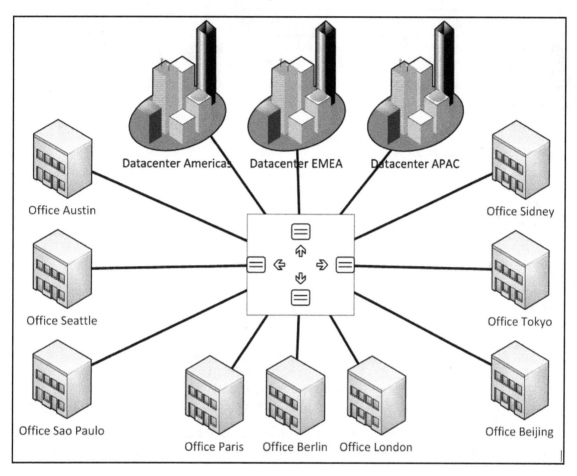

Currently, the customer uses the following IP ranges for his environment:

Region	Location	IP Range/Subnet (CIDR)
EMEA	Global	010. 000.xxx.xxx/8
EMEA	DMZ	010.010.xxx.xxx/16
EMEA	DC EMEA	010.011.xxx.xxx/16
EMEA	Office Berlin	010.012.xxx.xxx/16
EMEA	Office Paris	010.013.xxx.xxx/16

EMEA	Office London	`010.014.xxx.xxx/16`
Americas	Global	`010.100.xxx.xxx/8`
Americas	DMZ	`010.110.xxx.xxx/16`
Americas	DC EMEA	`010.111.xxx.xxx/16`
Americas	Office Berlin	`010.112.xxx.xxx/16`
Americas	Office Paris	`010.113.xxx.xxx/16`
Americas	Office London	`010.114.xxx.xxx/16`
APAC	Global	`010.200.xxx.xxx/8`
APAC	DMZ	`010.210.xxx.xxx/16`
APAC	DC EMEA	`010.211.xxx.xxx/16`
APAC	Office Berlin	`010.212.xxx.xxx/16`
APAC	Office Paris	`010.213.xxx.xxx/16`
APAC	Office London	`010.214.xxx.xxx/16`

> To implement a clean and well-structured WAN and LAN environment for the migration into the cloud is very important and can be a show stopper or could set any project on risk. So in the first step, analyze your current WAN and LAN environment and plan an environment and changes who fit your cloud migration needs.

The customer also has a point-to-site VPN in place that terminates directly in the regional data centers. Therefore, the current client has three configurations, shown in the following table:

Region	Location	DNS Name
EMEA	DC EMEA	`vpnEMEA.company.com`
Americas	DC Americas	`vpnAmericas.company.com`
APAC	DC APAC	`vpnAPAC.company.com`

Background information on Microsoft Active Directory

The customer uses a single-domain single-forest architecture with one domain controller per region, and in the offices with more than 200 users or with a bad connection he has positioned a **read-only domain controller** (**RODC**). The customer has one organization unit per region within the Active Directory. Currently the customer Azure AD yet. The Azure AD environment would be build up from scratch.

The following diagram shows the distribution of the domain controllers:

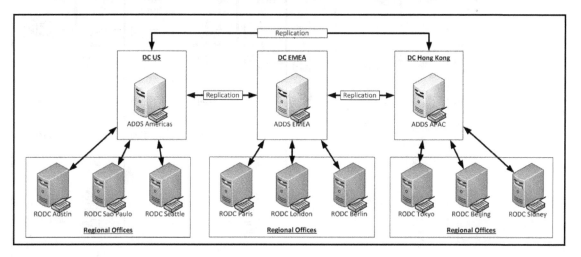

The following diagram shows the schematic organization unit topology:

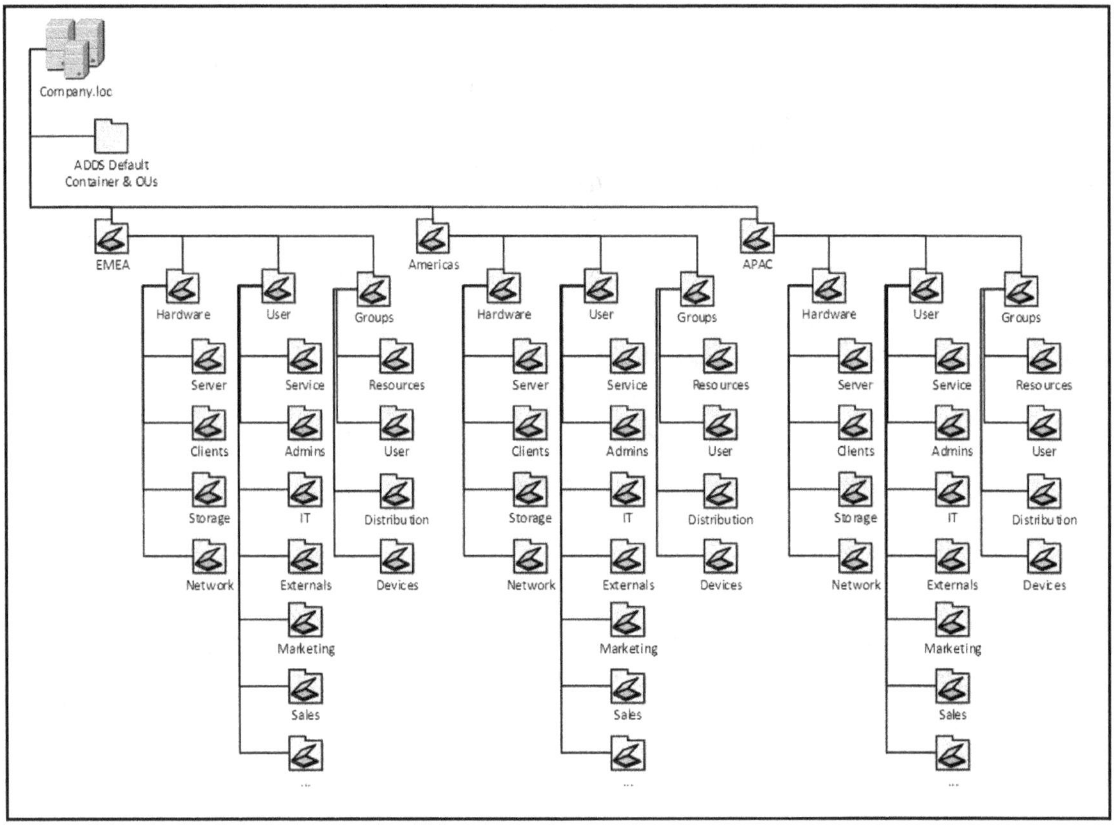

All domain controllers are on Windows Server 2012 R2 and the domain and forest function level is running Windows Server 2012 R2.

The customer has no Active Directory Federation Service in place yet.

Background information on Microsoft Exchange Server

Currently, the customer uses Exchange Server 2013 with a database availability group distributed in all three data centers. He has three mail databases with around 1,000 users for each database. Every user has a mailbox of around 300 MB size and an archiving mailbox of 1 GB size. All services from Exchange are running behind a Load Balancer cluster.

The following diagram shows a schematic view of the infrastructure:

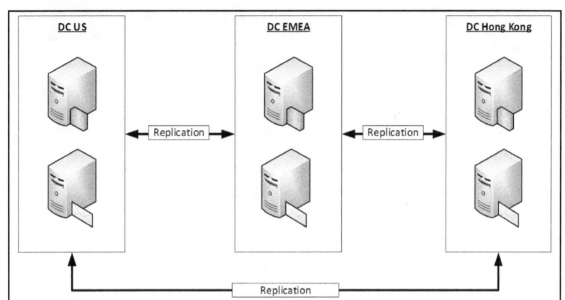

Background information on Microsoft SharePoint Server

The customer uses his SharePoint for internal websites and communities. He has a two-tier SharePoint solution with a three-node SharePoint cluster and a three-node SQL server cluster in the backend. The SharePoint Servers are placed behind a Load Balancer.

The following diagram shows the distribution of the servers:

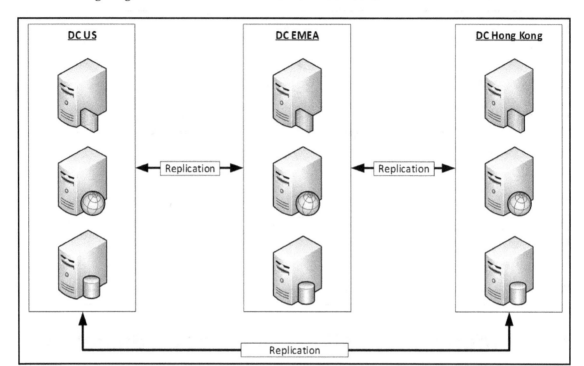

There are no special frameworks, workflows, or extensions installed with the current SharePoint installation.

Background information on Microsoft Skype for Business Server

In our scenario, the customer is using Skype for Business only as an internal chat and conferencing service. There is only one Skype server and one database in place at the moment:

Background information one document management system based on SMB shares

The customer is using a document management system that is storing its files on a File share. The system only uses one set of permissions on the File share and has full control over it. Every other permission is set within the document management system. The users don't have access to the File share.

The following picture shows a schematic overview of the current solution:

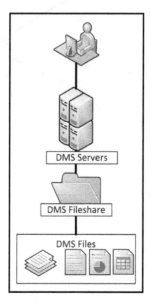

Background information on public website based on TYPO3 CMS

The public website of the customer is running on a single virtual machine with a TYPO3 installed on an Ubuntu Linux virtual machine with a MySQL database. The TYPO3 installation is based on standard Linux operating system components with no changes in Linux kernel or other OS components and the website is customized via the TYPO3 interface. There are no other frameworks installed for TYPO3 within the OS except a PDF creator, which is directly installed into the Linux system.

Background information on backup services

Currently, the customer uses a common backup software to back up all virtual machines from the hypervisor, and different machines are backed up with a client-based solution within the VMs and physical servers.

The following diagram shows the current backup environment:

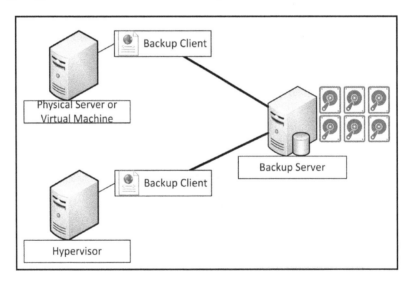

Background information on file servers

The customer has a classic file server infrastructure with shared folders for group work and homeshares for users. He is also using roaming profiles within his infrastructure.

The following diagram shows an example of the current file server structure:

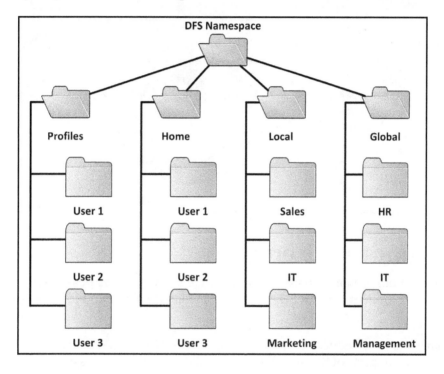

Every major office location has its own file server that replicates the data to its designated regional data center via distributed filesystem replication.

Global shares are replicated via all locations and data centers:

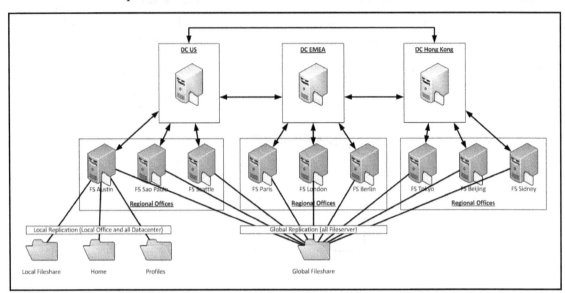

Customer requirements

The customer in our scenario wants to migrate as many services as possible to Azure and Office 365. Only services that have dependencies to latency and band location will stay on-site.

The customer wants to reduce complexity, and have as few virtual machines as possible. He also wants to move parts of his networking services to Azure, such as client point-to-site VPN.

In our case, the customer also wants to enhance Skype for Business usage by enhancing the environment with external meeting connection via the Internet and connection to MPLS network. The Skype system and connection should also be redundant.

In future, the customer wants to have the option to use single sign on and multi-factor authentication for all his enterprise applications, as well as password self-service for his Azure and Office 365 users. The identity and access management solution must be redundant.

The customer also wants to have a global point-to-site VPN solution that does not need any different DNS names and is based on a IP Geotargeting. That means that depending of the location of the client IP, the user will be connected to his regional nearest VPN gateway.

Solution in Azure

As you have learned so far, with Microsoft Cloud services, you have a wide range of services that are mostly integrated with each other. The challenge now is to put those parts together to match the expectations of your environment.

The next few pages are an introduction to a possible solution, with an explanation as to why some of the design decisions were made.

Solution for a wide area network

At the beginning of every Azure project, you need to plan your WAN environment and where to place your Azure instances.

So, you look at the company footprint and geographical distribution of the office and the users. If the company has only a few offices in Europe or another region, it is mostly enough to have one Azure instance in one region.

In our case, we have many offices of different sizes around the globe, so it is only necessary to have at least one Azure instance on each continent. In our case, we would need one in Europe, one in the US, and one in Asia, near China.

In the next step, you need to get in contact with your Internet service provider. Together with your ISP, you need to determine which edge site of Azure and which Azure Region would be the best. Your ISP would mostly decide between our location and the Azure edge site by latency.

To remember, Microsoft Azure Edge Sites and data centers aren't the same. Microsoft Edge Sites are separated to the data centers and mostly located on major Internet Exchanges around the global. Edge Sites are related to data centers but not the same.
As an example, if you only have locations in Japan, your ISP would prefer a Saitama edge. If you have locations in China too, your ISP would properly prefer the edge site in Hong Kong.
It also depends whether the ISP is able to peer in this location. Some ISPs are only able to peer in a global location.

Another very important factor to consider when choosing an Azure and edge location is which services you need. Some Azure services are not enabled in particular Azure Regions, so sometimes it might be necessary to choose a location by service and not by nearest location.

In our scenario, we will use the data centers and Azure edges in East Asia (Hong Kong), West Europe (The Netherlands), and South Central US (Texas).

The following diagram shows the chosen data centers:

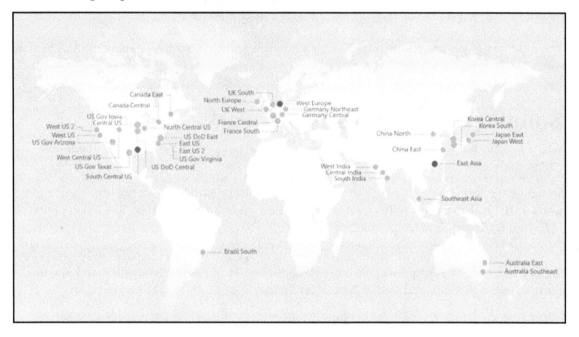

Source: https://azure.microsoft.com/en-us/regions/

As soon as you have chosen the Azure data center you want and can use, you need to identify whether you want to use a VPN or MPLS/ExpressRoute solution. In our case, we already have an MPLS in place, and we have high demand for low latency, so we will go with Azure ExpressRoute.

Now we need to figure out if we need one or more ExpressRoute circuits for our environment. Normally you would choose one high bandwidth ExpressRoute circuit with the premium add-on so that you can access all Azure data centers via one circuit. That might be a clever choice to save money, but it's a killer for our low latency needs.

Let us assume we have user in Seattle who wants to connect to a service placed in Texas, and our ExpressRoute circuit is in Amsterdam. The TCP packet will first travel via MPLS to the Netherlands, from there to Texas, then back to the Netherlands, and then to the user in Seattle.

The following diagram shows a schematic overview:

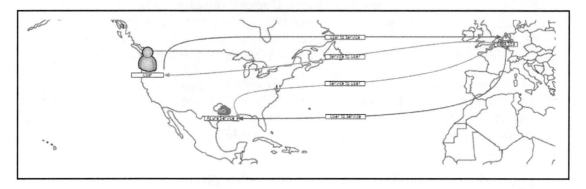

In our scenario, we placed at least three Azure ExpressRoute premium circuits, and then smaller circuits in every region to cover the local traffic, and to act as failover for another regional circuit.

In this way, our users reach their local service very quickly and connect to other services that are not in their region via an Azure backbone or MPLS network and another ExpressRoute circuit.

The following diagram shows the placement of the circuit:

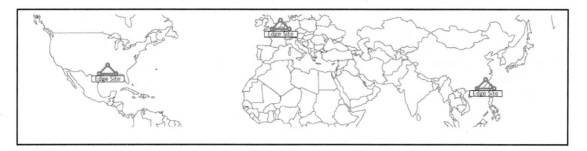

For our scenario, we only use an Azure ExpressRoute with private and public peering because we don't have the need for Microsoft peering at the moment. You mostly choose Microsoft peering via ExpressRoute when it comes to low latency and telephony, with Skype for Business, in combination with a telephone system or application communication via Internet is not permitted.

When you are working with Azure and you are in a project with ISPs, you need to learn some special *speech*. One of those phrases and words you mostly will here is the *peering* or *to peer*. These phrases only mean, that your ISP and in our case Microsoft will create an interconnect between their networks, also named **network-to-network interconnect** (**NNI**).

For most of the other use cases, it is more cost-efficient to let your ISP place an Internet breakout near your Azure edge site, which is mostly in the same data center, and do the last interconnect via public Internet and port `443(HTTPs over SSL)`. That last interconnect is mostly only one network hop, because most ISPs directly peer at the Internet Exchanges were Microsoft is peering too.

Please keep in mind that you need to route all traffic to Office 365 via those Internet breakouts. This routing must be done within your MPLS, and partly in your LAN too.

Solution for point-to-site VPN and GeoIP/DNS

In our scenario, the customer wants to connect to an Azure point-to-site VPN from all over the globe with one configuration and one DNS entry. He also wants his users to connect to the nearest Azure data center possible. To achieve this goal, GeoDNS and GeoIP need to be implemented.

To achieve a Geo available DNS record, there are different DNS providers, such as Microsoft with Azure DNS, Amazon Route 53 CloudFloorDNS. Those Providers operate DNS servers in any major public IP network which host customer DNS names and zones. Behind those DNS Names, the customer positions the IPs of his endpoints for example the point-to-site Azure VPN gateways we us in our scenario. Now the DNS provider analyses the public IP of the client device and pinpoints it to the nearest gateway, based on the IP of the point-to-site gateway.

In the first step, you need to create a point-to-site Azure VPN gateway in each of your Azure data centers and connect them to your Azure and company network.

The following diagram shows a schematic view on a possible solution:

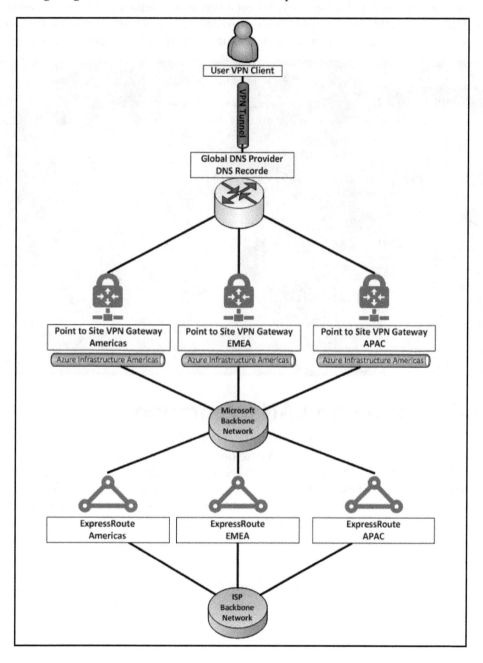

After you have configured the DNS and IP service at your GeoDNS/IP provider of your choice, you need to deploy the gateway. To get a consistent deployment for all clients, you need to deploy the same client certificate to all Azure VPN gateways. From there on, every client is able to use any gateway, and connects automatically to the nearest gateway:

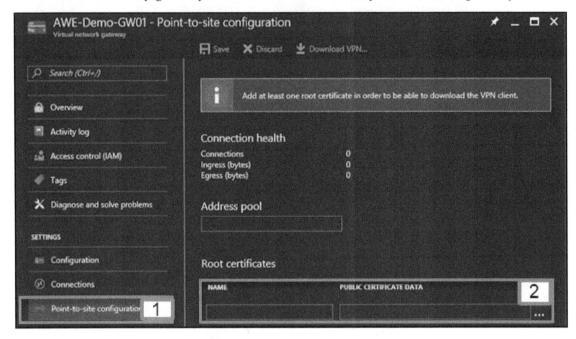

Solution for Azure LAN integration

For the LAN solution, we could go with a very classic environment where we would configure different subnetworks on our Azure network and connect it to the ExpressRoute or VPN gateway and the Internet. With such a network environment, you have a working Azure Network in the first place. But it might be not the best solution because the routing behavior within the Azure network. The default routing behavior of Azure routes *any to any* for every network traffic. That makes an Azure environment sometimes less secure or less performant than an on-premises network routing and firewall devices, especially when you have a demand for a DMZ.

For a more modern solution, we combine Azure networks with Azure VNet peering.

We would create two Azure networks, one for DMZ and one for internal services. Both are connected via VNet peering to the Internet. The internal VNet also has a connection to the on-premises environment. Within the Internet VNet we place all services that are used as internal services only with no outside connect or are backend services for services running in the DMZ. Within the DMZ VNet we place all services with external and Internet-facing services, as in a classic DMZ.

To secure the access and deny DMZ systems a connection to our corporate network, the gateway transit within the VNet peering would be disabled from both sites and **network security groups** (**NSGs**) will be defined which restrict or permit traffic between both networks. That means the services can only reach the other VNet, but nothing behind-for example, the on-premises network via VPN or ExpressRoute.

The following diagram shows a possible solution:

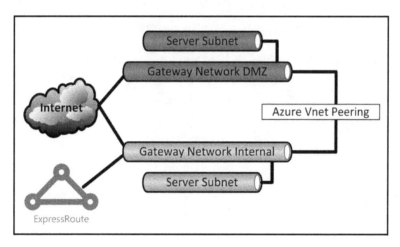

Solution for identity and access management

For the identity and access management in our scenario, we will use Azure Active Directory Premium P1 because our customer has two requirements that are only achievable with that level of plan. The first requirement is a single sign-on to third-party applications, such as Box and Salesforce. The other requirement is the password self-service for users, via the Office 365 portal https://portal.office.com. This is only available with Azure AD Premium P1 or P2 plan offered as additional Azure Active Directory Service.

With Azure AD Premium, there is an additional infrastructure requirement. Azure AD and the single sign-on with other applications and the password self-service requires Active Directory Federation Services to integrate the local Active Directory Domain Service. As a result, more systems are needed in our infrastructure.

Now you only need to decide if you want to implement a high available AD Federation solution or a single solution. A high available solution can look as shown in the diagram:

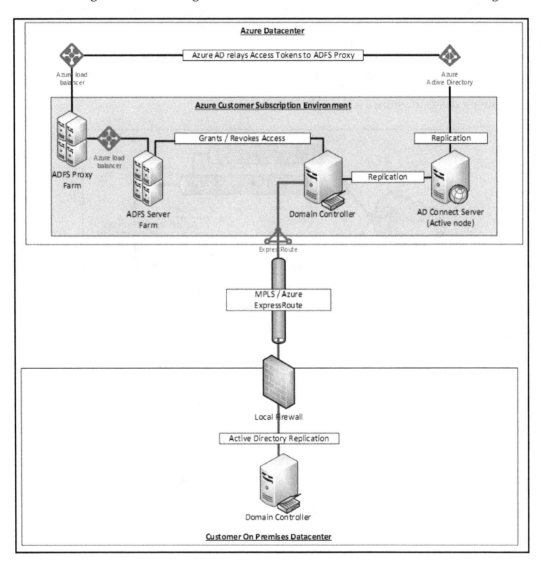

Solution for SharePoint services

When it comes to SharePoint, you have two options to choose. The first option is to run the SharePoint services as Azure virtual machines. Another option to migrate SharePoint into a Microsoft Cloud environment is to use SharePoint Online in Office 365.

The decision you make should be based on what you want to achieve with the SharePoint farm, if you have plugins that are not available or supported in SharePoint Online or if you need more performance than SharePoint Online can deliver.

In our case, we don't have any special plugins, and only use it for internal websites, the document library, and project sites. We don't break any SharePoint Online limitation.

So, we would go with SharePoint Online in Office 365. In that case, we don't need to set up any load balancer or virtual machines.

In the case, you reach certain SharePoint Online limitations, Office 365 SharePoint Online gives you the option to connect your SharePoint instance to Azure Resources like Azure SQL or Azure Storage.

The picture below shows the connection dialog to connect a SharePoint Online farm to Azure SQL:

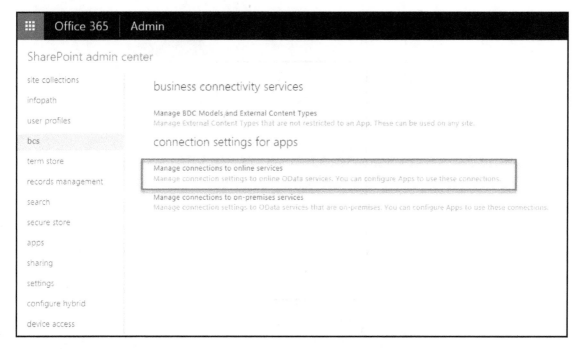

Solution for Exchange services

With Exchange, you have to make the same decision that you made with SharePoint. If you have no requirements for plugins or security, it is better to include Exchange Online with Office 365 in your solution. One reason for this is, for not hosting Exchange in Azure, you need to use premium storage, and in terms of gigabytes of data, that becomes very expensive.

 From the point of view of best practice and field experience, hosting Exchange within Microsoft Azure is mostly not very practical. In nearly all cases, it is more efficient to use Exchange Online in Office 365.

Solution for document management system

The document management system is based on Application Engine, which is distributed via two application servers, with the date stored on an SMB share. Those solutions are mostly based on VMs, and can't run as a PaaS application. One enhancement those DMSs have is that they mostly contain the permissions within the application interface and store the files on a share with full access.

That gives us the option to store the files on Azure Storage files as a PaaS service. The following diagram show a possible architecture:

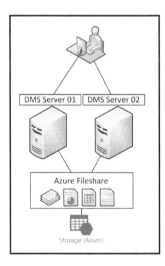

These configurations enable a solution that uses the cost-efficient and high available PaaS storage from Azure, together with legacy applications running in Azure IaaS services.

The solution is also able to be combined with other services based on Microsoft Azure Storage File—for example, backup solutions that are based on SMB and that are able to back up Azure PaaS services.

Solution for file services

The solution for file services is split into three parts right now. The first part is personal home shares, the second is the file shares for application server that have no need for **access control lists** (**ACLs**) and access controls, such as the document management system, and the third is the classic file services, which are based on NTFS, SMB, and ACL.

Personal homeshares

In a regular scenario, you would not use Azure File or Azure virtual machines because of the uncontrollable and very high downloads from users. Normally, you can also estimate that users store every kind of file within their personal folders. That's why Azure File storage is properly not the right solution for personal files.

For those files, Microsoft offers OneDrive for Business within Office 365, which enables your users to have up to 1 TB of storage for their personal files:

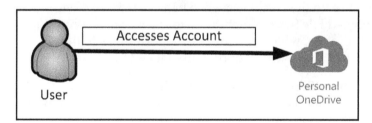

Storing profile data is not supported—for example, for roaming profiles on OneDrive. User profiles must still be stored on a classic file share.

No ACL shares

For shares that don't have any need for access control lists, and work with full control, you can use Azure Storage File accounts and connect the shares to the server directly via SMB. From there, the users can connect to the file share:

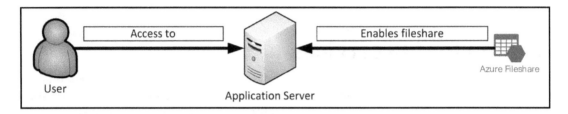

But there is a very important caveat. You need to take latency under consideration. Within an Azure data center, latency is no issue, but when you want to mount an Azure fileshare on a remote server, there could be a very bad user experience or failure during transfer because of high latency.

Classic shares

When it comes to a classic fileshare with a need of ACL, there is no Azure solution yet, but also in this case, you can use Azure to keep those fileshares available.

Sometimes there are use cases where you need to have caches for file servers and storage within a branch office. In the past, I needed expensive storage devices or complex software, or I used a Distributed File System replication to transfer files. With Windows Server 2016, we got storage replication, which gave us new opportunities to think about. You can use this kind of replication to move files or back up data into the cloud.

Windows Server 2016 storage replication
You can use Storage Replica to configure two servers to sync data so that each has an identical copy of the same volume. The following URLs below provide some background of this server-to-server replication configuration, as well as how to set it up and manage the environment.
Source: `https://technet.microsoft.com/en-us/windows-server-docs/storage/storage-replica/server-to-server-storage-replication`
Microsoft Azure VMs:
`https://azure.microsoft.com/en-us/documentation/services/virtual-machines/windows/`

Firstly, you need a file server as a source and a file server as target. You need to also ensure that the data you want to replicate is on a different volume than the data that stays onsite:

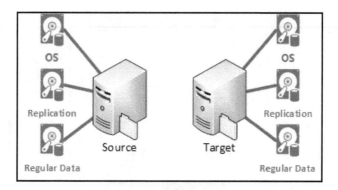

The Azure virtual machine should be at least VM Size DS3 or above, because you need at least two disks. If you want to replicate more disks, you should be able to add more disks:

From the network site, you need to implement VPN site-to-site connection between your offices and Azure. You need a performance gateway to get the necessary throughput and latency:

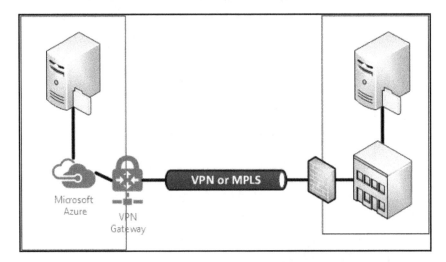

The on-premises server is the primary **Distributed File System-Namespace (DFS-N)** target for the clients. The file server in Azure is the secondary target. The secondary file server is disabled as the target for clients in the DFS-N. DFS-N is a common Windows Server Feature which enables admins to cover the regular name of a file share or its location and path behind a name label. If the admin needs to for example change the file server or the path of the file share. He does not need to change any DNS records or mess around with file server names. He only need to change the patch which is masked by the name label. There will be no impact on the clients, currently using the name label.

 If you want to learn more about DFS, you can fine more information in the Microsoft Documentation websites: `https://technet.microsoft.com/en -us/library/cc732006(v=ws.11).aspx`.

The access will be on the primary file server and the storage information will be replicated to the secondary file server:

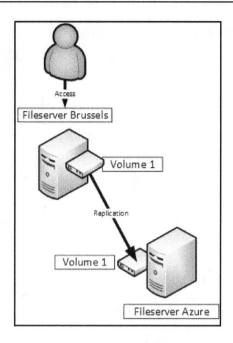

As long as everything goes fine, you will only have incoming traffic to Azure with no costs for traffic. If the primary volume or file server went offline, you can switch to the secondary file server by enabling the secondary file server in DFS-N and swapping the target volume to active. You can either do this manually or trigger it via automation services and monitoring, with, for example, the Azure Automation and Operations Management Suite or System Center Operations Manager:

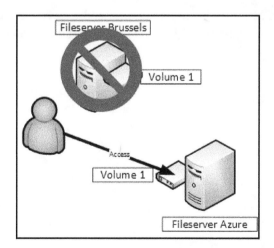

You can also use the file server as the target for different file servers:

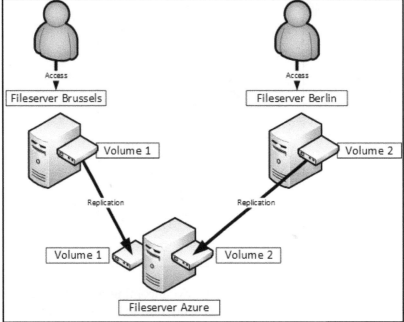

Solution for a public website with TYPO3 CMS

To provide the TYPO3 CMS solution in Azure we need to leverage Azure IaaS infrastructure. Currently there is no TYPO3 PaaS offering from Microsoft.

Many Publishers provide template with TYPO3 and MySQL installed in the Azure Marketplace.

Those templates are mostly a good and tested solutions but they have one major disadvantage. Often the user of the template has no access to the operating system which makes those templates unusable in our scenario. With the PDF creator installed in the operating system, we need to have access to the operating system.

So, the only solution for us in this case is to choose a template with an operating system matching our requirements and install and support TYPO3 and MySQL on our own.

Solution for backup services

When you are looking for a current backup solution to Azure and Office 365, you need to enable a three-part backup solution.

For Azure virtual machines, you can use Azure**Backup** to back up the virtual machine, but that is limited to files or databases. The following screenshot shows the service interface in Azure:

To back up single files, databases, and so on within a virtual machine, you need an additional product from Azure **Backup**. This product is a special server application, which will be installed on a backup server and works as a client-based solution, like System Center Data Protection Manager or Networker. The client is installed on every server where there are files that need to be backed up.

The following diagram shows such a backup solution:

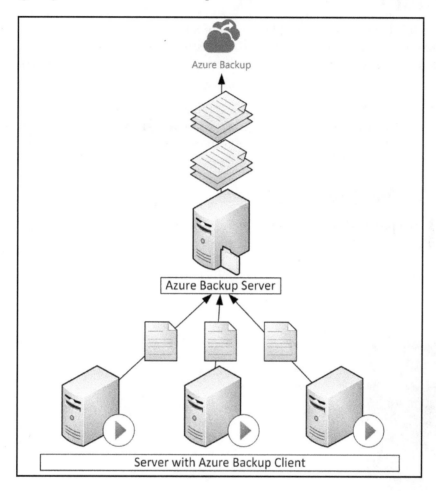

When it comes to the backup of Office 365, there is currently no option to do any backups for Office 365 with Azure. Therefore, you need a third-party backup application, such as Barracuda Networks.

There are plans to include Office 365 into Azure **Backup**, but there is no release date yet.

Summary

Having read this chapter, you should now know how all services integrate, and how you should approach an existing infrastructure and its requirements. You should now be able to identify basic Azure services and compare them to classic on-premises services and server systems.

If you go through such a scenario and you want to get a better understand what could be the estimated costs or what are the **Total Costs of Ownership (TCO)** and when you are reaching the return of investment, Microsoft offers two tools you can leverage.

Azure Price Calculator

First and from a personal perspective most important tool is the Azure price calculator. With the calculator, you can estimate the costs of your environment, running on Azure.

You can add any kind of Azure service from the product selector shown here:

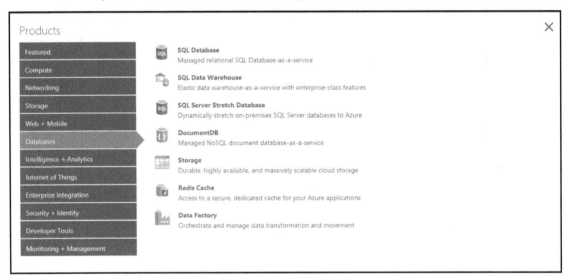

Change the sizing of the service:

And afterwards, you will get a complete estimate of your solution via web (**1**) or you can export it as a `.csv` file(**2**).

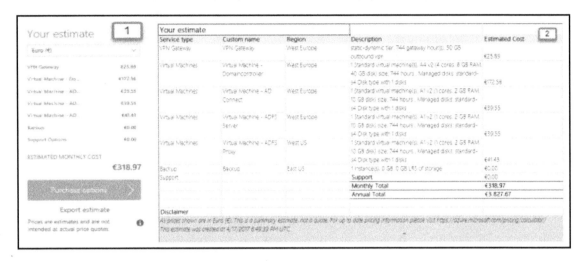

You can find the Azure Price Calculator at
`https://azure.microsoft.com/en-us/pricing/calculator/`.

Azure TCO and RIO Calculator

Together with the TCO Calculator you can simply set the Azure environment in relation to your on-premises environment.

As you can see on the following screenshot, the calculator is currently in preview but is already very reliable:

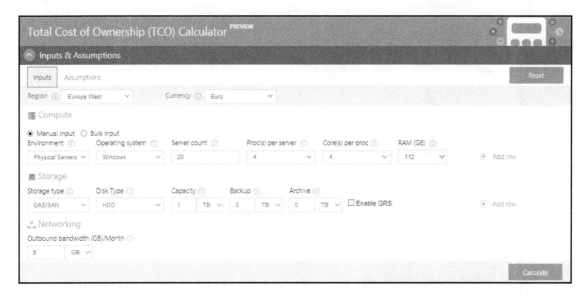

After you reflected your environment within the calculator, you can create a report get some insides in the estimated savings and RCO:

You can find the calculator at `https://www.tco.microsoft.com/Home/Calculator`.

Index